THE NAMES
OF KINGS

THE
NAMES OF
KINGS

THE PARISIAN LABORING POOR IN THE EIGHTEENTH CENTURY

JEFFRY KAPLOW

BASIC BOOKS, INC.
PUBLISHERS
NEW YORK

The author is grateful for permission to use the following material:

Bertolt Brecht, "A Worker Reads History," from *Selected Poems of Bertolt Brecht*, trans. H. R. Hays, copyright 1947 by Bertolt Brecht and H. R. Hays. Reprinted by permission of Harcourt Brace Jovanovich, Inc. and the Ann Elmo Agency.

George Rudé, table from *The Economic History Review*, by permission of the editors and George Rudé.

All photographs were used by permission of the Bibliothèque Nationale, Paris.

In Memory of Vera

and

for Leo

A Worker Reads History

Who built the seven gates of Thebes?
The books are filled with the names of kings.
Was it kings who hauled the craggy blocks of stone?
And Babylon, so many times destroyed,
Who built the city up each time? In which of Lima's houses,
The city glittering with gold, lived those who built it?
In the evening when the Chinese wall was finished
Where did the masons go? Imperial Rome
Is full of arcs of triumph. Who reared them up? Over whom
Did the Caesars triumph? Byzantium lives in song,
Were all her dwellings palaces? And even in Atlantis of the legend
The night the sea rushed in,
The drowning men still bellowed for their slaves.

Young Alexander conquered India.
He alone?

Caesar beat the Gauls,
Was there not even a cook in his army?
Philip of Spain wept as his fleet
Was sunk and destroyed. Were there no other tears?
Frederick the Great triumphed in the Seven Years War. Who
Triumphed with him?

Each page a victory,
At whose expense the victory ball?
Every ten years a great man,
Who paid the piper?

So many particulars.
So many questions.

BRECHT

If I have a fair opportunity to pass much of my time in good company at Paris, I have also no small trouble in turning over books, MSS. and papers, which I cannot see in England: this employs many hours a day, with what I borrow from the night, in making notes. I have procured also some public records, the copying of which demands time. He who wishes to give a good account of such a kingdom as France, must be indefatigable in the search of materials: for let him collect with all the care possible, yet when he comes to sit down coolly to the examination and arrangement, will find, that much has been put into his hands, of no real consequence, and more, possibly, that is absolutely useless.

ARTHUR YOUNG

PREFACE

The work presented here has been in gestation for a long time, for it deals with a subject in which I first became interested while still a graduate student more than ten years ago. No doubt there will be those who will find the baby still premature, lacking flesh on his bones and squealing where he cannot reason. I leave that to the judgment of my fellow historians and readers in the sure and certain hope, as the Book of Common Prayer has it, that I will agree with them only in part.

My purpose has been to understand how and why the Parisian masses were led to take so active a part in the essentially bourgeois French Revolution, as historians like Lefebvre, Soboul, Rudé and Cobb, among others, have shown them to have done. Hence, the plan of this book. In the first chapter, I attempt to locate the laboring poor in their city, both physically and socially. I then go on to define their several strata; to discuss how they lived, worked, and died; what they believed and how; and finally, how the sum of their life experience first prevented and then prepared them to take part in the politics of the age. The approach has been informed by the conviction that the concept of the laboring poor is an appropriate one for analyzing preindustrial capitalist societies and that the laboring poor as a coherent social unit had to disappear with the advent of a modern capitalist social formation. Hopefully, it will be possible at some later date to continue this investigation with a view to producing a book about the making of the French working class.

Because my point of view is (I think) a Marxist one, I will undoubtedly—inevitably—be accused of displaying too much sympathy for my "heroes," as one reader of the manuscript put it. Let me make it clear that there are no heroes in this book. That I have a certain sympathy for my characters is obvious. Furthermore, I explicitly reject the unreal objectivity which, under the guise of value-free science, would have the historian stand aloof from involvement in his analysis. The laboring poor of eighteenth-century Paris do not, at this late date, need anyone to judge them or to distribute praise and blame for moral or immoral behavior. They had an integrity of their own, keyed to their life style and set of values, that is, to their class situation. That is what I have tried to chronicle and, to some extent, explain. Vice and virtue have nothing to do with the case, whether defined by twentieth-century American society in general, or the class to which I belong, or myself in particular.

The question I started with was: How and why did the laboring poor develop a political consciousness in the course of the eighteenth century? So far, it has been impossible to come up with a complete answer. Much remains to be studied, especially in regard to the dynamics of change. One day I hope it will be possible to distinguish the stages, the ups and downs of the process more clearly than I have yet been able to do. But one point must be stressed at this juncture. If I have chosen this procedure, it is not because of any belief in the inevitable growth of consciousness in a given class or social group. Still less is consciousness a reified thing pre-existent to the needs which it expresses and ready to be assumed by a set of men. No, the question was asked, because it appeared evident that it constituted the missing link between the relatively passive laboring poor of the prerevolutionary period and the mass of participants in the revolutionary actions of 1789 and the following years. Need it be said that not all individuals or strata of the laboring poor were equally involved in the Revolution? Because it is so obvious, to point it out at every opportunity would be to kick in open doors. Soboul has shown how much the leadership of the sans-culottes fell to master artisans and petit-bourgeois shopkeepers rather than to the men we study here, who remained followers and not leaders.

There are paragraphs in this book that might be developed into full-scale treatises. As it now stands, the book is intended to be a series of essays in a hitherto neglected field. I hope by publishing now, at this stage of the research, to solicit the interest and aid of other scholars, for work in this kind of social history can only be carried out by collective effort. It is not merely a matter of the quantity of material to be considered, despite the fetishistic attachment to ever-growing piles of paper and notecards displayed by some historians. Were that the only problem, it might well be solved by a couple of computers and an army of programers. There is another dimension. To study the laboring poor is to study the entire society in all its multitudinous aspects, and that in turn presupposes a variety of interests and talents in addition to the advantages to be derived from a hydra-headed collective wisdom. I do not mean, however, that we ought to dispense with the need for a common point of view, the lack of which has too often turned published volumes by groups of authors into bargain basements of the mind, rather than what they should be, disciplined reflections hammered out in common on problems of significance.

I confess that in writing this book, contemporary problems have never been very far from my mind, particularly those having to do with the formation of revolutionary situations and actors. So far from apologizing for these preoccupations, I think them to be the *sine qua non* for the writing of meaningful history.

I have been helped in bringing this book to term by the financial aid of the American Philosophical Society and the Columbia University Council for Research in the Social Sciences, whose generosity made possible several trips to France for research in the early stages of this project. Fellowships of the National Foundation for the Humanities and the Social Science Research Council in 1968–1969 enabled me to complete the research. The Wenner-Gren Foundation for Anthropological Research showed the catholicity of its interests with a grant for the study of the family life of the laboring poor, only some of whose results have been incorporated here.

The research was carried out primarily at the Archives Nationales and the Bibliothèque Nationale. The staff of both institutions have been unfailingly helpful and pleasant despite the difficulties imposed upon them by lack of both money and space. I would also like to express my gratitude to the archivists and librarians of the Archives de la Seine (and especially Mme. Felkay), of the Seine-et-Oise at Versailles (M. Lions), and of the city of St. Denis, as well as of the Bibliothèque Historique de la Ville de Paris, the archives of the Public Assistance Administration, and of the archives of the Prefecture of Police. I must, on the other hand, record with regret the fact that I was refused permission to consult the archives of the former foundling hospital, on grounds of family interest. It would appear that nobody loves a bastard, or at least would rather not have it known that there was one in the family. It is a pity that historical research should be stymied by such considerations.

I have benefited from the advice of my friends Harvey Goldberg and Helmut Gruber, and if they have not always succeeded in saving me from myself, it is I who must assume the entire responsibility.

JEFFRY KAPLOW

Paris
May, 1972

CONTENTS

THE NAMES
OF KINGS

[1]

PARIS: THE URBAN ENVIRONMENT

❦ I ❧

To name this city is, in a sense, to say what it is, since there is no one who does not know that it passes, and with reason, for one of the most beautiful, the richest, the most populated, the most flourishing, and one of the biggest cities of Europe. It is also known that it is second to no other city in the world in the prodigious number of superb buildings, the wisdom of its government, its relationship to the sciences and other arts cultivated there, its conveniences and pleasures, as well as the prodigious commerce carried on within its boundaries.[1]

So wrote the Abbé Expilly in 1768, with pardonable pride in an era when all Europe, with the possible exception of the British, looked towards Paris and France as the center of the arts, of science, and of progress. But there was another, more nuanced, side to the story. Rousseau was less enthusiastic about the glories of the city:

To what degree did Paris, at first, give the lie to the idea I had conceived of it. . . . I had imagined a city as beautiful as it was big, of the most imposing aspect, where one saw only superb streets, and palaces of marble and gold. Entering through the faubourg Saint Marceau, I saw only small, dirty and stinking streets, ugly black houses, an air of filth, poverty, beggars, carters, sewing women, women hawking tisanes and old hats. All this struck me to such a degree at the beginning that everything I have since seen in Paris of real magnificence has been unable to destroy this first impression, and there has always remained in me a secret distaste for living in the capital.[2]

Finally, the Russian traveler Nikolai Karamzine saw Paris for the first time in March 1790, and his reaction was little different from that of thousands of his predecessors. All were impressed by the grandeur of the city, its vastness, color, and all-pervasive sense of movement. All noted the size and density of the population (well over 600,000 on the eve of the Revolution), the animation of the streets, and, above all, the sharp contrasts between extreme luxury and abject poverty, the opulence of the noble and the financier, the mediocrity of the artisan, and the starving faces of the ubiquitous beggars. Karamzine wrote:

Soon we entered the faubourg Saint Antoine, and what did we see there? Narrow, dirty, muddy streets, evil-looking houses and people in tattered rags. "So this is Paris," I said to myself, "the city that seemed so magnificent to me from afar."—But the decor changed completely when we arrived at the banks of the Seine. There arose before us magnificent edifices, six-storey houses, rich shops; what a multitude of people! What variety! What noise! One carriage follows on the heels of another. Constantly one hears the cries: "Take care! Take care!" and the people roll about like the sea.[3]

To anyone seeing Paris for the first time, it must have seemed, as it did to Marianne in Marivaux's novel (*La Vie de Marianne* [1731–1741]), like the moon, another world difficult to understand and still more difficult to accept. The Burgundian peasant, the city dweller from Provence, and even the rich businessman from Lyons, Bordeaux, or Rouen, would be equally impressed and not a little confused by what they saw. Paris was large in eighteenth-century European terms, second only to London, although relatively small by our standards. The inexactitude of measurement accounts for discrepancies found in contemporary accounts, but it was generally agreed that the city within the boulevards covered an area of approximately 2,400 *arpents* (an *arpent* being equal to a little more than four-fifths of an acre), and about 4,000 *arpents* with the faubourgs. The new limits fixed by the construction of the Farmers General wall of 1786 increased the figure to 3,370 *hectares*, or 9,000 acres.[4]

Paris was divided into 20 quarters, to which several faubourgs were appended for administrative purposes. The threefold division among the ville, the faubourgs, and the banlieue had grown up over the centuries. The first was the city proper as defined before 1786 by the ramparts of the inner boulevards to the north and somewhat smaller than the area enclosed within the boulevards to the south. The second covered the area from the boundaries of the ville to the barriers of the General Farm. The banlieue comprised the suburban communities—some, like Auteuil, Passy, Montmarte, Belleville, and Vaugirard that would be annexed to the capital in 1860, and others, like Ivry, Montrouge, Boulogne and Saint Denis that remain administratively separate to the present day. Contemporaries knew that there was no longer any valid reason to maintain the distinction between ville and faubourgs in the eighteenth century, and they were in fact treated as a single urban unit. Two examples will suffice: all legislation was drafted to cover both sections, and guild membership was open to inhabitants of the faubourgs as well as to the population of the ville (with the exception of the faubourg Saint Antoine before Turgot's reforms of 1776).

Eighteenth-century authors thought of Paris as a well-populated city, having neither too many nor too few inhabitants. According to Charles René de Fourcroy, a city was properly supplied with people when there were 200–250 per *arpent* (400–500 per *hectare*). "With this proportion," he wrote, "streets can be laid out without overdoing it, and buildings constructed to a height of two or three storeys at most, which is an advantage essential to health."[5] The problem, however, was the uneven distribution of population in the several sections of the city. The quarters of the Halles, the Ile de la Cité and several others in the center of the city sheltered as many as 400–500 persons per *arpent*, while the western districts and certain faubourgs, where the streets were wider, the houses smaller and fewer, the gardens and courtyards more numerous, had a density of only 100 per *arpent*.

All roads led to Notre Dame, the symbol since its construction in the late twelfth century not only of Paris but of Christian France. The seat of the Archbishop of Paris, its great Gothic mass dominated the original hub of the capital, the Ile de la Cité. The Island in the eighteenth century was a microcosm of the city, its ecclesiastical, judicial, and administrative center, dotted with world-famous monuments—not the cathedral alone, but the Palace of Justice where the sovereign court of Parlement met, surrounded on either side by the delicate spire of the Sainte Chapelle, built by St. Louis to house a fragment of the crown of thorns, and the Conciergerie, the prison where captives stayed while awaiting execution in the Place de Grève. Immediately in front of Notre Dame stood the buildings of the Hôtel-Dieu, the hospital in which thousands of Parisians were treated every day. At the opposite end, the Island was traversed by the Pont Neuf, built in 1610, with its majestic equestrian statue of Henri IV, the legend of whose good deeds lived on in Parisian folklore. Of all the 14 bridges that crossed the Seine, it was the busiest and most popular, with no fewer than 178 stalls and shops until they were pulled down in 1756.[6] During the day activity on the Pont Neuf was constant and intense, and anything that money could buy was for sale. It was thought to be extremely dangerous to walk in this neighborhood at night because of the presence in the environs of thieves and criminals of every description.

To the casual observer, the Cité was an impressive architectural ensemble and a turbulent maze of narrow, winding, crowded streets at the same time. All sorts of commerce were carried on there, but the luxury trades were dominant. The Pont Notre Dame linking the Ile to the Right Bank epitomized the activity of the Cité as a whole. Its 68 three-story houses, torn down for reasons of safety in 1786, lodged no fewer than 14 goldsmiths' shops in 1769, in addition to numerous jewelers, mercers, embroiderers, and dealers in art and religious objects. The workers who produced the luxury goods often lived in the worst imaginable conditions, a single room serving as both home and workshop. The population density in this and the immediately surrounding quarters was among the highest in the city, the inhabitants being literally piled on top of one another and lacking the most elementary forms of comfort.[7]

Across the Pont au Change on the Right Bank were the quarters of St. Jacques de la Boucherie and the Halles, home of the great markets. Here, too, lived a varied population of wage-earners, master artisans and bourgeois who engaged in all branches of trade, with the accent once again on luxury items: the goldsmiths and gilders of the rue and quai de Gesvres are a case in point. In close proximity to these merchants to the upper classes stood the stalls and shops of the butchers and fishmongers, whose merchandise gave the area a particularly foul odor. In addition, clothing was sold here in great quantities. The quai de la Mégisserie was also known as the quai de la Feraille (Junk Wharf) because it was the place where itinerant pedlars offered for sale hardware of all sorts: buckles, knives, and pots and pans. Of the public monuments, no doubt the most famous were the Grenier à Sel or salt depot of the despised state monopoly and the Cemetery of the Holy Innocents with its open pits for the mass burial of the poor, which was finally closed in 1780 after more than half a century of complaints. Until the late seventeenth century, the French counterparts of Macheath and Peachum used to gather in the Cour des Miracles behind the cemetery, so called because fraudulent beggars made it their headquarters, where they could remove their disguises, abandon pretense and emerge able-bodied after a day's labor. Beggars of this kind were fewer in number in our period than they had been in the sixteenth century, and their hiding places were less notorious.[8]

East and north to the boulevards lay the remainder of the core of Paris as it had developed from the thirteenth to the seventeenth centuries. The quarters of St. Denis, St. Martin, the Grève (Hôtel de Ville), the Marais, and St. Paul were physically similar to those already discussed, although the streets grew wider and more regular and the population somewhat less dense as one moved toward the city limits. St. Paul was very commercial and filled with manufactures of printed cloth and tapestries. St. Denis was another center of the luxury trades—ribbons, laces, and gold braid being among its principal products.[9] Further to the east, the quarter and faubourg Saint Antoine were famed for the manufacture of furniture and, secondarily, of mirrors and pottery.

In these quarters large tracts of land belonged to religious establishments, like the Benedictines of the Abbey of St. Martin des Champs and the convents of the Filles Dieu and the Madelonettes. The area as a whole, and the Marais in particular, had been the center of aristocratic life in the seventeenth century and, even now that many nobles had opted for the newer faubourg Saint Germain, still remained a desirable place for solidly established bourgeois, both mercantile and judicial. The old mansions, whose names—Sully, d'Ormesson, Lamoignon, d'Albret, Le Pelletier— read like a catalogue of great families, remained, although not always in the best of repair. And the place Royale (des Vosges), that beautiful and expensive trinket of Louis XIII, was in even poorer condition, its houses having early been leased out and left to the tender mercies of private maintenance.

The expansion of Paris in the eighteenth century had moved in an east to west direction on both banks of the Seine. Next to the markets on the Right Bank lay a more opulent area. In the district around the great palaces of the Louvre, the Tuileries, and the Palais Royal, lived the rich merchants and financiers, that is, tax farmers and investors in the privileged commercial companies. The former, many of them members of the Six Corps or great merchant guilds, centered around the rue Saint Honoré,[10] and the latter in the streets surrounding the place des Victoires, built to celebrate the magnificence of the Sun King. The rues Saint Honoré, du Roule, and de l'Arbre Sec in the parish of Saint Eustache were the preferred locations of dealers in objets d'art, near the homes of their rich clientele.[11]

Westward beyond the Tuileries Gardens, open to the public who liked to stroll in its shaded walks, was the newly laid out place Louis XV, later successively known as the place de la Révolution and the place de la Concorde. The rue Royale connected the place to the Madeleine, whose construction was begun in 1764. Here began the great boulevards that formed the limit between the city proper and the faubourgs. Still further to the west were the Champs Elysées, as yet unmarked by construction of any kind.

On the Left Bank across from the Ile de la Cité was the university, or the Latin Quarter, corresponding to the quarters of Saint André des Arts and Saint Benoit. It, too, was a tangle of old streets occupied by great religious establishments and the largest agglomeration of educational institutions of any city in Europe. On its southeastern limits, on the sloping streets of the Montagne Sainte Geneviève, the Church of Sainte Geneviève, the patron saint of Paris, rechristened the Panthéon during the Revolution, was built in the 1760s. To the east, the quarter of the place Maubert contained one of the great local markets and was the dwelling place of a large artisan and laboring population. To the west, the Latin Quarter was bounded by the quarters of the Luxembourg Gardens and the faubourg Saint Germain, the aristocratic districts par excellence. To the south lay the populous faubourgs Saint Jacques and Saint Marcel (Marceau). The first was the center of the printing and bookselling trades, their practitioners being obliged by law to reside here. The second was traditionally identified, along with the faubourg Saint Antoine on the Right Bank, as the center of artisanal activity. St. Marcel's great industries were brewing and tanning (the latter in rapid decline in the last quarter of the eighteenth century), both of which depended on the waters of the Bièvre, a tiny river that ran through this part of the city.[12] It may well have laid claim to the title of the poorest area of the capital, for its vicar reported in 1743 that 12,000 out of 15,000–18,000 parishioners old enough to take communion were "so poor that they could not subsist, either in illness or even in health, without the help of charities."[13] Furthermore, its population was much more mixed than that of the faubourg Saint Antoine. In addition to artisans of all sorts, it contained an extraordinary variety of unskilled workers, street merchants, and floaters, sufficient to give it the reputation of being the most unsettled and most seditious part of Paris.[14]

The northern boulevards, especially their easternmost section between the porte Saint Antoine and the rue du Pont aux Choux bordering on the faubourgs Popincourt and Saint Antoine, became a popular place to visit in the 1740s after the municipality had had a neighboring sewer covered over. The boulevards were always thick with people out for a ride or a stroll. Satirists in the 1750s had a field day at the expense of the pretentious aristocrats and social climbing bourgeois who liked to outdo one another in ostentatious display. Thus, one character is made to say that it is safer to drive a carriage on the boulevards where one need not fear running into "those boors who inundate the Tuileries"; and another woman exclaims: "What, Marquis, you know women who frequent the Tuileries? . . . I would like to know where you go to dig up women who go to the Tuileries. I knew you were a little naive about certain customs, but it never would have entered my mind that you would be capable of betraying your nobility and acting like a bourgeois."[15]

After 1760, the character of the northern boulevards began to change. The center of activity moved northwestwards to the boulevard du Temple, and entertainments of various kinds—theatres, puppet shows, acrobats, menageries, scientific demonstrations—became all the rage. Mansions were built on the side of the boulevards facing the faubourgs in the 1770s and 1780s, and soon the quarter was on its way to becoming a mixed residential and theatrical district, while people of fashion took to frequenting the gardens of the Palais Royal. The southern boulevards were not completed until the 1760s and never enjoyed the same kind of popularity.[16]

Beyond the boulevards lay the faubourgs. Still largely rural in aspect at the beginning of the century, they began to succumb to urban sprawl after 1750. From west to east, on the Right Bank, the faubourgs bore the names La Roule, Saint Honoré and La Ville l'Evêque, Les Porcherons, Montmartre, Nouvelle France, Saint Denis, Saint Lazare, Saint Martin, Saint Laurent, La Courtille, du Temple, Popincourt, and, last but not least, Saint Antoine. On the Left Bank, the faubourgs Saint Victor, Saint Marcel, Saint Jacques and Saint Michel lay within the ramparts. Outside those limits were the districts of Gros Caillou, Grenelle (including the Invalides and the newly constructed Ecole militaire), Montparnasse and the area around the hospitals of La Pitié and La Salpêtrière. The landscape here was dotted with farmhouses and fields whose most important products were vegetables for the Paris market. Even the faubourg Saint Honoré was still inhabited only by "gardeners, truck farmers and the *menu peuple*" at the end of

Louis XIV's reign. And although this began to change very rapidly in the 1720s, the area beyond the Hôtel d'Evreux (now the presidential palace of the Elysée) was not allowed to be built up before 1765 and then only subject to royal control until the city gates were moved north and west in the 1780s. Gros Caillou was an uncultivated terrain until the early part of the century, when gardeners and launderers (who worked on the banks of the river) moved in. They were soon joined by their employees, soldiers, whose wives worked in the fields, and tavernkeepers, many of whom lived in great misery. In the north, Nouvelle France underwent a similar evolution.[17]

As the faubourgs became urbanized, they tended to become extensions of the quarters to which they were administratively attached. The western districts, like La Roule and Ville l'Evêque, were invaded by bourgeois. A memoir written by Aguesseau de Valjoing in 1733 in favor of allowing inhabitants of the faubourg Saint Honoré to build houses worthy of their station in life spoke of the area as "the most suitable for persons of distinction . . . it contains no manufactures; situated between the Louvre and the promenade, one can compare it to the faubourg Saint Germain." He may have anticipated reality by a few years, but he was essentially correct as to the future of the neighborhood.[18] At the same time, the eastern faubourgs started on their way to becoming artisanal centers. In 1738, the faubourg Saint Antoine was described as "a place of delights in which one tastes at one and the same time the pleasures of the city and of the country." It had market gardens, orchards and beautiful houses, many of them occupied only in the summer. Only the presence of a port for unloading wood and plaster for use in the building industry hinted at the future pre-eminence of the place in the production of furniture, mirrors, cheap earthenware and wallpaper. There was as yet no indication that it would be one of the centers of popular activity during the Revolution, to the point that the inhabitants of the district and the sans-culottes are, to the historian of the period, all but synonymous terms.[19]

Where the faubourgs ended, the banlieue began. By the end of the eighteenth century it had grown to include most of the communities that belong to it even today. They were not yet dormitories for Parisian workers but rather farming villages specializing in the production of wine and vegetables (*cultures maraichères*), together with a little grain. Industrialization of this area did not begin in earnest until the 1840s.

Despite roads that left a good deal to be desired, the proximity of the urban market made it possible for even a small holder dealing in agricultural produce of high yield per surface unit and/or costly in relation to its bulk to survive and even to prosper. Such items included eggs, butter, milk, vegetables, fruits, flowers, tree seedlings, and, above all else, wine. In 1807, more than 47,000 *arpents* in these districts were planted in vines, producing a poor quality brew that was nonetheless eagerly sought after for the poor man's table.[20]

The amount of land in peasant hands varied greatly from place to place. As a general rule, the peasants' share increased the further one moved away from Paris and Versailles and also in the less wooded regions (forests were the preserve of the crown and the aristocracy). Studying nine subdelegations of the Parisian region covering 460,000 *arpents* in 438 parishes during the years 1784–1788, Louchitsky found that 380,000 *arpents* (82 percent) belonged to noncultivators, that is, 35 percent to nobles, 20 percent to the clergy, and 27 percent to bourgeois. Peasants owned only 5.4 percent of the land in the subdelegation of Gonesse, 9.9 percent in the subdelegation of Versailles, but as much as 44.4 percent in the subdelegation of Enghien. The variations among the parishes were also very great, and in districts where vineyards were numerous, peasants owned as much as 15 to 20 percent of the land. The cultivation of the vine was a poor man's activity, for it demanded only a small amount of capital investment, little land, few animals, or little materiel of any sort.[21]

The taille rolls for the suburban communities show that although there were some quite substantial winegrowers heavily taxed in proportion to the value of their land, there were many more who held very small parcels. The listing of *vignerons-manoeuvriers* (persons who combined the cultivation of their little plots with working for a wage) or *vignerons-artisans* (for example, coopers who made casks for the wine they produced) is most common. Aside from persons directly engaged in rural labor of one sort or another, the suburban communes were populated by the usual range of artisans and petty commercial traders as well as by unskilled laborers and indigents. There were a few particularly large groups, like the launderers who worked along the banks of the Seine and the quarrymen at Ivry and the Buttes Chaumont. In Belleville, there were a number of persons employed in the manufacture of tile, brick and porcelain, and a little further north, in the garbage dumps of Montfaucon, horseskinners were at work. The majority of suburban workers eked out a meager living as best they could under conditions of great insecurity. They formed a vast labor pool for the Parisian market and accounted for a significant portion of the nondomiciled poor always to be found in the capital.[22]

The marketing of their wine was, naturally, of great concern to the inhabitants of the suburbs. The normal outlet was through the *guinguettes* in the neighboring communities, where the wine could be sold free of excise taxes. In places like Belleville and Vaugirard, tavern keepers and wine merchants formed a very important part of the population, and their establishments, with their evocative names like *Au Deserteur, Le Puits de Jacob*, and *A l'Ami du Coeur*, were famed far and wide. (The cabaret founded by Ramponneaux in the middle of the century made its proprietor a character of local folklore.) It was normal, then, that they should resist any attempt to change the tax system to their disadvantage, like the proposal to include their villages in the new city limits established on the eve of the Revolution. Taxes on wine, they argued, would have resulted in a loss of income while taxes on consumer goods were raising their own cost of living. The matter was settled only by the abolition of entry duties by the National Assembly in 1791. In the meantime fraud was commonly practiced to avoid taxation.[23]

✎§ II §✎

A series of royal edicts of 1724 and 1726, renewed in 1728 and 1765, attempted to restrain the growth of Paris by forbidding construction beyond a fixed point, generally the last extant house on streets already laid out. No new streets could be created, and it was forbidden to build houses on lots other than those with frontage on the existing streets. The ostensible reason for these measures was that great houses, the ornaments of the city, ought to be kept as near its center as possible and that the substantial citizens should be discouraged from moving to distant quarters, to which they would attract so great a number of other inhabitants that the center of the city would become depopulated.[24] In reality, these prohibitions were inspired by a set of more reasonable fears. Primarily, the government was troubled by problems attendant on maintaining and increasing the food supply in proportion to the growth of population. Should it fail to meet its responsibilities, there would be the threat of bread riots.[25] There was also a moral prejudice: those who inclined to the physiocrat-cum-corruption school of thought were certain that the wicked city would attract the unsuspecting and gullible peasant and would ruin him and French agriculture, source of all wealth and goodness, at the same time.[26] Finally, Léon Cahen has suggested that administrators were worried about the inability to police a city in which criminals seemed to be running wild—seemingly more so every day.[27]

An anonymous contemporary commenting in 1762 on the building restrictions showed how unlikely they were to achieve their goal. One by one he examined and countered the objections raised against new construction. New buildings, it was argued, would necessarily take land now used for planting food crops, notably vegetables. True enough, but there was more than enough land available for all purposes. Building materials would become scarce and more expensive, but why not use other materials? In a city allowed to grow at will, the quarters would be far from one another and communication among them would be difficult; yes, but was this really significant, if each section had all the essential services and there were good roads? And then he came to the crux of the matter. If the city were difficult to supply or police, it was not because of the number of buildings, but because of the number of people. Rational planning (an increase in agricultural production, creation of roads and canals) would solve this problem, indeed would have to do so. There was no other alternative: "So long as the arbitrariness of the taille, the fear of the militia and the horrors of corvées continue to oppress the countryside, one must expect that the cities, where one is sheltered from these evils, will continue to grow at the expense of agriculture. . . ."[28]

The fact is that Paris did seem too small to a fair number of its citizens. For the rich, a move to the faubourgs meant the opportunity to construct substantial, comfortable houses on suitably large plots of land (generally cheaper the further one went away from the city center) or to make income-producing investments.[29] For the less prosperous, the housing conditions there were often more attractive than those prevalent in the densely populated center, and certainly the atmosphere was more pleasant and more healthful.[30] In addition, construction was encouraged by the demand for lodgings of a continual flow of immigrants, both seasonal and permanent, since nothing was done to stop them from coming to the capital. The result was that Paris became a more and more expensive place to live. Throughout the century, rising real estate prices, both for sales and rentals, provided an incentive for new construction, but this was somewhat counterbalanced by the increasing costs of labor and materials as well as by government policy. The lack of solid foundations made it impossible to add storeys to older buildings, especially in the core area from the

Halles to the rue de Richelieu. The only alternative (and one often used) was to build houses one behind the other, in a series of courtyards. In this way, some 250 to 300 houses were built each year from 1720 to 1750 and substantially more from mid-century on. Even so, housing remained scarce until the Revolution and the subsequent emigration created a supply greater than the demand.

The Cassandras could not carry out their plans to limit the growth of Paris.[31] By 1786, when the Farmers General built a 10-foot-high wall around the city to insure proper collection of indirect taxes, it was too late. Parisians strongly protested its construction which, by cutting off one part of the urban agglomeration from the other, interfered with their commercial activity and their supply of food and cheap wine.[32] Doggerel protest verse abounded:

> Pour augmenter son numéraire
> Et raccourcir notre horizon
> La Ferme a jugé nécessaire
> De nous mettre tous en prison.*

And better still, the celebrated pun: *"Le mur murant Paris rend Paris murmurant."***

By attempting to stop all growth, the royal adminstration missed the chance to develop the capital according to a centrally directed master plan. A few major public works projects were undertaken such as the place des Victoires about 1720, the Ecole militaire, the place Louis XV, the Madeleine, and the Church of Sainte Geneviève in the 1750s and 1760s. Monumental architecture flourished, but urban planning of any significance was totally absent. In the 10 years starting in 1772, one contemporary noted, a new city grew up between the Madeleine and Saint Lazare. Its development was totally anarchic. For lack of government action, there was no plan and no regulation of street layout nor of the size or height of buildings. The provision of open spaces, fountains, and markets had been totally neglected.[33] And so it was for every new district promoted by private investors rather than public authority—for example, the Duc de Choiseul in the district near the boulevards,

---

* To increase its coin
  And cut off our view
  The Farm has thought it necessary
  To put us all in prison
** "The wall walling Paris makes Paris a wailing wall."

the Comte d'Artois (the future Charles X) on the rue Royale, the banker De Laborde on the rues de Provence, d'Artois (now Laffitte), Taitbout, and du Houssaye, all three in the area known as the Chaussée d'Antin behind the present-day Opéra. In 1783, the Comte d'Angoulême in his capacity as grand prior of the Temple opened up a new quarter, which he modestly christened the Ville d'Angoulême. And these are only a few examples.[34]

‬ III ‭

For all the differences of class and status, occupation and wealth that divided them, there was a certain physical environment that all Parisians shared in common. To begin with, there was the river. Its aesthetic value aside, the Seine supplied Paris with most of the necessities of life: food to eat, wine and water to drink, wood for fuel, and stone and wood for building materials. Water transport, in general cheaper than shipment over land, especially for goods sold in bulk, was so common that Arthur Young found the roads leading to Paris "deserts, comparatively speaking, with those of London."[35] There were no fewer than 20 ports established along the banks of the river, each one specializing in the handling of certain commodities. In the east, the Port Saint Bernard received wine for the Halle aux vins, and the Port Saint Paul was the landing stage for fresh water fish. The Port de la Conférence dealt in stone from nearby quarries. Near the center of town, the Port de la Grève handled grain, coal, and wood, while opposite the Louvre, the Port Saint Nicolas enjoyed a mixed trade in soaps, oils, pepper, coffee, oranges, fish, wine, and liqueurs.[36] The Seine was also crowded with a multitude of flat boats on which washerwomen carried on their laundering. When the river froze over, as it often did, or flooded, as was more rarely the case, a most difficult situation was created. The miserable state of the roads made it impossible for wheeled transport to assume the entire burden of supplying the city, and some products, like wood, could only be shipped by water.[37] Historians have perhaps been overhasty in attributing *all* eighteenth-century supply crises to inadequate production or to a high rate of demographic growth. In the case of Paris, it seems that it was often not only a lack of goods, but also, and sometimes more significantly in the short run, the inadequate means of getting goods to market that lay at the heart of the difficulty.[38]

The streets in the city proper were maintained by the royal administration, while the boulevards and streets of the faubourgs were the responsibility of the municipality, which in turn taxed the residents. The streets were paved, but that is about all that could be said for them. The maze of culs-de-sac, alleys, and narrow passages hindered the creation of arterial roads capable of handling a heavy burden of traffic. In an east-west direction, there were the Champs-Elysées on the one end, and the rue du Faubourg Saint Antoine on the other, but as yet no rue de Rivoli to connect them. Running north to south the situation was somewhat better as the rue du Faubourg Saint Laurent-Saint Martin was continued on the Left Bank by the rue du Faubourg Saint Jacques, and the rue Saint Denis by the rue de la Harpe, but both were interrupted by the congestion of the Cité.[39]

Sidewalks were virtually unknown, except on a few bridges and along the newly constructed quais. In the 1780s, provision was made for them on some new streets then being laid out. The lack of sidewalks was a great inconvenience for pedestrians—that is to say, the laboring poor—because they continually ran the risk of being ridden down by a carriage passing at breakneck speed. One critic ventured to maintain that children could not go out on the streets alone to play and that the consequent lack of exercise contributed greatly to their early deaths.[40] The Dickensian image is manifestly exaggerated, but the observation is nonetheless basically true. Poor boys and girls had nowhere to play but the streets, and it seems that they were deprived of even this resource. In fact, there existed two classes of men, the *écrasans* and the *écrasés*, those who had carriages and those who did not.[41] And although the second category was not synonymous with the poor alone, it was they who felt the distinction that existed between those who rode and those who walked, in the sense that going on foot was for them a matter not of choice but of necessity. This distinction was re-enforced by the fact that Paris was essentially without mass public transportation in this period. The last attempt to establish a system toward the end of the seventeenth century was a failure. To be sure, a sedan chair or a carriage might be hired, but the expense was prohibitive. Even a place in a coach for the suburbs cost between 10 and 15 sous per league (2.2 miles), more than what three-quarters of the population could afford. Water transport was less expensive but still not cheap. One paid 7 sous in 1787 to go from the center of the city to Saint Cloud and proportionately less for the nearer suburbs along the Seine. The ferry across the river cost sixpence (one-half a sou), but there was always the alternative of making a detour in order to walk across one of the 14 bridges.[42]

Complaints about the filth of the streets came from the highly placed as well as from the people. A German visitor spoke of the foul-smelling gutters,[43] and Arthur Young wrote:

This great city appears in many respects the most ineligible and inconvenient for the residence of a person of small fortune of any that I have seen: . . . Walking, which in London is so pleasant and so clean, that ladies do it every day, is here a toil and a fatigue to a man, and an impossibility to a well dressed woman. The coaches are numerous, and what are much worse, there are an infinity of one-horse cabriolets, which are driven by young men of fortune and their imitators, alike fools, with such rapidity as to be real nuisances. . . . If young noblemen at London were to drive their chaises in streets without footways as their brethren do at Paris, they would speedily and justly be well thrashed, or rolled in the kennel.[44]

Three sorts of streets were distinguished in eighteenth-century Paris: the few avenues 42 to 60 feet wide, the ordinary streets measuring 18 to 30 feet, and the narrow winding backstreets and alleyways of 6 to 18 feet. It was not until 1783 that a royal edict fixed the minimum width of new streets at 30 feet and set the maximum height of stone houses at 60 feet in streets at least 30 feet wide, 48 feet in streets less than 30 feet wide, and 36 feet in the narrowest streets. Previous to that time, builders had often agreed among themselves not to put up stone houses taller than 50 to 60 feet and wooden houses taller than 48 feet, but there had been no way of legally enforcing the custom.[45] The narrowness of the streets and the height of the buildings combined to keep the sun from reaching the hovel of many a poor man, and doctors considered that to be one of the primary causes of poor health, particularly in the Cité and its environs, where so many of the most miserable unskilled workers lived—or existed. Menuret de Chambaud wrote in 1786:

The same room, often windowless, serves as shelter for 20 bootblacks or porters. It is in these dirty quarters, among the lower classes, that the inconveniences of humidity and the corruption of the air are greatest. The tendency to scurvy is universal in this city, but it is here that it is the basis of many chronic illnesses: it manifests itself in acute diseases and becomes the very principle of that malignant decomposing fever that is observed almost exclusively among this species of people who gather and pile on top of one another in great numbers in small hovels. . . . The sun and the winds scarcely penetrate there. . . . The pavement of these streets is always wet and muddy. The houses are humid and dark, all the inconveniences resulting from overcrowding are provoked and increased by their arrangement, their elevation, the smallness of the rooms, the multiplicity of households,

the great number of people, the establishment of markets, and of
workshops.[46]

Regular lighting of the streets of Paris began under the administration of the first lieutenant-general of police, La Reynie, in
1667. It was financed by a tax imposed on all householders and,
furthermore, until 1759 it was their duty to elect one of their
number to be the lamplighter. Needless to say, the burden generally fell on artisans and small shopkeepers, for the others used
their influence to shirk responsibility. A bourgeois who had the
bad fortune to be elected to the post normally hired a workman
to take his place.[47]
The light furnished came from candles set in lanterns attached
to the front of houses 14 feet above the ground, at intervals of
approximately 60 feet. That they were not placed in the middle of
the street limited their utility. They also were regularly blown
out by gusts of wind, and the burning candles spread a thick black
smoke that dirtied the lanterns to such an extent that, after a while,
the light hardly shone through. In short, the lanterns were clearly
inadequate, and visitors were still being advised, in 1727, not to
walk about at night without hiring a torchbearer to guide them.[48]
Improvements in street lighting were, however, made throughout
the century. By 1770, the only sort of lamps used were oil burning
and equipped with reflectors. They were hung 16 feet above the
middle of the street, out of range of lantern smashers, and at intervals of 180 feet. By 1789, the city and faubourgs counted 3,528
street lamps. (The only persons who complained of their introduction were the prostitutes who now had, in Hardy's words, a
little more difficulty "going shopping.")[49] If the light thus provided was nearly sufficient for the city's needs, there still remained
the question of when to use the lamps. They were lit only on
nights when there was inadequate moonlight, and they remained
burning only until 3 A.M., a particular disadvantage to the market
workers who moved provisions into the city during the early hours
of the morning. From June to September, no light at all was provided, and the bourgeois sometimes complained that this made it
difficult to enjoy a walk in the pleasant summer air.[50]

⋙ IV ⋘

Given the variety of population estimates in the eighteenth century, I will take as my starting point the assumption that Paris
contained at least 700,000 people and perhaps 50,000 more on the

eve of the Revolution, floating population included.[51] Of the total, some 7,000 families formed the *Tout Paris* or the high society, noble and bourgeois, whom Georges Lefebvre designated as the effective rulers of the old regime.[52] There were also 35,000 master artisans in the mid-1760s, a figure which we may take to have remained relatively stable in the last half century.[53]

What part of the population belonged to the laboring poor? On the basis of information found in marriage contracts, Furet estimates that in certain quarters, like the faubourg Saint Antoine, 56 percent of the contracting parties were salaried, to which we would add at least part of the 30 percent who married without contracts—in other words, about one-half of the total population.[54] Leon Cahen counted 100,000 salaried persons in his estimated population of 550,000 in 1750. If a substantial number of those 100,000 are counted as heads of families, then his estimate could be made to coincide with that offered by Furet.[55] The most recent and most convincing estimates have resulted from the investigations of George Rudé, and they seem to bear out what earlier authors have said.[56] Starting from Braesch's figure of 73,455 male workers in 1791, Professor Rudé shows that numerous categories of wage-earners were ignored in the questionnaire concerning assignats needed to pay salaries, which was the basis of Braesch's documentation. First among them, by definition, were the unemployed and the inmates of hospitals and other charitable institutions. Furthermore, no attention was paid to workers in the food industries, domestics, and the porters of the markets and the docks. On the assumption that 10 percent of the wage-earners were women and that 25 percent were unmarried men, the following figures come to light:

Of Braesch's estimated 73,455 workers:	
Male employed workers (including bachelors)	65,700
Female employed workers	7,300
Together with:	
Housewives	47,450
Unemployed children	94,900
To which should be added the supplementary categories:	
Food industries	10,000
Clothing and textile industries	6,500
Domestics	20,000
Market and dock workers	5,000
Sub-total of above, with families	94,000
Unemployed	32,000
In hospitals, hospices	14,000
Total	355,350

Only the number of domestics appears to be underestimated, perhaps by as much as 50 percent. This may, however, be due to the fact that Rudé is speaking of 1791, by which time many servants had fled with their emigrant masters or joined the ranks of the unemployed.

The laboring poor were unevenly distributed throughout the city. If we speak only of categories other than journeymen-artisans (that is, of those who most closely approximate the condition of a modern proletarian or lumpenproletarian) we find that true workers' districts were exceedingly rare. Only two areas really merit the name: the streets near the Seine around the Port au Bled (rues des Jardins and de la Mortellerie in the section de l'Hôtel de Ville) where river workers, porters, chimney sweeps, Auvergnats, and Savoyards congregated, and the old streets near the place Maubert, where migrant building workers were particularly numerous. On the other hand, if we speak of all wage-earners, we find them concentrated mainly in the north and center of the city. In the seven sections of Bonne Nouvelle, Beaubourg, Gravilliers, Ponceau, Mauconseil, Poissonnière and the faubourg Saint Denis, there were 21,884 wage-earners (Braesch's estimate) who, with their families, accounted for 65,000 persons in a population of 80,000 to 100,000. Similarly, the four sections of the Louvre, Oratoire, Marché des Innocents and Lombards contained 5,897 workers (18,000 with their families) in a total population of 36,000 to 45,000. Surprisingly enough, the percentage of wage-earners in the faubourgs Saint Antoine (4,519 = 13,000 of 35,000–40,000), and Saint Marcel (5,557 = 17,000 of 62,000–70,000) is somewhat smaller. Comparisons of this type are, in my view, misleading. The laboring poor, which I take to be the most useful category of social analysis in this regard, were not synonymous with wage-earners, but included also petty but independent merchants and even master artisans no longer functioning as such because they had fallen on evil days. For that reason, Braesch's figures as corrected by Rudé, although they are the closest approximations we have, do not tell the whole story.

Contemporary political arithmeticians were fond of simple calculations about the population of Paris. Thus, they would divide the number of inhabitants by the number of houses and come up with a number representing average density. Messance gave this figure as 24.5 (23,565 houses for a population of 576,630 in 1755), and we might make it 29.3 if we start with an estimate of 700,000.[57] The exercise seems, however, to be a complete waste of time for it in no way comes to terms with the reality of population distribution in the capital. One-half of the sections had a population density of 200 or more persons per acre, one-half less.[58] The extreme limits stood at 580 (Arcis) and 11 (Champs-Elysées), a ratio of 53:1. The center of the city was most crowded: 555 in the Halles, 444 in the Section of the Oratoire (Gardes-Françaises),[59] and 438 in the Section of the Lombards. A little further to the north, there were 388 in Mauconseil, 364 in Gravilliers, 360 in Bonne Nouvelle and Ponceau. As one moved away from the center to the west and south, the densities diminished significantly. The section de la Bibliothèque, the center of the financial bourgeoisie, had 147 inhabitants per acre, and the three sections of the faubourg Saint Germain had 86, 67, and 17 respectively. The section of the Tuileries was noted at 74 and the place Vendôme at 75, and the figure in the last case would have been even lower had the calculation applied only to the more bourgeois part of the section, south of the boulevards.[60] In the east, only the Panthéon had a dense population (320), while the three sections of the faubourgs Saint Marcel and Saint Victor had only 60, 35, and 32. Similarly in the faubourg Saint Antoine, the figures were 45, 27, and 17—very low indeed. The explanation of the low density of the popular faubourgs is that the measurement is based on total land area, and there was still much open space in these districts. If only the built-up area had been measured, the figures for the faubourgs would have been considerably higher, while those for the center of the city would have remained substantially the same.

In certain sections, densities differed greatly from street to street, in accordance with class division. In the faubourg Saint Marcel, the densities varied in the proportion of 1 to 12, but this once again may have been exceptional because of the fact that some streets were still virgin territory. Nonetheless, the Ile Saint Louis, which was entirely occupied, showed variations in density of 1 to 6, with the quais, the preserve of the nobility and the upper bourgeoisie of the robe, more favored than the interior streets inhabited by a mixture of working people and traders.[61] In the section of the Bibliothèque, the financiers had their mansions in the rues Louis le Grand, Vivienne, Notre Dame des Victoires and Sainte-Anne, but the approximately 20 percent of the population designated by Braesch as workers mixed with the other classes and lived in the same houses but on the upper floors in the immediate company of apprentices and domestics. It is difficult to say if this practice had any significant effect on the patterns of density.[62] In a few areas, like the Section de l'Homme Armé, the population was either so homogeneous (in this case, preponderantly small artisans) or so equitably distributed that no variation in density by street is to be observed.[63]

There is a general, but not an absolute, correlation between high population density and poverty. In the same way, there were quarters which were predominantly popular, although none was exclusively the preserve of the laboring poor. The north and north central sections were the loci of most intense misery together with the faubourg Saint Marcel, "that seat of obscure poverty" that gave birth to so many rebellions. The faubourg Saint Antoine and the neighboring parishes probably had a slightly higher standard because of the presence of a greater number of master artisans. The further one went to the west, from the Ile Saint Louis through the Latin Quarter to the faubourg Saint Germain on the Left Bank, from the Palais Royal and the rue Saint Honoré to the place des Victoires and the Champs-Elysées on the Right Bank, the more the city took on a monumental aspect and the tone of the *classes aisées*.

❧ V ☙

Paris was a relatively well-policed city. Administration was, however, troubled by a network of overlapping jurisdictions: the Crown (both the Contrôle-général and the Maison du Roi, in which there was a minister responsible for the affairs of the capital), the Parlement, the Bureau des Finances, the seigneurial courts of the princely *apanages*, the great abbeys and royal establishments, and the Bureau de la Ville and its executive arm, the Conseil Particulier de la Ville, formed in 1767, which made decisions on municipal expenditures and other financial matters but was always and increasingly subject to royal control. The Bureau also claimed jurisdiction over the navigation of the Seine and everything related to it, that is, the supply of Paris by water and the activities of the persons engaged in the trade, as well as over the city guard.[64]

In practice, the most powerful figure in the day-to-day administration of the city was the lieutenant-general of police, a royal appointee whose office had been created in 1667 and whose powers were considerably extended throughout the eighteenth century. Assisted by 48 *commissaires du Châtelet* and 20 police inspectors who purchased their offices, he had charge of all manner of things. First, there was what was termed *la police générale*: the supply of the city with foodstuffs and other necessities, the lighting and cleaning of the streets, the regulation of printers, pedlars, nurses, hospitals, fairs, the prevention and extinction of fires, the care of prisoners taken by the police, and the supervision of the tax farmers; second, the control of the guilds and of the police court (Châtelet) with all that it implied; third, the execution of the king's orders and the administration of the prisons; fourth, surveillance over trade and manufactures, brokers, lotteries, and the stock exchange, and the hunting down of proscribed merchandise; and fifth, the responsibility for the security of the population, watching over hotels and rented rooms, and making certain that foreigners were not engaging in illicit or injurious practices.[65] Mercier was correct to call the job "terrible and difficult" because its essential purpose was to "contain so many men consigned to want while they see others swimming in abundance."[66]

To carry out the services required of him, the lieutenant-general of police could call on his armed force: the *guet* (1 5o men) and the *garde* (approximately 1,000 men). The former patrolled the city gates and ramparts, while the latter were stationed in groups of 12 throughout the city. As they served on alternate days, one-half of the total manpower was available at any given moment. They made the rounds of their districts in groups of six, while six others remained at their station in case of need. In this way, they relayed each other every two hours through the night. Five-man cavalry patrols also rode about in the small hours. In case of serious trouble, a regiment of French guards and two companies of Swiss guards could be called upon to restore order. They made up a force of perhaps 5,000 men.[67] There were also the *sergents* and *exempts de police* (constables) who made arrests and broadcast royal ordinances. The *Maréchaussée* was controlled by the prévôt de l'Ile and functioned primarily in the suburbs. Only one of its eight brigades of the Generality of Paris (17 men) was resident in the city. All the policemen were assisted by a large number of informers called *mouches*, members of the lowest order of the manhunting trade. All in all, the surveillance exercised by the police over every aspect of life was extraordinarily great.[68]

The reputation of the police was not a happy one. They were criticized from all sides. The bourgeois charged that they neglected their duty, scarcely deigned to deal with vagabonds and thieves, and were "rude and brutal" to persons soliciting their aid.[69] It was the last point that really rankled, and at least two assemblies of the third estate took the trouble in 1789 to include demands in their cahiers calling for the reform of the police. The district des Barnabites asked that both officers and soldiers be held responsible in law for any deaths they caused, and the district des Théâtins demanded that "the policing of the City of Paris be henceforth carried out with the greatest exactitude, not that insidious policing which, seeking out only the guilty, is always ready to infringe on the freedom of citizens, but one which protects them, which insures them the peace and tranquility they ought to enjoy."[70]

Popular dislike for the police was never more clearly shown than in the tendency to believe anything and everything that might be said of them, to which several instances of suspected kidnapping bear witness. In April, 1720, there had been two days of rioting in response to the abuse of royal orders to pick up vagabonds and beggars for shipment to the colonies, which had resulted in the arrest of innocent persons. In 1769, the police had to ask the vicars of Paris to calm their flocks who were once again convinced that their children's lives were in imminent danger.[71] But the most spectacular and dangerous of these episodes took place in May, 1750. Before it was over, 15 to 20 people had died in the rioting, and 3 persons had been hanged for taking part in it.

First of all, it ought to be made clear that there was a basis in fact for the charge of kidnapping. Berryer, the then lieutenant-general of police and cordially hated by the *menu peuple* for his harshness, ordered his agents in March to arrest "vagabonds, libertines, and vagrants who play ball and cards, and who throw stones at street lamps." The constables were paid 12 sous per arrest. Most of those picked up were young boys and men aged 13 to 25, both apprentices and unskilled workers, and some were the sons of master artisans. It is impossible to determine whether the police made a series of honest mistakes or were, as many witnesses in the subsequent inquiry testified, trying to extort money from parents who went to the prisons to claim their offspring. Be that as it may, it soon became evident to the *menu peuple* that their children were not safe from arrest—and for no good reason. To this evidence, they added the suspicion that the victims would be (1) shipped to the colonies, (2) emptied of their blood for the care of a sick princess, or (3) suffer torments unknown. The result was first protest and then riot.[72]

As early as May 1, 1750, there had been a small skirmish in the St. Denis quarter. But it was not until two weeks later, on Saturday, May 16, that matters came to a head. At the Port Saint Paul, on the rues Geoffroy Lasnier and Nonnains d'Hyères, a crowd led by a certain Lebeau, a coal heaver, roughed up one Labbé, a clerk of the *domaine*. Labbé had been seen in conversation with a young girl, the daughter of a local upholsterer, and her mother had been told that he was a child thief. The force of rumor was in this way unleashed. The next day, Sunday, there were incidents at the

Porcherons, where two bourgeois were attacked on the same grounds. After a four-day hiatus, trouble broke out once again on the following Friday, this time in several places at once: in the rue du Gros Chenet of the faubourg Saint Denis, at the Croix Rouge of the faubourg Saint Germain, and at the house of the Commissaire Delafosse on the rue de la Calandre near the Pont Neuf. In each case, the crowd wanted to get hold of a suspected kidnapper. On Saturday, May 23, the crowd caught up with Labbé, dragged him from under a bed in the rue Saint Honoré and murdered him. The Parlement now took a hand in the affair and ordered an investigation. The popularity enjoyed by the magistrates enabled them to calm the people.[73]

Until the murder took place, the authorities seemed to have reacted to the rioting in a very mild way. After all, "it was common," as one observer noted, "for the people of Paris to attribute to the police much more than they actually did, and to make a mountain out of a molehill."[74] The protest would run its course, and things would then return to normal. The prediction was correct, for the people who participated in the riot were incapable of acting politically. They could not threaten the stability of the regime, nor had they any desire to do so. All they wished to do was to take out their accumulated frustrations on someone, and the police had made themselves a convenient target. For example, a bookseller on the Pont Saint Michel who had been forbidden by them to ply his trade was seen to be one of the persons most active in urging the crowd to attack Commissaire Delafosse's house. To be sure, the issue at hand, the kidnapping of children, was such as to excite the *menu peuple* to an even greater extent than did a shortage of bread. Barbier, good bourgeois that he was, found it normal that they should react in this way and even sympathized with their anger at the hanging of three persons convicted of being ringleaders. The executions, he thought, were not the sort that would bring disgrace to the families of the condemned.[75]

There was a definite, if limited, social content to the riots, and it was made manifest by the way the participants identified one another. To the party of order, the rioters were *gens du plus bas peuple*, while the rioters tended to attack any person carrying a sword or otherwise "looking like a bourgeois," by which they meant anyone who was not of their own status. In fact, the participants were a mixed bag, not all the lowest of the low. Apprentices and journeymen were involved alongside street merchants, shoeshine boys, watercarriers, coal heavers, militia men (one of whom was a coachman in civilian life), and beggars. Many women took part and distinguished themselves by their passion and hardness of heart.[76] It was a motley crew, representative of all the sections of the laboring poor. As yet the only idea they had in their collective head was to set right a single glaring abuse, a feeling not entirely separable from a strong desire for revenge.

[2]

THE LABORING POOR

⋥ I ⋤

I do not think there can be a Hell upon earth more terrible than to be poor at *Paris*, to see oneself continually in the center of all Pleasures, without the power to taste any of them.—Amidst all this great Plenty, are seen an infinite Number of miserable Objects, who beg in a Tone, as if they sung; They seem frozen with Cold in the Winter; and in the Spring, they present you with Flowers, to obtain your compassion.[1]

The poor in a state are like shadows in a picture; they create a necessary contrast, which humanity sometimes bemoans, but which does honor to the intentions of providence. No doubt it was ambition, vanity and the eccentricity of men which created the distressing distinction found among them: but it is wisdom that maintains it. It is therefore necessary that there be poor people; but there must not be *misérables*. The latter only exist to the shame of humanity, while the former, on the contrary, are part of the order of political economy. Through them, abundance reigns in the cities, all conveniences are found there, the arts flourish, etc.[2]

"The poor ye shall always have with you." But who are they? It is clear that in the second passage Philippe Hecquet, a doctor and moralist, was not referring to a group of people distinguished only by their chronic lack of money. Rather, the poor are all those who are obliged to work in order to make a living. In a well ordered society, the poor ought to be able to survive, provided only that they be industrious. However precarious their conditions of life and labor, they ought not to be allowed to become *misérables*, perpetually without means of support because unintegrated into the social organism. The role of charity was to prevent this from happening, not only because the *misérables* might be dangerous, but because they were a mortal stigma upon the society that permitted them to exist. Only the idle poor, those who would not work and showed (inevitably) a tendency to debauchery and immorality, were to be punished by the workhouse and prison. Eighteenth-century moralists believed it proper that the poor should sweat all day for a single loaf of bread but improper that they should be tempted by need or their evil propensities to steal that same loaf. A precapitalist Christian paternalism still permeated their thought and made the kind of exploitation—or would they have said disintegration?—typical of nineteenth-century capitalist industrialism inconceivable to them.[3]

The distinction between the laboring poor and the *misérables* was not so clear-cut in the realities of eighteenth-century Paris. Workingmen and women did, for the most part, live in abject poverty, and when there was no market for their labor or the products of their labor, few alternate means of getting a living were open to them. They could leave the city, beg, or turn to crime. They suffered, mainly in silence, and they knew what it was to live with the constant fear of indigence. They were not proletarians in the modern sense, for some of them were self-employed (street merchants), others operated as independent contractors (porters and carriers of various descriptions), while still others worked for a wage but were not totally separated from ownership of the means of production nor subject to the exigencies of the developed capitalist market place (journeymen). Who the members of this highly disparate group were and what role they played in Paris in the half century before the Revolution is our task here to determine.

For our purposes, it will be assumed that master artisans, or at least master artisans who effectively functioned as such by running their own enterprises and employing labor, even in small quantities, did not belong to the laboring poor. Their status in the eyes of the community, the power they exercised in the guilds, and the relative potential for upward mobility that they enjoyed were three essential points that distinguished them from their journeymen, who stood immediately below them on the social ladder. The differences did not preclude cooperation of the two groups on trade or political matters. In all these questions of stratification, shadings of one group into another were often imperceptible, the more so when mobility was, at least in principle, built into the system, as in the guilds. If there were as yet no real barriers of class between master and not-yet-master artisans, they were nonetheless engaged in a master-servant relationship that by definition made equality impossible and justifies our treatment of them as separate groups.

This was certainly the point of view shared by contemporaries. The anonymous author of a police report of 1709 listed the members of Parisian society in the usual order: nobility of the robe and sword, the old and rich financial and commercial bourgeoisie, the members of the liberal professions, the great merchant guilds of the Six Corps, retail merchants, and master artisans. Only then did he add the following:

Finally . . . there are port workers, industrial workers, the journeymen joiners, carpenters, plasterers, masons, locksmiths, tanners, bookbinders, parchment makers, tailors, tinsmiths; in a word, of all estates and professions, laborers, to whom must be added the Auvergnats, the Savoyards, the watercarriers, coal heavers, butchers.

There are, moreover, lackeys, grooms, pages, domestics, runners, servants, huntsmen, guards, kennelmen, stablemen, ostlers, apprentices, bakers' boys; surveillance of them must be active, for, led astray by the examples set them by their masters, these unfortunates often end up on the scaffold, the wheel, or at the stake, and lucky they are, when the outcome takes them only to the galleys.

The slime of Paris, despite its blackness and infection, contains nothing as infamous as the race of men called crooks, cheats, Greeks, Egyptians, astrologers, fortune tellers, English. All this pack of rabble gets up in the morning not knowing where or what they will eat, where they will warm themselves or sleep. They live only on swindles, thefts, rapine and wrong doing; they kill, burn, rape or poison for their own account or for others; happy with an *écu* or asking their weight in gold to commit a crime, in accordance with the state of their purse, whether it be empty or full, and their appetite more or less strong.

Such are . . . the different classes of which Parisian society is composed. One must add the whores, public or hidden, all devoured by evil and vice; they live with thieves whom they support most of the time with the fruit of their debauchery, and who *blackmail* them, a slang term, that is, who force them to give them money, when these creatures refuse to do so.[4]

The laboring poor, in this view, were made up of at least three principal groups. The eighteenth century knew them as *ouvriers*, *manoeuvriers* and domestics, who, according to the Lieutenant-general of Police Lenoir, together made up more than two-thirds of the population of the capital on the eve of the Revolution.[5] The word *ouvrier* implied a skilled laborer and in particular one who worked within a guild structure, either as a journeyman or an apprentice. *Manoeuvrier* designated a semiskilled or unskilled worker—"les hommes de peine et de main"—like the bargemen, longshoremen, coal heavers and market workers. Their occupations were mainly free, not incorporated into guilds, although some of them were directly regulated by the police of the General Farm. This group included the Auvergnats and Savoyards, generic names for men and boys who shined shoes, ran errands and in general were jacks of all the unskilled trades. The real Auvergnats, Savoyards, Normans, and Limousins formed so many regional subgroups of the whole.[6] The domestics were also present in bewildering variety—cooks, butlers, chambermaids, lackeys, grooms —all arranged in a hierarchy of their own.

To this classification we ought to add a fourth group, the ubiquitous street merchants who sold everything from old hardware to lemonade, anything, in fact, for which there was a market. Besides the respectable, if humble, orange sellers, fishwives, and ragpickers, this category included the less respectable habitués of the Pont Neuf and other ill-famed quarters, the fortunetellers and the quacks and charlatans who sold balms and unguents guaranteed to be good for what ails you.[7] They sold products like *orviétan*, a mixture of roots, leaves, plant seeds, clay, honey, and theriac, so called for its having been invented in Orvieto in the sixteenth century. It was supposed to be a sovereign remedy for the plague and various contagious diseases. Although it went out of large-scale popular use on the eve of the Revolution, it was still sometimes hawked on the streets in the nineteenth century.[8]

Finally, at the bottom of the ladder stood the beggars and criminals, both professional and amateur, whose personnel was recruited largely, if not exclusively, from the ranks of the laboring poor.

⋘ I I ⋙

The distinction has to be drawn between the domiciled poor and the floating population, between those who were truly Parisian, either by birthright or through prolonged residence, and those who used Paris as a place to make a living only, staying there for longer or shorter periods and maintaining strong ties to their places of origin. The floaters were more likely to be found among the *manoeuvriers*, street merchants, and domestics than among guild artisans. This was so, first, because the latter's training demanded that they stay in one place for a number of years and, second, the exercise of their professions were commonly supposed to take place in the city where they were trained, although Parisian artisans did enjoy the special privilege of being permitted to work in other places. Finally, membership in the guild tended to anchor the artisan in his situation and to protect him against misfortune in a way for which the worker outside the system could not hope. The journeyman might suffer low wages and still lower mobility, but he did not normally, once his *tour de France* was over, take to the road.

We know about this floating population from several sources. One has only to thumb through the bundles of the Y series in the Archives Nationales to examine the interrogations of persons accused of diverse crimes in order to get some idea of its extent. Immediately, one is struck by the constantly repeated question concerning the place of origin of the accused and the length of his stay in Paris. The answers given show that internal migration toward Paris was most common and that the majority of the respondents had passed through the capital once or twice before settling there definitively, if settle they did. It is thus evident that immigrants often came to Paris without any fixed idea of staying there permanently. They seem to have come to Paris to try their luck, ready, if need be, to return home temporarily or once and for all. So long as they remained in the city, they formed separate groups distinguished by their patois (many did not speak French[9]), their habits, perhaps also by their dress, and certainly by their occupations. The Auvergnat was often a water carrier or chimney sweep, the Limousin a mason, the Lyonnais a porter or chair carrier, the Norman a stonecutter, paver or thread seller. The tie between each provincial group and a given occupation was so strong that we find neologisms created that identify one with the other, as in the case of the Savoyard, already cited. Prejudices grew up about the special features of character of the migrants. Burgundians were said to have no conscience, men of Champagne to be arrogant, Limousins to be easily excitable.[10] All this was yet another factor in hindering the development of a unitary class consciousness among the laboring poor.

There is evidently no means of knowing how many floaters lived in Paris at any given time. Census reports are nonexistent and the tax rolls have disappeared. The repeated attempts in the old regime to force innkeepers and others who rented rooms to keep records of the names, qualities, places of origin, and even the nature of business of travelers failed more often than not.[11] Under the circumstances, the best we can do is to make an educated guess on the basis of certain discrepancies that exist in contemporary estimates of population.

At the beginning of the eighteenth century, Saugrain guessed (it is the only suitable word, since he does not inform us of his procedures) that there were about 700,000 Parisians. Later, Messance multiplied the average number of births (in reality baptisms, 20,020 for the years 1771–1780) by 30 and concluded that there were 600,600 residents of the city.[12] Necker raised the figure to 660,000, and La Michodière fixed it at 670,692.[13] Even Expilly, the most conscientious of observers, is incapable of supplying an exact number. He tells us that the use of the coefficient 30 indicates a population of 576,639 in 1768, but he recognizes elsewhere that the most common estimates by parish suggest that 661,200 is closer to the truth.[14] The officially recorded number of baptisms per annum (1781–1783) averaged out to 19,679, or 593,070 when multiplied by 30.[15] And to complete the survey: of 26 contemporary authorities, one thought the population was 500,000, 8 opted for 560,000–700,000, 8 suggested 700,000–800,000, 2 stood firm at 900,-000, and 7 said one million.[16] So far, historians have been content, for lack of more precise information, to estimate the population of Paris on the eve of the Revolution at between 550,000 and 700,000.[17]

But can one ignore the other observers, a majority, who believed this estimate to be too low? Is it not just as valid to suppose that they had in mind the very people who would not be taken into account by the process of multiplying the birth totals by a fixed coefficient, precisely because they were geographically mobile? If this is true, we can assume the presence in the city of a group of some 100,000 or more persons representing the floating poor, certainly not a negligible part of the *classes inférieures*. This figure coincides with contemporary estimates of the number of persons "lodged in furnished rooms, foreigners or not, counted as foreigners and not subject to the capitation tax."[18]

"Paris . . . is the refuge of a quantity of *honnêtes gens*, and at the same time of a quantity of *misérables* who come from all parts of the realm to settle there and to seek employment or work, but not all of them can succeed."[19] They worked as agricultural laborers, in the building trades, as pedlars and street workers, and as petty artisans: tinkers, shoemakers, and lanternmakers, to cite only a few examples. Young girls between the ages of 10 and 20 came to town to work as domestics for persons of the same provincial origin, but relatively few adult women were to be found in the ranks of migrant labor.[20] All were moved by the need to supplement the income they drew from the land. For some of the younger men, an additional motive was the desire to avoid being present at the annual drawing for the militia, convinced as they were (wrongly) that temporary emigration would excuse them from service.[21]

Migrants came to Paris at all seasons of the year, but mainly at times when their attention to agriculture was not required. Auvergnats of the wine-growing country were less free to move about than their fellows of the mountainous districts of the same province, where agricultural work was more or less at a standstill from November to March.[22] Conversely, the masons, stonecutters and carpenters from La Marche left their homes in the good season between the early spring and the approach of winter, which meant, presumably, that a good deal of the agricultural work was done by their wives and children.[23] Seasonal migration was often the beginning of a process of uprooting which sooner or later, in how many cases we do not know, made the wanderer into a permanent migrant. This was as true for the Limousins and Auvergnats, who "come back each year to the same place like swallows," as for the Alsatians and Lorrainers who "come every year to cultivate the marshes in the environs of Paris."[24] On the other hand, at least some of them eventually returned to their native grounds, like the water carriers who "after 20 tiring and thrifty years return, with a small capital, to the bosom of their family."[25]

In general, migrants arrived in the city from areas relatively nearby and of easy access. In every survey of migrant labor carried out for the last years of the old regime and the Revolution that I know of, the pattern is always the same. Normandy, the north and the east, together with the Parisian region itself, account for a majority of the individuals concerned. Large contingents also come from the center (Auvergne, Haute-Vienne, Creuse, La Marche, Vienne) and Savoie, areas of high birth rates and limited agricultural resources.[26] The part of Paris in which they chose to settle was often determined by the availability of work, but there is some evidence to suggest that they took lodgings in the district where they first entered the city—migrants from Orleans and other localities south of Paris in the faubourg Saint Marcel, for example.[27]

The illnesses and accidents to which migrant workers were subject in the course of their travels made many commentators denounce seasonal migration as a great evil. But worse still, in their eyes, was the threat to the maintenance of the agricultural population, the moral and economic backbone of the realm.[28] Their economic fear was that there would soon no longer be enough people on the land to cultivate it properly. Their moral sensibilities were strained by the prospect of the eternally seductive city destroying respect for parents, the family, and, hence, the entire authority structure. Together, the twin results of prolonged urban residence would be responsible for the decline and fall of France.[29]

Most of the urban moralists who spilled enormous amounts of ink in dealing with these themes of the bucolic countryside and the noble (if not entirely savage) peasantry probably would not have known how to distinguish a stalk of wheat from one of rye. Still, they were not completely wrong in their prognoses. Their moral science was better than their economics, for in the latter their perspective was a static one, while in the former, they fully allowed for, indeed expected, change. And that was what they feared, at least when they were not in charge of it. The removal of men from their traditional cadres could lead to the development of a whole range of anomic, and therefore dangerous, behavior. Geographical mobility only expedited the process in a most dramatic way. Even before the countryside could feel the effect of the migrants' change of attitude, the city would suffer, delivered up to the assaults of men without masters. Fear of the uprooted, of the unintegrated mass of floaters, was as great in the eighteenth century as it was in the period 1815–1848, analyzed by Louis Chevalier. In the words of one publicist:

Who are the agents of these public calamities [assemblies, riots, seditions]? They are always men whose names and addresses are unknown; they are individuals who seem to be strangers in the very city that furnishes them means of survival; beings who live only for the moment, and who disappear as easily as they had appeared; men who hold to nothing, who have no property, and who flee with the speed of lightning, to escape from the pursuit of justice. . . . Night, which ordinarily covers with its veil their entry into the capital, favors their escape; and it is thus that an immense proportion of the men who make up the population of Paris live there anonymously and can at any moment spread alarm through the city by infringing on the public safety and the security of the citizens.[30]

ᦟ III ᦟ

The major distinction between the apprentice and journeyman in the guilds, on the one hand, and nonincorporated workers on the other, was twofold. First, the guildsmen were subject to the paternal discipline of their masters. Second, they could, in principle, hope to become masters themselves one day.[31]

In a society whose entire concept of order was based not on any notion of consent but rather on the authority emanating from a natural and organic chain of being, the idea of each person having someone to watch over him was of paramount importance. As the king watched over his people and the father, his family, so the master artisan controlled his workers, to whom he stood *in loco parentis* "in regard to his person only and not his goods."[32] A man who had no master, especially one who was far from home and thus free from paternal control, was subject to the gravest suspicion.

From the moment a child was bound as an apprentice, at an age that varied from 13 to 18 or thereabouts, certain duties were imposed on him. He had to promote his master's interests in every way possible, conduct himself honestly and morally, and, above all, apply his labor to any task that might be set, provided only that it did not contravene the laws of God and the state. If he was ordered to do something he thought to be injurious to his master's interest, he might protest, but he was expected to do the deed unless the order was rescinded.[33]

The apprenticeship contract imposed mutual obligations on the signatories. If the apprentice could not leave his employment at will, neither could his master send him away without sufficient cause as determined by the local police judge.[34] The master still had the upper hand, but this regulation is symptomatic of the fact that society and the law conceived of the relationship between the master and his apprentice as reaching beyond the purely economic. The typical formula of indenture made this clear:

François Vigneron, a mason's helper, binds himself to serve Louis Fauchez, a master wheelwright, for a period of two years. He promises "not to absent himself from the said Mr. Fauchez's home during the said two years and not to go to work elsewhere, to learn everything that he will teach him, to obey him in all things honest and licit that he will order him to do, to seek his profit, avoid his loss and to warn him if he should have knowledge of such loss." In return, Vigneron is to receive lodgings, light, and 20 sous a day, in addition to instruction in his master's trade.[35]

Or another, even more explicit, example:

Philippine Angélique Bonne Desgois is apprenticed to Marie Anne de France, a seamstress and mercer, who promises for a period of six years "to show her the trade of seamstress and all other things she does, without hiding anything from her, to treat her humanely, to give her food, lodgings, heat, and light, and to pay for her laundry; in particular, to teach her religion and to send her to religious instruction so that she may be able to take first communion."[36]

The apprentice lived in the master's house, most often ate at the master's table, and functioned as a member of the master's family, with all that that implied for the formation of a dependency syndrome. It was probably more important that the apprentice be assiduous and obedient than that he be bright or do his work well.[37] The exchange of money between apprentice (or his patron) and master, always subject to negotiation, was of distinctly secondary importance and was most often intended to indemnify the master for trouble taken should the youngster fail to finish out his term.

The term of apprenticeship normally varied from three to six years. The cost of the *brevet d'apprentissage* was low, rarely exceeding 50 livres. A journeyman worked for two to five years before becoming eligible to present his masterpiece and to obtain mastership, provided also that he could pay the high admission costs. In 1760, these ran from 200 livres (gardeners, china and glassmakers), 300 livres (tanners, potters), to the 600–800-livre range (embroiderers, bookbinders, wine merchants, papermakers, cutlers) and upwards to milliners and goldsmiths at 1,200 livres, masons and carpenters at 1,400, and drapers, who stood at the head of the Six Corps, at 2,500 livres.[38] These were enormous sums and must have effectively excluded many a candidate from the masters' ranks. The theoretically easy progression from journeyman to master was made still more difficult by the tendency of many guilds to favor sons of masters by requiring less of them than of an outsider in the way of apprenticeship and the production of a masterpiece. In addition, many guilds restricted the number of apprentices a master might have at a given time so as to keep the trade in the hands of a limited number of families.[39] Numerous otherwise qualified persons were in this manner prevented from becoming masters and were forced to remain journeymen throughout their working lives. They stayed on as wage-earners in their masters' shops after their time was out, or they set up more or less clandestinely in their own homes working as small contractors directly for merchants or the public at large. In the printing trades the system was formalized by the replacement, increasingly common in the eighteenth century, of apprentices by *alloués*. The latter resembled the former in every way, except one, which, from the point of view of social mobility, was the most crucial: they specifically waived the right to become masters.[40]

Whether as eternal journeymen or *chambrelans*, the poverty of these workers was likely to be extreme and their mobility nil, a condition they may have resented even more intensely than did their brothers outside the guilds, for they had been promised advancement that was not forthcoming. There is no evidence that Turgot's short-lived reform of 1776 or the subsequent reformation of the guilds did anything to alter the situation.[41] The *chambrelans* were, furthermore, subject to constant harassment by the masters, who wanted to escape their competition. Whenever guild statutes made mention of them, it was to prohibit masters from giving them work. And in 1789, the master wigmakers included in their *cahier* a demand that all landlords be forbidden to give shelter to "worker *chambrelans* who take all their work away from the masters and who, by reducing them to unemployment, make it impossible for them to live and to pay their taxes, under penalty of a 3,000-livre fine for the offenders."[42]

Journeymen, at least those among them who worked more or less steadily and who hoped for advancement to mastership, were known for their conservatism, that is, their attachment to the guild system.[43] Even during, and for years after, the Revolution, when the guilds had been totally abolished, there would be an occasional recrudescence of this sentiment among workingmen in reaction to the first advances of industrial capitalism and the consequent development of alienated labor in the full sense of the term. Men who had been used to the complex relationships and familial atmosphere of the workshop were not so easily convinced to sink or swim in the icy waters of the cash nexus.[44] But in the course of the eighteenth century, before anyone could know what the future held in store and as the dysfunctional nature of the guilds became ever more apparent, some of the junior members began to have doubts about their viability. When Turgot's reform went into effect in 1776, journeymen bakers, roofers, watchmakers, and others celebrated their liberation by dancing in the streets. For Hardy, it was a scandal that could only be explained by the machinations of Jews and Protestants, now free to practice their several trades. Right-thinking people, he said, knew that this change could only bring about "disorder and general confusion," for proof of which he cited fights that had broken out between masters and journeymen in the faubourg Saint Honoré. Soldiers of the *gardes françaises* had been called in because the police had been unable to handle the situation, and numerous "rebels" had been imprisoned.[45] The joyous reaction of the journeymen is easy to understand when we remember the discipline to which they were bound and from which they now expected to be set free. Among the wigmakers, for example, any workers *"vaquans et non-placés"* could be arrested by the syndics of the guild. And in the furniture trade, even the so-called privileged artisans who could ply their trade freely because they lived in places like the faubourg Saint Antoine where the guild's writ did not run, were subject to inspection.[46]

So much has been written in recent years about the sans-culottes, and so much emphasis has been laid on their tendency to identify themselves, before and during the Revolution, as consumers rather than producers that we have quite lost sight of the fact that certain of their constituent elements in individual industries did band together from time to time to defend their common interests. It could be argued that in the period prior to the Industrial Revolution, the only consciousness available to the urban poor, the only element that could bind them all together, had to be based on their nonproductive roles, but these conditions did not preclude the emergence of group consciousness among smaller sets of producers. Perhaps there was not yet any concrete assertion of the dignity of labor, certainly there was no conscious separation of men into categories based on their relationship to the means of production, but workingmen did assert themselves to demand higher wages and improved working conditions in an *ad hoc* manner and sometimes on a more durable basis.

The tradition of militant defense of corporate interests by journeymen was centered in the *compagnonnages*, which existed in some 27 trades at the end of the old regime. They were mutual-aid societies whose chief purpose was to provide help for members on the *Tour de France*. Organized into three rival associations (Les Enfants du Père Soubise, Les Enfants du Maitre Jacques, and Les Enfants de Salomon), they spent as much time fighting one another as in finding work for their members or in negotiating with the masters. Their operations were secret and overlaid with heavy amounts of ritual intended to bind them together and to insure security.[47] The *compagnonnages* do not seem to have been particularly important in Paris, although the authorities exhibited fear and disapproval of their potential activities by forbidding them—and for that matter, any organization of workingmen, to exist.[48]

Strikes were frequent throughout the second half of the century. They were usually of short duration, and the government and the courts did all in their power to break them.[49] Nonetheless, the strikers sometimes won the day. In 1756, gauze workers struck for a wage increase and forced nonstrikers to make contributions to a strike fund.[50] Twenty years later, in 1776, the journeymen bookbinders demanded a reduction of hours to 14 a day instead of the 16 "they have been in the constant habit of working since time immemorial."[51] Hardy, who was a bookseller directly affected by their action, expressed the bourgeois reaction: punish the ringleaders and wait for the others to run out of food. They would eventually return to work "as hunger almost always chases the wolf from the woods."[52] In July, 1785, there was a one-day strike of masons, stonecutters, and their laborer-assistants against a two-penny per day pay cut set by the Chambre Royale des Bâtiments. They quit work and went in a group of 700- to 800-strong to protest to Lenoir, the lieutenant-general of police. Two or three hundred also demonstrated in front of the Château of Brunoy where the king was staying. On the following day, the Parlement declared the offending order null and void, and the strikers returned to work immediately.[53]

Demands of this nature were not limited to journeymen. The unincorporated and unskilled workers sometimes—more rarely—were able to make their strength felt. In October, 1785, workers concerned with the shipment of firewood in the Port of Sens and all along the Seine, Yonne, Marne, Oise and Aisne Rivers demanded an increase in pay for loading wood from 6–9 sous to 10–12 sous per cord. They chose their moment well, for there was then a shortage of labor and winter was about to begin. But all they got for their trouble was the threat of imprisonment and corporal punishment as disturbers of the public peace.[54]

On December 28, 1785, the government inaugurated in Paris a privileged company for the carriage of parcels. This gravely prejudiced the interests of the messengers and street workers who usually undertook distributions of this kind. It was the worst possible time of year for this to happen, for employment was short, and the seasonal migrants and other *gagne-deniers* were suffering from the cold. They had difficulty getting jobs with the new company, which demanded that they post a bond of 150 livres and pay 2 sous a day for their uniforms. They were the victims of what amounted to a lockout, and they struck back at their enemies. On January 2, 1786, company drivers were attacked in the rue Gallande, necessitating the intervention of the city guard. The attackers were arrested and taken to a commissaire's house in the rue des Noyers to be charged. A crowd of *menu peuple* from the faubourgs Saint Marcel and Saint Antoine soon gathered there and threatened to break down the doors to release the prisoners. Five more arrests were made. On January 11, a crowd of 700 to 800 persons marched on Versailles to petition the king (who was not there). A substantial number reached their destination despite a massive deployment of police along the route. Two persons were sentenced to the pillory and nine years' banishment from Paris. Despite public sympathy for the demonstrators and a collection of 236 livres taken up in their behalf, they obtained no satisfaction.[55]

Numerous incidents involving journeymen carpenters, blacksmiths, and masons and other building workers in 1786 and 1787 seem to indicate a great willingness on the part of workingmen to take risks in order to defend their rights.[56] Restif de la Bretonne, to whom popular unrest was little short of treason, explained: "In recent times, the workers of the capital have become unmanageable because they have read in our books a truth too strong for them, that the worker is a precious man."[57] Taken literally, this analysis sounds like the purest Taine: the contagion spread among the lower classes by the intellectuals. But another interpretation is more suggestive. The laboring poor, and not last among them the journeymen building workers involved in these outbreaks, had a long history of professional self-consciousness. As early as 1725, we find them composing protest songs against their bosses:

> Tout ce qui me chagrine
> C'est que les maîtres-macons
> Ont toute la farine,
> Nous n'avons que le son,
> Et souvent rien du tout,
> Voila ce qui me fâche;
> N'est-ce pas avec raison
> Que le proverbe dit sans façons
> Au plus pauvre la besace?
>
> Aucun apprentissage
> Ils n'ont fit de leur metier;
> Le deffaut de l'ouvrage
> Ils ne connaissent point
> S'il s'en trouve quelqu'un
> Il y en a plus de cinquante
> Qui ne scavent que raisonner
> Ou barbouiller du papier
> Voilà toute leur science.*[58]

---

* What makes me sad
  Is that the master masons
  Have all the flour,
  While we have only the bran,
  And often nothing at all.
  That's what angers me;
  Is is not with truth
  That the proverb says straightaway
  Au plus pauvre la besace

The last expression is impossible to translate directly. Literally, a *besace* is a tramp's knapsack, here used to symbolize the fate of the poor. The sense is: the poor get poorer.

No apprenticeship
Have they had of their trade:

The increased tempo of their protests in the last years of the old regime may be attributed not only to the ongoing economic depression, but also to the generalized discontent with government and society which they heard and felt on all sides. It was an ambiance that made the assertion of their demands legitimate, and the result was a limited *prise de conscience* parallel to the much more extensive politicization of 1789 and the following years.

⋘ IV ⋙

In the 1761 edition of Savary's *Dictionnaire du commerce, gagne-deniers*, the urban equivalent of the rural *journaliers*, were defined as "strong and robust men, who are hired in Paris (and elsewhere) to carry burdens and merchandise in return for a certain sum mutually agreed to."[59] The definition is fine as far as it goes, but it gives us no idea of the extraordinary division of labor that existed even among these unskilled workers. In fact, it is curious to observe that the division of labor at this time was more developed among unskilled workers, where it had no technological or economic basis, than among the skilled.

There were at least four kinds of *gagne-deniers*. The first group went by many names (*commissionnaires, crocheteurs, hommes de peine, portefaix*), but what they all had in common was that they were porters and messengers; they were the most miserable of all the categories, unprotected as they were by privilege against competition. The second group was made up of men who worked on the ports as stevedores. They were in turn divided by function: the *débardeurs* unloaded wood that had just been brought down the Seine by floatage or boat. The *garçons de la pelle* took coal off the boats and filled the sacks of the *plumets*, who then delivered them to customers in town. A third group consisted of porters specialized in the carriage of certain types of goods: wood, chalk, hay, plaster, salt, and grains. The fourth group, and probably the most economically successful, was the *forts de la douane* and the *forts des Halles*.[60]

The lack of work
They know not
If there's one
There are more than fifty
Who know only how to reason
And to fill paper with scribbling
That's the extent of their knowledge.

Only the nonprivileged porters were free to sell their labor where and when they saw fit, but it was a specious kind of freedom, for they were not allowed to come into competition with the privileged groups. The latter were organized into work gangs in each place, and membership in them was conditional on acceptance by the administrative authorities. In this way, the *forts de la douane*, who had a monopoly on the carriage of all goods passing through the customs, depended on the Farmers General. Those who worked in the Halle aux Draps were named by the masters and guards of the mercers and drapers' guild, those in the Halle aux Toiles by specially appointed officers. The longshoremen were named by the *prèvôt des marchands* and the municipality or, in the case of the *plumets*, by the *officiers-porteurs du charbon*. In each instance their number was limited (28 *garçons de la pelle* and approximately 550 *plumets*), and sometimes one had to pay for an appointment. At the customs, a place cost 800 livres and a recommendation was necessary.[61] Only the *gardes françaises* and the *gardes suisses* could infringe on these monopolies with impunity. The former were particularly privileged to unload wood used for construction, while the latter did all sorts of menial work, like porterage and hod carrying. Neither hesitated to use force in order to impose their services on a reluctant employer. And on occasion, as in January, 1736, they would come into conflict with one another, and riots would ensue. *Le peuple*, particularly the civilian dock workers, divided their support between the opposing factions, and the result would generally be a couple of deaths and the intervention of the police.[62]

In Savary's opinion this work was "lucrative and honest, and of much trust, which is why only people of proven loyalty are employed."[63] Nonetheless, the workers had a reputation for being wild and troublesome, always out to hold up the merchants for high fees, sometimes abandoning their loads to get drunk in a local cabaret. In consequence, the police kept a close watch over them.[64]

Furet and Daumard have called these laborers "salariés à clientèle" because they normally worked for several employers and were thus freer in the execution of their tasks than they would have been under the supervision of a single master. The argument is plausible, and it is consonant with Lenoir's previously mentioned contemporary distinction between workers who had masters and those who had none. But freedom may be a misleading concept in this case. No doubt, they were not subject to the same kind of discipline as guild workers, but the combination of police surveillance and economic necessity kept them under effective control.

Other unskilled workers included water carriers (who were known to climb seven flights of stairs as many as 30 times a day), chair carriers, shoeshine boys, hod carriers and chimney sweeps.[65] The *décrotteurs* were young boys who worked in groups of five or six. They ran errands, washed dishes, cleaned chimneys, and shined shoes. Some of them had fixed places of business, which were jealously guarded, while others walked the streets in search of employment. Workers from the same province joined together to defend their turf against "foreigners," that is, all those who came from outside their province, not to say the canton or the diocese. Natives of the vallée de la Barcelonnette in Dauphiné lived in the faubourg Saint Marcel with their fathers, who were organ grinders and held magic-lantern shows in the streets. The Savoyards lived in the quarter of the Ville Neuve near the Porte Saint Denis, as well as in the faubourgs Saint Jacques and Saint Marcel. Lyonnais chair carriers preferred the faubourgs Saint Germain and Saint Jacques, while their Norman brothers stuck to the quarter around the rue Saint Honoré and the Marais. The Auvergnat water carriers lived in the place Maubert and the faubourgs Saint Honoré and Saint Antoine. Norman pavers and roofers stayed in the rues des Gravilliers and des Vertus and on the Left Bank outskirts of the city near the gates of Sèvres and Montmartre. Quarrymen lived near the Observatoire and the Gobelins, within easy reach of their work at Arcueil, Montrouge and the La Salpêtrière. In the 1730s, 1,100 to 1,200 laborers from the Limousin lived in the rues de la Vannerie and de la Mortellerie, the place Maubert, and the rues Traversine, de Versailles, du Bac, and des Brodeurs in the faubourg Saint Germain, just then undergoing a great building boom. But they were divided among the several streets according to their place of origin.[66] The examples could go on ad infinitum, but the point to remember is the exclusivity of each group and the jealousy with which its members sought to protect their hold on a given trade. In this they were acting just as guildsmen did, and provincial loyalties served the same purpose that guild rules did for the artisans.

The street workers from the provinces, many of them seasonal migrants, lived together in *chambrées*, that is, from 8 to 10 to as many as 50 to a room, under the guidance of a leader, usually an older man. It was his task to keep the peace and to safeguard the mutual loyalty without which living at such close quarters would have been impossible. According to a priest who went among them dispensing religious instructions in the 1730s, the system worked very well: "They live," he wrote, "in harmony and view

the small successes of their comrades without jealousy." The
prime sanction against a wrongdoer was the very effective one
of ostracism from the group. He was denounced to all his fellows
currently in Paris. Shunned by them, it became impossible for
him to make a living, and he had sooner or later to take to the
road. Given the common origin of the members of the group and
the closeness of the ties that bound them to their native villages—
many of them eventually returned home to settle down—one may
wonder what fate awaited the miscreant back in the provinces.

❧ V ☙

The street merchants of Paris sold everything imaginable from
matches to guns, including hardware, food, old clothes and household goods. The *crieurs de vin* offered samples of wine available
in the taverns, the *oublayeurs* sold sugar and spice cookies (*oublies*),
and the *marchandes de plaisir*, despite their name, sold waffles.
There were pedlars of notions and brooms, men who would repair
a worn bellows, mend a pot of china or porcelain, or fix the
weight on a clock and the bars on a door. In principle these trades
were free and not organized into guilds, but there were exceptions. The pedlars of old hardware were limited in number to 80.
Although there were no apprentices, the unincorporated community elected successors to members who died, and they had a
right to confiscate any goods illegally sold by others. The only
competition they could not protect themselves against was that
afforded by the off-duty soldiers of the *gardes françaises*, whose
reputation for nastiness and brutality led people to give them a
wide berth.[67] All tradesmen were, as always, subject to police
intervention. On occasion there existed a real hierarchy among
the vendors of a single set of goods. The *crieuses de vieux chapeaux*,
for example, were divided into three categories: (1) those who
dealt by wholesale and owned a shop, (2) those who walked the
streets purchasing hats to resell to the wholesalers, and (3) the
novices who paid a fee of 12 to 15 écus to be allowed to accom-
pany the others on their rounds and thus to learn the business.[68]

A certain number of these street merchants had a fixed place
of business, usually a stall rather than a store, which was supposed
to be, but rarely was, taken down at the end of each day. Others
merely occupied the same piece of ground day after day for years,
using the earth as a counter on which to display their wares, like
the hardware sellers of the Quai de la Mégisserie. The great ma-

jority, like the knife grinders or food sellers, carried their shops on their backs, and went from place to place seeking to attract customers by calling out their wares.[69]

An Order in Council of August 23, 1767 ordered all "merchants selling by weights and measures, and all others whose profession involves any sale of merchandise, or craft, or trade, either in shops open to the public, warehouses, rooms, workshops, or otherwise, or who follow a profession having to do with commerce, or which concerns the food, lodging, clothing, or health of the population," and who are not members of guilds to register at the Châtelet within three months. Either the order was not rigorously enforced or records have been lost. In any case, a single register has been found containing the names of 1,760 persons with their occupations and places of origin. This is no doubt only a small part of the total and covers the period from October 5, 1767 to May 10, 1768. Still, it may be used for purposes of sampling.

Of these 1,760 persons, an occupation is given for 1,263 women and 486 men. Most of the women were retailers or repairers of old clothes and hats (823), of rags (78), and of old ironware, buckles, and hardware (33). Two hundred and seven women were designated as "retailers" without further qualification. The only group of any importance that did not sell something tangible were the 76 rooming-house keepers. Among the men, there were 240 retailers— 35 repairers of old clothes, 33 sellers of old ironware, and 19 sellers of medicines for eyes, corns, and assorted afflictions. One hundred and sixty-three kept rooming houses.

If it is impossible to make any statement about the presence on this list of a seller of astrological books or of a charlatan whose trade it was to go about the streets curing assorted maladies, the list itself does lead to certain conclusions. Of the total, 60 percent dealt in old clothes, which is symptomatic of the fact that so many Parisians were never able to afford the luxury of a new suit or dress.[70] The *fripiers* of the Halles and the quais had the reputation of never letting a customer escape them, even if it were necessary to apply a bit of force. They kept their shops open on Sundays in violation of the law, but the soldiers of the watch company never bothered them because there were numerous ties of kinship between the two groups. On Mondays, the wives and female relatives of old-clothes hawkers sold their goods at the place de Grève at the Foire du Saint Esprit, where their principal clients were "petites bourgeoises, wives of *procureurs*, and excessively economical women."[71]

Thirteen percent of all those listed rented out rooms, a total of 239. Only 82 of them were proprietors or principal tenants. We have here the phenomenon of sub-subleasing. Those who let rooms lived, together with many other street merchants, in the homes of butchers, bakers, mercers, glaziers, cabinetmakers, etc. The proprietors and principal tenants were, in other words, recruited from among artisans and in the higher strata of the population.[72]

A large number of these petty merchants (47.6 percent) were natives of Paris (625) or of its diocese (113). But more than one-half were provincials. Many were recruited in the Parisian region taken in the widest sense of the term. Thus, 63 were natives of the Ile de France, 55 of the Brie, the Gâtinais and the Beauce, 28 from the Orléanais, and 61 from the dioceses of Sens and Auxerre. The north (Artois, Picardy, Flanders, Hainaut) furnished 130 recruits, while 134 came from Normandy. From the east came 107 Champenois, 99 Alsatians, and 86 Lorrainers. These were the regions of most intense recruitment. Burgundy with 45, Franche Comte, Dauphiné and Savoie with 64, and the west, from the Touraine to the sea, with 38, were still not negligible sources of immigrants. The center of France, from Poitiers to Nevers and Bourges to Rodez, furnished 71 persons, of whom 27 were Auvergnats. Brittany (18), the south from the Lyonnais to Provence (15), and the southwest (15) were less important. It is true that this distribution may in part be a function of the kind of tradesmen called upon to register, but it is nonetheless permissible to note that three great regions (the area bordering directly on Paris, Normandy and the north, and the northeast) were the prime suppliers of this kind of manpower to the capital.[73]

Women outnumbered men on this list almost three to one. This raises the possibility that for many families, street merchandising was the source of a second income for the household. In fact, we find many women of this category married to journeymen, unskilled workers, and domestics, which suggests just how closely they were tied to the bulk of Parisian wage earners and why their participation in the revolutionary *journées* was to be of such great importance. They, and in particular, the *poissardes* or market-women, were able to mobilize fairly large popular armies:

Because they [the *poissardes*] are linked by blood or clientage relationships to all the respectable men of Paris who shine shoes, carry coals, clean out sewers, build or tear down walls, set up clamors in their ranks, etc., their joy or anger is shared by thousands in a moment and so in the space of a few minutes they can recruit an army that counts among its members the roughest and strongest fists and the harshest voices and can in that way create an extraordinary feeling of terror. One cannot prevent these very honorable people from giving themselves out as the Nation and from being convinced that what they want and do should be wanted and done by the entire Nation. In this way a great number of phenomena of the recent Revolution can be explained.[74]

The street merchants did not always enjoy governmental favor. Just as artisans and merchants were forbidden to sell goods anywhere but in their shops,[75] so periodic attempts were made to prohibit *forains*, nondomiciled persons, from selling goods in competition with them. Pressure on administrators to act in this way was particularly strong when the merchants or artisans were organized into guilds. The *forains* were, on occasion, offered the possibility of buying masterships and settling down in Paris, but this was not a real alternative, since most of them had not sufficient capital to do so. The Auvergnat *chaudronniers* (braziers and coppersmiths) were a case in point. They claimed the right to buy, sell, and repair used items, arguing that they were not really in competition with the masters, who didn't care to do their sort of petty work— or who would charge double for it, if they did. In short, they were "very useful to the poor citizen" of both town and country and ought to be allowed to carry on. Conflicts of this kind sometimes became very acute, but no legal principle applicable to all disputes seems to have evolved before 1789.[76]

VI

According to Expilly, the capitation rolls of 1764 (which have unfortunately not come down to us) accounted for 37,457 employed domestics, about equally divided between men and women. Men outnumbered women by only 2 percent in the city as a whole but were far and away the majority in the quarters of Saint Eustache, the Louvre, the Palais Royal, the place Royale and Saint Germain des Pres, the centers of aristocratic and upper-bourgeois life. On the other hand, women outnumbered men by 50 percent in Saint Martin, Saint Marcel, Saints Innocents and the Hôtel de Ville. There were three times as many womenservants as men in the faubourg Saint Antoine and the Saint Denis quarter. In other words, the wealthier the family, the greater the likelihood that it would employ a manservant. Modest establishments, which could afford only a limited number of domestics, preferred to hire women, presumably because they were paid less and/or were willing to perform a greater variety of tasks.[77]

Of taxed families, 17,657 of 71,114 employed one or more servants. The proportion is one family in four, but the figure is somewhat misleading. The very families least likely to pay capitation were those without servants, so it is possible that families employing domestic help were fewer in proportion to the total population than this statistic would indicate. There were, however, a great many persons who worked for foreigners who were not subject to inclusion on the tax rolls, and others who engaged in more transient employment by serving tourists. Expilly estimated that their number was equal to one-sixth of the settled domestics.[78]

Domestic workers were divided into many categories according to their function and responsibilities within the household. The maître d'hôtel or steward, whose task it was to supervise the entire establishment, was a man of some importance and considerable power in the backstairs world. His nearest equivalent, in terms of status, among the women, was the governess and, perhaps, the cook. Although all three were, like the other domestics, entirely subject to the master's will, their posts required training and skill sufficient to set them apart from the majority of their fellows— the valets, porters, dishwashers, coachmen, postillions and grooms among the men, and the chambermaids, maidservants, and laundryworkers among the women. The former might even accumulate enough capital to quit domestic employment and to set up as petty merchants. The latter were likely to remain servants or unskilled workers throughout their lives. There seems to have been some possibility of advancement within a household, but it is impossible to say how often this did, in reality, occur.

Domestics had a reputation for wiliness and corruption. The English doctor and novelist Tobias Smollett was struck by their behavior:

You cannot conceive [he wrote] with what eagerness and dexterity those rascally valets exert themselves in pillaging strangers. There is always one ready in waiting on your arrival, who begins by assisting your own servant to unload the baggage, and interests himself in your affairs with such artful officiousness that you find it difficult to shake him off. . . . The Truth is, those fellows are very hardy, useful and obliging, and so far honest, that they will not steal in the usual way. You may safely trust one of them to bring you a hundred loui' dores from your banker; but they fleece you without mercy in every other article of expense. They put all your tradesmen under contribution

. . . even the Bourgeois who owns your coach pays him twenty sols a day. His wages amount to twice as much, so that I imagine the fellow that serves me, makes above ten shillings a day, beside his victuals, which, by the bye, he has no right to demand.[79]

No doubt, the permanently employed servant was subject to closer surveillance by his master and, in the case of a large household, by the maître d'hôtel. He had, consequently, little opportunity to supplement his wages in this way. When critics spoke of domestics in the eighteenth century, it was less to their abuses than to their very existence that they referred. The lackeys or personal servants in particular were the objects of their wrath. They were the most visible of domestics, for they wore their master's livery and did, or were expected to do, his bidding in all things. Like Leporello, and in addition to their more mundane tasks, they acted as confidants and procurers and protected their employers against the importunings of creditors through their skillful use of lying and deceit.[80] And their chief function was to celebrate their master's status by a display of his colors and by their insolence toward men of lower rank.[81]

Domestics were also legally under their master's control. In the case of a dispute between master and servant over pay or conditions of work, the master was believed on his oath alone. A domestic who insulted his master could be punished by being made to stand in the pillory, followed by three years' banishment from Paris. A police ordinance of 1720, renewed in 1778, made it necessary for a domestic, when he was dismissed or left a household on his own initiative, to have a certificate from his ex-employer, stating whether or not he was satisfied with the servant's conduct and whether or not the servant had served him loyally. For lack of this certificate an unemployed domestic was to be considered "a libertine and a vagabond" and treated in consequence. It was as much a crime to falsify these certificates as it was to leave work without one. The employer, who since 1759 was civilly responsible for his servant's actions, might not hire a person whom he did not know, that is, one who did not have a certificate. Unemployed domestics had no right to remain in Paris for more than a week (after 1778, a month). A 500-livre fine was to be imposed on anyone who gave them asylum after the expiration of the time limit, and innkeepers who did the same might lose their licenses.[82]

The ordinances here cited, together with the laws governing domestic theft, indicate that all was not well between master and servant. Mercier thought that the good old days when servants had been "part of the family" had long since gone, to be replaced by a relationship which emphasized material well-being but neglected to make servants feel necessary and wanted. "They are scorned; they feel it and have become our greatest enemies. In the old days, their life was laborious, hard, and frugal, but they were accounted something of value, and the domestic died of old age by his master's side."[83] The golden age of domesticity may have been a myth, but the fact remains that domestics in the eighteenth century were more and more *déracinés*, perhaps even *déclassés*. For every servant who lived out his life in his employer's home, many more passed through one or more households, alternating between work and unemployment, often turning to beggary and theft when necessary. Lenoir thought they were responsible for a larger share of Parisian crime than any other category of the laboring poor.[84] The arrogance and insubordination of which they were so often accused may have given them comfort but did not save them from endemic poverty.

In the years immediately before the Revolution, there were more jobs for servants than ever before. But there were also more people looking for work than ever before and greater numbers of peasants unable to make a living on the land and, therefore, ready to migrate to the city. At the same time, servants were being employed by a greater range of social classes, notably bourgeois of one sort or another, many of them *nouveaux riches*. These people had no tradition of feudal master-serf or master-client relationships, hence their tendency to treat domestics as simple wage earners, and their willingness to dismiss them with little or no ceremony for relatively minor infractions of the code of behavior. At the same time, domestics, once uprooted and having left their agricultural occupations behind them, had nowhere to turn. There would be no role for them to play in urban society until the development of industry in the middle of the nineteenth century. Domesticity can be seen as a kind of transitional stage between the peasantry and the proletariat, but only in the long term. In the short term, which alone has any significance for biological individuals, domestics were coming to be subject more and more to the same disabilities as the rest of the laboring poor.

Insofar as they remained domestics, they lived differently, and to some extent separated, from the other sections of the *menu peuple*. Settled domestics were to be found in every quarter, it is true, but they tended to congregate in the areas near the Palais Royal, the faubourg Saint Germain, the Louvre, Saint Eustache and the place Royale. On the other hand, only 295 of 5,568 families in the faubourg Saint Antoine employed servants, for a total of 429 individuals. This semi-isolation may perhaps have been overcome by family ties between domestics and other working people, but of this we cannot be certain. On the other hand, domestics were separated from their fellow workers by a difference in lifestyles. Their family organization is a case in point. Sometimes husband and wife were both servants, either working together or in different households. This was not always the case, and we have no reason to assume that it was true of the majority. If one of the partners was not a domestic, what did he or she do? Did the nondomestic live in the house where the spouse worked? (The decline of feudal patterns would make this unlikely.) Were they able to live together at all? And the children? What was to become of them in the absence of a settled home? The answer to these questions is, I suspect, that domesticity compromised, if it did not destroy, the possibility of constituting a family on the accepted model and thereby re-enforced the loneliness and distinctiveness of the domestic in the midst of the laboring crowd. The children were early left to fend for themselves and were lucky indeed to find places as servants or apprentices, the parents being in no position to help them.[85]

All of these matters deserve further investigation. Still, it is even now possible to see in them the bases of the distrust felt for domestics by the other sections of the laboring poor. Domesticity had long since been considered by the opinion makers to be a vile and unworthy occupation. Domestics gave up not only their independence but also part of their characters as human beings. They descended into the lower orders, where they might still be useful but could no longer be respected. They were, furthermore, lovers of debauchery and haters of work, for what else could ever make them give up the land to become a bunch of unproductive parasites? As Des Essarts wrote on the very eve of the Revolution:

Hatred of work, the desire to enjoy the pleasures of the cities, a taste for laziness, the habit of vice, indifference to the ties most dear to the heart of men, the hope of getting rich, and lastly, the most decided and most shocking egotism, are the motives which cause domestic work to be cherished; it is they which cause men to prefer the baseness of this state to the honorable and useful fatigue of the farmer. One may thus correctly conclude that the class of servants is composed exclusively of the scum of the countryside.[86]

Freedom and productivity are values dear to the bourgeois and typical of the Enlightenment. They are also highly abstract ideas,

which seem unlikely to have affected the laboring poor. Freedom
was an unknown quantity to them, and it is a question as to whether
they had as yet any conception, modern or ancient, of its meaning.
Similarly, men who did not define themselves primarily according
to their roles in the process of production could not have been
expected to make productivity, whether conceived of technically
as efficiency or spiritually as a justification of life, their watchword.
It may have been that this reflection of bourgeois ideology trickled
down to the laboring poor, thus establishing a prejudice in their
minds against domestics. It is more probable, however, that the
distrust of servants arose from different life-styles,[87] the fact that
they were exempt from taxation (their masters paid) and from
militia duty, and, above all, on account of their tendency to ape
their masters and to identify with their interests.[88] That it was
possible for a domestic to serve his master loyally insofar as his
orders were not antisocial and at the same time to defend his own
interests was a rather new idea, first bruited at the beginning of
the Revolution.[89] It was difficult no doubt for domestics, especially
those who had spent a lifetime in the service of a single family, to
make the distinction, and equally so for the *menu peuple* to break
old habits and have confidence in the *valetaille*. The revolutionaries, no doubt preferring not to take any unnecessary risks, refused to recognize domestics as citizens.

⤳ VII ⤶

The poor worked long hours, 14 to 16 a day. By 5 o'clock in the
morning, the Savoyards and unskilled laborers were in the streets
ready to start a new day. Building workers labored from 5 A.M.
to 7 P.M. in summer, and from 6 A.M. to 8 P.M. in winter in 1787.
Journeymen and others who went to work at 6 or 7 A.M. left their
ateliers between 8 and 9 P.M. The streets were filled with returning
workers at that hour, and shops stayed open as late as half-past
ten.[90]

Parisian workers labored not only long but hard. They were
poorly paid, especially if we take into consideration their often
chronic state of underemployment due to the many holidays and,
in particular, the inability of the economy to absorb them all. The
twin specters of the hospital and beggary must have constantly
haunted ordinary men despite their best efforts to remain solvent.
A short period of illness or unemployment due to another cause
was enough to lay them low, for they were unable to put aside

any money to protect themselves against these misfortunes. As Mercier put it:

The people of Paris is, of all the people in the world, the one that works the most, is the worst fed and appears the saddest. . . . The poor Parisian, bent under the eternal weight of toil and work, erecting, building, forging, plunged into quarries, perched on the rooftops, transporting enormous burdens, abandoned to the mercy of all the men of power, and crushed like an insect as soon as he wishes to raise his voice, makes a meager living—and then only with difficulty and in the sweat of his brow. It is sufficient only to keep him alive, but incapable of assuring him a serene life in old age.[91]

No doubt the best-paid workers in the last decades of the old regime were those in the building trades. A skilled mason was paid between 2 livres and 2 livres and 10 sous a day, and a brick-layer's wages might vary from 2 livres and 10 sous to as much as 4 livres. Stonecutters and quarrymen were paid at the same rate as masons, while laborers in construction gangs received between 1 livre and 1 livre and 15 sous a day. A skilled engraver made between 12 and 18 livres a week (2 to 3 livres per day) in 1780–1781, while a worker in the Réveillon wallpaper factory was paid 25 sous.[92] All of these rates had risen somewhat since the middle of the century, but none, as far as I can determine, increased in such a way as to contradict Labrousse's calculation of a rise in nominal wages of 22 percent between 1726–1741 and 1771–1789.[93]

What was true of the skilled and semiskilled workers was equally true of domestics and petty entrepreneurs like water carriers and gardeners. Male domestics earned between 150 and 180 livres per year (10 sous per day), and women often got less, as little as 90 livres a year. Much depended on the nature of the job and the status of the employer, so female domestics were not always at a disadvantage in comparison to men. It should be remembered that domestics were fed and lodged in addition to their meager wages. A water carrier was paid between 1 livre and 10 sous and 2 livres a month by his regular clients. Assuming that he could make thirty trips a day (a high estimate), this would mean a monthly income of 45 to 60 livres.[94] Water carriers who were less fortunate and did not have steady customers made considerably less. The Savoyards and other *salariés à clientele* were unlikely to be better off in terms of wages, and they totally lacked the security of regular employment. Competition among them was strong and not always tempered by the corporate spirit for which they were so roundly praised.

The great majority of the laboring poor thus had to make do with about 1 livre and 10 sous a day or less. This was little enough, even had it been available 365 days a year. The situation was all the more likely to become disastrous because there were so many days when no work was done (111 in Rudé's estimate), and in light of the phenomenal rise in prices in the last part of the century. Labrousse has shown that the rise in the price of food and other essentials of popular consumption (lodging, heat, and light) was of the order of 62 percent between 1726–1741 and 1771–1789, and this does not take into consideration the seasonal or short-term crises, which were the ones most sharply felt.[95] In 1789, a man whose daily wage was 25 sous had an effective wage of 15 sous if he worked only a little more than 250 days a year. When the price of bread rose to 9 sous for the four-pound loaf (which was more or less normal), he was obliged to spend 60 percent of his income for bread alone. At 12 sous, the percentage rose to 80, at 13½, to 90, and at 14½ (as in the spring and summer of 1789), to 97. The following table drawn up by Professor Rudé is a measure of how easy it was for a poor man to become indigent:[96]

| | | Expenditure on Bread as Percentage of Income | | | |
Daily Wage	Effective Wage	9 Sous	12 Sous	13½ Sous	14½ Sous
25 sous	15 sous	60	80	90	97
30 sous	18 sous	50	67	75	80
40 sous	24 sous	37	50	56	60
50 sous	30 sous	30	40	45	48
100 sous	60 sous	15	20	22½	24

Only artists like sculptors and goldsmiths could attain a wage of 5 livres a day, and they were hardly members of the laboring poor. For the rest, it is impossible to conceive of most workingmen actually earning the 435 livres needed annually to support a family of four at the barest subsistence level. The labor of their wives and sometimes of their children was necessary for survival.

Under the circumstances, Restif's moral preachments ring singularly false. Like the good burghers who wanted to do away with the popular theatricals they considered the source of idleness and bad habits,[97] he blamed the poor for their lack of industriousness. They were too well paid, he wrote:

The populace, like savage hordes, lives only for the present: if they are able to earn a sufficient amount to live on [for a week] in three days, they work only three days, and engage in debauchery for the four others. But then they do not have enough to live on, and live in poverty; they borrow, do not pay, ruin the baker, the shoemaker, the wine merchant, although the latter poisons them in order to get his own back: everything is in disorder. But, contrarywise, keep the cost of labor low, and the populace, ever malleable, works for six days, because they need the work to meet the amount of their expenditure; they do not become unsettled and are less burdened with debt, when making 9 livres a week than when able to earn 18."[98]

This was an indictment much worse than the remarks that earned Réveillon an attack on his factory in April, 1789. There is, however, a kernel of truth in it, despite its sovereign contempt for the idle poor. Parisian workingmen did tend to think only of present gratification, and they had little sense of work discipline. If, as Edward Thompson has said, the workers of the Industrial Revolution could not live on articles in the *Economic History Review*, neither could the men and women of Paris be much affected by strictures from the pens of the classical economists and their disciples, for whom work had become the *summum bonum*. Restif's normative prescription of an iron law of wages could come only from a man who believed that "you are obliged to work in order to pay for your needs with its produce, and if you do not, you are the bane of the commonweal and subject to punishment by it."[99] The laboring poor, for whom a man was first a man, a husband, a father, or even a regional patriot before he was a producer, could not agree.

❧ VIII ❧

It is difficult, for all intents and purposes impossible, to give an estimate of the number of women who worked in eighteenth-century Paris. We know that they were very numerous, and unless we wish to neglect the very important contribution of one-half of the population to both economy and society, we must try to give at least a qualitative description of their activity.

Few women were active in the productive sector. Even those trades organized into guilds and exclusively reserved for women were mainly devoted to merchandising: for example, the flower vendors and fruit sellers. For Restif, it was proper to say that "the women of the populace were uniquely employed in peddling useless things, like flowers."[100] Although we need not share his philistinism, it is true that the single exception among the guilds that comes to mind is that of the seamstresses, who were constantly in competition with the tailors, on the one hand, and with the *ravaudeuses* or sewing women who were not members of a guild, on the other. In a society that sought to organize work on the basis of monopolies of production, women were singularly neglected. Mercier, among others, was scandalized by this state of affairs, which he believed to be contrary to the dictates of nature:

Is it not ridiculous to see [men working as] women's hairdressers, men pushing a needle, handling a shuttle, and usurping the sedentary life of women; while women, deprived of the trades they could exercise, unable to support themselves, are obliged to take up arduous tasks, or abandon themselves to prostitution.[101]

Except for the widows of masters who were allowed to take their late husband's places, access to the men's guilds was a strictly masculine prerogative. In other words, a woman's role in a guild was always acquired through her relationship to a man, except where the guild itself was exclusively feminine in composition. The widow who remarried a man of another trade generally lost her privileges. With the restoration of the guilds after the abandonment of Turgot's reforms, widows were theoretically granted equal rights with other masters, and other women were allowed to join on condition that they neither vote nor hold office. In reality, women were no more frequently admitted to guilds after 1776 than before.[102]

Women were thus limited almost completely to activities outside the guild structures. Some of the jobs that had traditionally been theirs now no longer existed, casualties of the great metropolis. If they still functioned as midwives and nurses, they were no longer very often called on to act as professional mourners, the *pleureuses* whose function it had been to march in funeral processions and "to give to the relatives of the deceased that sadness of tone suitable to such an occasion." In the main, they had to work as domestics and as retailers of food, clothing, and other assorted items. Many of the dealers in second-hand clothing at the Halles were women, and the Foire du Saint Esprit at the Grève was their exclusive preserve. The latter was a kind of bargain basement before its time where, as Mercier noted

Since it is women who both buy and sell, cunning is about equal on both sides. From very far off, one can hear the high, false, discordant voices quarreling. From close up, the scene is even more curious. When the female sex (which is not the fair sex on this occasion) contemplates feminine clothes, there is in their faces a most particular expression.[103]

The general term for a woman who sold small amounts of goods in the markets or streets was *regrattière*. This included the *graillon-neuse* who sold leftovers from the tables of private citizens and caterers, as well as persons who bought fresh food in the market for resale, and the coal hawkers, among whom the wives of the longshoremen who unloaded the coal had a particular advantage. They could keep a larger stock than their competitors because their husbands were paid in kind. All the *regrattières* had to be licensed, and their number, in theory, was limited to 3,000 by an edict of 1694. It seems doubtful, however, that the limitation was observed.[104]

The strong, male-dominated family was the common ideal of all classes in eighteenth-century Paris. A woman who married gave up her freedom, insofar as she had acquired any through emancipation from paternal control. An unmarried woman was theoretically the equal of a man in civil affairs, but in fact she was subject to all kinds of disadvantageous legal exceptions. A widow was closer to equality of rights with a widower, than a wife with a husband, or an unmarried woman to an unmarried man. But complete equality never truly existed, for even the widow was subject to control by a family council and/or the courts.[105]

The husband controlled his wife's person and property. She could appeal to the law against his abuse of either, but she could only obtain a separation of community property if she could show that her husband was guilty of willful abuse of the goods entrusted to his care and that her dowry was in danger. Legal separation was granted on the grounds of physical abuse or defamation only. In any case, going to law was a long and expensive process, not generally available to a poor woman or to any woman for that matter, unless she had the support of her father or some other male relative. Divorce did not exist, and annulment was infrequent. A double standard of sexual behavior persisted. A certain permissiveness mutually granted among aristocratic couples at this time should not allow us to forget that a husband continued to have legal recourse against his wife's adultery, a right that was refused her when he was the guilty party. The Council of Trent had reaffirmed the sacramental character of marriage, and throughout the old regime church tribunals had competence to deal with marital disputes, while royal courts were, in theory, limited to dealing with the civil effects of marriage as arranged in the contract made by the two parties. There was, however, a steady tendency to increase the role of the state by granting appeal jurisdiction to the Parlements.

Freedom to make a marriage contract as one wished was formally recognized, but its most ordinary form under Parisian law, and the one that prevailed unless express arrangements to the contrary were made, was that of community property. The partners combined their holdings, present and future, and the husband was given the right to administer the joint estate. The wife's consent to his actions was not required, except insofar as he might appear to be manipulating matters in order to cheat her or her heirs of the rights due them at the dissolution of the contract. The wife was, on the other hand, absolutely forbidden to make a contract engaging any community property without her husband's consent. There was one exception to this rule: if the wife conducted her own business, she could enter into a contract on her own, it being assumed that she was acting jointly with her husband and that he had stated his agreement. The wife also possessed dower rights over a portion of her husband's estate at the dissolution of the community. If she predeceased him, this right passed on to her heirs.

The married woman could not, unless she was in business separately from her husband, alienate her property (that is, property remaining outside the community), make a contract, or sue. She could make a will, for it was reasoned that the will went into effect only after the community had come to an end. She could not act for her husband, even in the case of his being absent or incapacitated, except upon the authorization of the courts.[106]

The laboring poor, having little property to dispose of, were perhaps not directly affected by these provisions, although they did marry under the system of community property, either expressly or by default in the absence of a contract.[107] But the lack of substantial wealth did not in any way loosen the husband's control over his wife's person or style of life.

Husband and wife were obliged to live together until death did them part. Theirs was hardly an equal relationship, the very conception of which was unknown at this time. In the words of a tract published in 1782, women were expected to feel respect for their husbands, whom "they ought to regard . . . as their chiefs." Affection, tenderness, and benevolence should make them able to render whatever services, both spiritual and physical, were asked of them. Courage and generosity should enable them to bear all the faults to which their husbands might be subject, while religion and a spirit of penitence ought to be called into play to soften any bad treatment received. Finally, charity and zeal should cause wives to take an interest in saving their husbands' souls. Docility was expected in all things, to which a husband was exhorted to respond with friendship, esteem, attachment, justice, and condescension (he ought not to demand his rights absolutely). Women are weak and inferior, and men ought to remember to treat them with indulgence, while encouraging them zealously to perform their religious duties.[108]

It is no exaggeration to speak of women in this relationship as objects. They were supposed to have no will of their own, or at least none that could escape subordination to their husbands.[109] Although it was considered wrong to have sex too frequently, a woman had no right to refuse her husband's demands, even during the menses or pregnancy. Refusal might lead her husband into libertinage, for which sin she would bear the entire responsibility.[110]

The father also had complete authority over the person and goods of his children until they reached their majority or were otherwise emancipated, as by marriage. He was obliged to raise and support them, and they, in turn, had to look after their parents, should the need arise. If a man under 30 or a woman under 25 married without parental consent, they and their children could be disinherited absolutely. Indeed, current jurisprudence at the end of the old regime allowed a father to disinherit a son who married after 30 the woman the parent had previously refused. The concern here was twofold and affected primarily members of the nobility and the upper bourgeoisie. First, there was the need to defend the family patrimony, and second, perhaps even more important, the political desirability of protecting society against *mésalliances*. Renoul de Bas-Champs argued:

The marriage of a citizen of the first class with a citizen of the last ought to be . . . proscribed, in a government based on *inequality*, such as is monarchical government.

Inequality among the different steps which form the ladder of a monarchical government cannot be altered beyond a certain point without altering at the same time the form of the government. The consideration attached to the first ranks supports the subordination that safeguards the harmony of the body politic. One ought thus to avoid, insofar as possible, weakening this consideration by marriages too lacking in proportion, which would fill in the space found between the first and last order of citizens. Such marriages are a weakening of the state. They sow discord and division within the most illustrious families, and alter the fundamental constitution, by causing the disappearance, little by little, of the inequality which is its basis.[111]

We have here stated in fine the justification for all honorific rights in the old regime. It was because they functioned as a support of a rigid hierarchical structure that any exception made constituted a danger to the whole. For the same reason, marriage was seen, not as a matter for individual decision, but as a domain reserved to the family and, if need be, to society. These were the arguments used against the social-climbing bourgeois rather than against the laboring poor, who did not constitute a danger. The romantic attachment of a young nobleman to a serving girl led to concubinage rather than to clandestine marriage because his sense of family honor was likely to triumph over any momentary whims he might have. The little information we possess about nuptial patterns among the master artisans and members of the laboring poor indicates that marriage was rarely a means of significant social mobility. In the faubourg Saint Antoine between 1791 and 1795, 50 percent of the fathers-in-law shared a common socio-professional identity with their sons-in-law. And the figure would no doubt be higher if we conceived of the matter in terms of class.[112]

To what extent, if at all, did the norms relating to marriage and the family affect the behavior of the laboring poor? Sturdy beggars were constantly charged with practicing the "community of women" and of peopling the countryside with bastard children whom they left to fend for themselves.[113] An offended sense of propriety overdid and misunderstood what in fact did take place. The "community of women," if it had any meaning at all, meant that the beggars lived in concubinage and that they changed partners on occasion. Mass promiscuity does not seem to have been the rule. As for the children, they were less likely to be abandoned than to be integrated into a gang of beggars, where they fulfilled a function as objects of pity or acted as petty thieves. Although they may not have had a family in the ordinary sense, they were part of what may be called an extended kinship group and enjoyed the company of numerous mothers and fathers.

In all probability, most settled workingmen and women did marry. There is, however, intriguing evidence to the effect that some never bothered with a formal ceremony, perhaps because they had not the money to pay for it. In 1770, the police discovered "a great number of poor people who had not been joined together in the eyes of the Church," and their immediate response was to get the parish vestries to authorize the marriages of indigent persons without charge. Some of these common-law couples were happy to legalize their relationships, but most, according to the same source, ignored the whole thing. Inspection showed that not only the poor but "wives of bourgeois, who had recently got rich and become church wardens, had been living in this flagrantly irregular situation for a long time, with no one the wiser."[114] It was a habit that persisted, for in the 1820s there still existed a group of *bien-pensants* called the Société de Saint François Régis, whose special goal was to regularize "illegal unions [that are] so frequent among the people."[115]

It is possible that these extralegal arrangements were subject to a certain etiquette. Where marriage involved a contract and a transfer of property, concubinage may have required payment, not to the woman, since she did not own the use of her own body, but to her father or former lover. Of this we have no proof but only this passage in the memoirs of a journeyman glazier, writing of the 1750s. [He had been seen with a girl. A man approached him to ask:]

if it were really true that I was seeing this girl, and that it was good for me to know that she belonged to a French Guard, and that he might give her to me for 40 *écus*, and that [an illegible word, probably a name] had been obliged to do as much, and that it was in this manner that most of the girls of the faubourg [Saint Marcel] are bought.[116]

The existence or absence of a formal marriage tie probably did not make much difference in the way men and women lived together. There is no evidence of flagrant family instability among the laboring poor. Households were not constantly made and unmade in the fashion of the contemporary ghetto. Because there was no need to protect property in the interests of the ongoing family community, the poor could do without the certification of church and state. The disabilities visited on bastards were indifferent to them.[117] Women still remained subordinate to their men, in or outside of marriage. Insofar as workingwomen could feel some advantage over their socially superior sisters, it was because they were not obliged to live forever on a pedestal of dependency. Down to earth, in the streets, they earned their own living, and this may have given them some greater weight in running their households, albeit within a limited scope.[118]

How did family unity fare in the face of grinding poverty? To this there is no simple answer. In 1778, Faydit de Tersac, the vicar of Saint Sulpice, accused the poor of abandoning their children at a very early age. At best, he said, parents gave them food but little or nothing else.[119] Aside from the case of foundlings, who were abandoned in the full sense of the word, what did this mean? That they were denied love or attention? That they were not appreciated? That they were turned out of the house? The possibilities are infinite. Restif reported that it was "quite usual in Paris among the working class to allow children to fend for themselves as soon as they can get along alone."[120] His example was a young girl working as a *brocheuse* (book stitcher) for a mistress and living alone in a rented room. Her situation may have been due to the location of her job or the exigencies of the apprenticeship system and may tell us nothing about the solidity of family ties. Children went to work at an early age, but that does not mean they were abandoned nor that they were no longer subject to paternal authority. For those away from home in another city, much would depend on the presence of persons who stood *in loco parentis*, the master artisan or the head of the *chambrée* of migrant workers, and also upon the extent to which the children had not only accepted but internalized that authority before departure from their fathers' houses.

The real cases of abandonment are found among newborn and very young children. There were some instances of infanticide, particularly by unmarried mothers, but the crime seems rarely to have been committed with premeditation. The death of an abandoned infant was usually the result of the exposure of the newborn without proper precautions. The mother's motive for abandoning her child was conditioned in the first instance by her poverty, also by the law which obliged unmarried women to declare their pregnancies and thus expose themselves to the shame of the community and possible loss of livelihood, particularly if they were domestic servants. Failure to make the declaration was a punishable offense but, worse still, the death of a concealed child before baptism and without public burial might bring capital punishment down upon the mother.[121] The solution was to get rid of the child as quickly as possible, to conceal the evidence so to speak. In this way, the law effectively destroyed the lives it was intended to protect. One can imagine the panic of the maidservant, scarcely recovered from labor, as she contemplated her screaming offspring. The open sewer or the river must have been tempting, indeed.[122]

There was an alternative, and it was one that a majority of parents who intended to abandon their children preferred: the Foundling Hospital. In the three decades before the Revolution, children abandoned there numbered 6,000 to 7,000 annually.[123] A very large percentage of them died in short order for lack of care and because they were exposed to all sorts of infectious diseases during their stay either in the hospital or in the countryside where they were put out to nurse.[124] By no means were all the foundlings illegitimate. In his report to the Comité de Mendicité of the Constituent Assembly in 1790, La Millière estimated that as many as one-third were legitimate children abandoned by parents too poor to support them.[125] The figure is open to considerable discussion, but a glance at the registers of foundlings kept by the commissaires du Châtelet shows that children were often brought to the hospital by midwives who declared them to be legitimate, mentioned the names of the parents, and produced baptismal certificates as proof. To be sure, there were also many children recorded as having unknown fathers (and mothers!), and still more who were clandestinely left on the doorsteps of churches and hospitals with no record of their identity whatsoever.[126]

Many of these children were sent to Paris from the provinces. Between 1772 and 1776, 10,068 out of 32,222 children admitted to the Hôpital des Enfants Trouvés, or about one-third, were born outside Paris, for an average of 2,000 a year.[127] This fact led the royal administration to take action: on January 10, 1779, an Order in Council commanded that, from October 1 of the same year, all persons to whom parents confided their children would be expected to take them directly to wet nurses or to the nearest foundling hospital, but not to Paris.[128] Despite this measure, provincial children continued to arrive in the capital, 768 in 1781, but only 222 in 1788. The Hôpital des Enfants Trouvés also accepted children from the Generality of Paris beyond the city limits, a total of 618 in 1788.[129]

The mortality rate among foundlings varied according to age group. The highest was for children less than one month old. In 1751, 68 percent of the children admitted before their first birthday died within a year of entrance, and in the year V (1796–1797), the figure was 92 percent.[130] The few who survived were destined for work as domestics, agricultural laborers or apprentices. We have a record of the entry into a foster home in 1783 of the foundling Louis Leroy, aged 7. He was bound out to one Etienne Delagneau of the diocese of Sens, who promised to keep and support him until age 20, to raise him in the Catholic religion, to send him to school to learn to read and write, to take him to Church on Sundays and holidays, to teach him a trade or to keep him busy with agricultural work so that, at his majority, the young man would be able to make a living. The administrators of the Foundling Hospital would keep a constant watch over the guardian and his ward and would pay an annual allowance of 40 livres until the boy reached age 16. From 16 to 20, Delagneau was to pay Leroy 80 livres per annum inclusive of room and board. Leroy might have to serve in the militia in place of Delagneau's son, should the latter draw a short straw.[131] Leroy was at least dealt with as an individual instead of as part of a great mass of foundlings sent off to work in a provincial factory, a more and more frequent practice in the last years of the old regime.[132] Oberkampf employed 900 such children at his textile factory in Jouy-en-Josas around 1780. Others worked at carding and spinning wool in the Holland cloth manufacture of the faubourg Saint Marcel and in the printed cloth factories throughout the Generality of Paris, at Saint Denis, Arcueil, Claye, Beauvais, Meaux and Corbeil.[133]

Two-thirds of the children born in Paris were not abandoned, and husbands and wives and unmarried couples continued to live together. The arrangements were not always peaceful, but they were stable. Furthermore, there was a sense among the laboring poor that the family was a unit that ought to be defended, even if this sometimes made necessary the intervention of public authority. Complaints of "dissoluteness and loose living" on the part of a spouse are numerous, and the usual remedy sought was to have the offender locked up in Bicêtre or La Salpêtrière, although men also indulged in the more direct action of wife beating. Quite a few mothers and fathers, including some of very modest circumstances, asked for royal orders to imprison or ship off to the colonies an errant son, on the claim that his conduct was likely to dishonor the family.[134] A case in point is that of Louis Pirouel and his wife, Marie Jeanne Prévot, who had worked as domestics for the same employer for 14 years. In December, 1777, this stable and proud couple appealed to the lieutenant-general of police to lock up their 15-year-old daughter at Sainte Pelagie because she could not keep a job, stayed out regularly until 10 or 11 at night, and was a suspected thief. They pleaded:

It is in these circumstances that we dare to hope, My Lord, that, although we are domestics, you may heed our prayer and make it possible for us to safeguard the honor we have acquired by our conduct and irreproachable probity. We would make the sacrifice, for this unfortunate, of six-months' board at Sainte Pelagie, so as to bring her back to the straight and narrow path; we still have two other daughters, My Lord. You may judge our position by the burden of three children, but one must safeguard one's reputation and have nothing to reproach oneself.[135]

The citation reveals a highly developed sense of personal honor and a desire for the maintenance of reputation. To be sure, these are domestics speaking, and they may have absorbed the dominant social values through close association with their masters more easily than did other working people. Still, other evidence allows us to speculate that honor among the poor sometimes took the place of more material blessings. It was the only patrimony they had to protect, and this they did with a will, both in and outside the family. Eagerly they brought their domestic quarrels and cases of minor insults to the attention of the police who could do nothing more than arrange an apology or perhaps reprimand the guilty party.[136] There was also the more effective appeal to public opinion, when the community was called upon to note and disapprove of the conduct of a spouse, child, customer or neighbor, or to referee a trial by combat. Petty violence of this sort was endemic to the quarters inhabited by the laboring poor. Their well-deserved reputation for being short tempered and quick to take offense was just another sign of their indigence and frustration. They could not attack the social order, so they turned their hatreds and dissatisfactions inward upon themselves and their fellows.[137]

The map of Paris drawn in 1787 shows the successive enclosures from Roman times through the middle ages and down to the end of the eighteenth century. In 1786 a wall ten feet high was built to provide a customs barrier for the General Farm. Its construction gave rise to much protest on the part of Parisians, and one of their first revolutionary actions in 1789 was to attack and destroy these hated symbols of oppression.

These drawings of street merchants and itinerant workers were done by Bouchardon in the 1740s and published under the title *Les Cris de Paris*. They constitute the best record of what the Parisian laboring
poor actually looked like. Like all Parisians, they were small of stature. Their clothes, second hand, old
and sometimes bearing the distinguishing marks of their trade, tended to set them off from the rest of the
population.

The place Maubert on the Left Bank, at the edge of the Latin Quarter and bordering on the populous
faubourg Saint Marcel, has always been a center for the activities of the laboring poor. Here we see a
market scene with the typical accumulation of minuscule enterprises, mainly hawkers of fruits and vegetables. Note the animated discussion of poorly dressed marketwomen. On the right, a crowd is being entertained (or edified) by a street singer recounting what appears (from the picture displayed) to be a
highly moral tale.

Gagne-Petit Auvergnat

One of the numerous migrant workers found amongst the floating population of the Parisian laboring poor. This man no doubt circulated in the streets of the capital with his grinding wheel, calling out for scissors and knives to be sharpened.

Carpe Vive—Fresh Carp for Sale
Cotterets—Firewood
La Vie, La Vie—
The cry of the brandy merchant,
from the name of the drink,
eau-de-vie.
Peaux de Lapin—Rabbit Skins for Sale

These subjects, drawn from life by Bouchardon for his *Cris de Paris* (1737-1741) are a good sample of the peripatetic merchants who offered their goods for sale in the streets of Paris. The other prints show their companions in poverty, an old mason and a porter.

The promenade on the ramparts of Paris in the 1760s where the elite met to take the air and engage in worldly conversation, to see and, especially, to be seen. The poem speaks of the striking contrast between "stupid opulence" and poverty, the latter represented by the apple seller, accordion player, and coffee vendor in the foreground.

Here we see the nursing sisters of the Hôtel Dieu performing their morning exercises—making up the beds with straw pallets, cleaning the ward, feeding the sick, emptying bedpans, and carrying a dead body off to the morgue. The picture is somewhat idyllic when compared to reality, but even so it shows us that conditions were rather less than perfect. Note especially the presence of several patients in a single bed.

The pillory to which criminals were sentenced for petty infractions, of which theft was the most typical. This punishment was often accompanied by branding and exile from Paris, more rarely by commitment to the galleys for a period ranging from three to nine years.

Nine scenes from the life of Antoine François Desrues, master criminal. Desrues is shown watching the poisoning of Mme. de la Motte and her son. He then carries off their bodies and arranges for their disposal. He seeks to convince M. de la Motte that he should honor a debt contracted by his wife. The last four scenes are typical of the *cursus honorem* of persons convicted of capital crimes. Desrues is tortured to make him confess, he is required to beg forgiveness in front of Notre Dame, he is confronted with his wife (who, of course, faints), and he is burnt at the stake, while the crowd looks on.

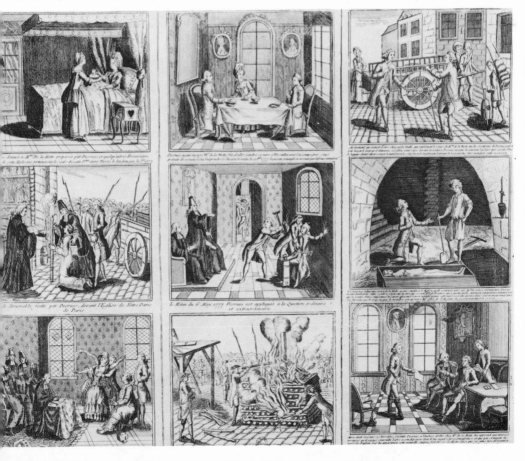

The whores of Paris were numerous in the eighteenth century. They were divided into many categories from the equivalent of present-day call girls on down the scale. But it would seem that the myth of the whore with the heart of gold had not yet been invented.

The first engraving shows the whores of Paris about to be shipped off to America. It is done deliberately in a flashy primitive style, reminiscent of a sixteenth-century woodcut. The apothecaries and surgeons are shown as losing their most constant and important clients.

The second picture shows the whores having their heads shaved and being shipped off to the hospital, the usual punishments. Posters on the wall advertise hats for bald heads and offer hair for sale. The man on the left holds a copy of the new police order in his hand, and a streetsinger recites a moral tale for the crowd.

[th]e picture at the top shows the Jansenist convulsionaries in the midst of their religious exercises. The [ma]n in the right-hand corner is being beaten with a heavy stick, his ecstasy being a proof of the grace [th]at had been communicated to him.

The picture at the bottom shows Jansenists praying at the tomb of the Diacre Paris. His reputation [fo]r holiness had given rise to the belief that miraculous cures could be obtained by prayer through his [int]ercession. Both pictures testify to the multiclass nature of this form of Jansenism. But note the presence [in] the second picture of simply dressed lower-class women.

At the end of August 1788, there were a series of demonstrations held in the place Dauphine and throughout the neighborhood of the Pont Neuf in support of the exiled Parlement. The Parlement of Paris had succeeded in presenting itself as the champion of the people's interests against the monarchy on numerous occasions throughout the eighteenth century, and this was yet another example of what was by now an almost traditional alliance. The participation of considerable numbers of the laboring poor made this the first stage in the development of a revolutionary mass movement.

ntons à perdre haleine | Après un long Carême | Vous mon Tuteur avide | Vous Marchandes de Modes
ureux événement, | L'appetit est meilleur | Voyons, comptons nous deux | Plaiseuses de Rabats,
qqement nous ramène | Faisons donc notre Thême | Ou le Juge décide | Regarnissez vos Cordes,
e bon Parlement. & bon, bon | Chante mon Procureur. & flon | Si vous êtes un queux. & flon | Riez aux Avocats, & flon, flon

nneur et l'innocence | Notre Femme sera sage, | Les Normands par le coche | Tout dit la Chansonnette
tre leurs oppresseurs, | Ou grace au Parlement | Rapportent leurs procès. | Fini par des chansons
eurvient sans défense, | Je le fais mettre en cage, | Alerte la Bazoche, | La preuve en est complette
s ils ont leurs vengeurs. & flen | Et ça dans le moment. & flon | Et vous aussi Greffiers. & flon | Chantons donc et dansons. & flon

The people celebrating the return of the Parlement of Paris in September
1788. Throughout the eighteenth century, the Parlement had managed to
maintain a reputation for the defense of popular interests against the undertakings of government policy. As a result, the laboring poor often supported
the pretensions of the Parlement to play a legislative and political, and not
merely a judicial, role. The events of 1788–1789 are the last instance of this
kind of alliance, for the laboring poor were soon to learn that the robe
nobility did not, in fact, have its welfare at heart.

The laboring poor went to drink in the cabarets or *guinguettes* located in the suburbs beyond the cus toms barriers. The wine was cheap and the play was rough. The most celebrated of these establishmen around 1760 was called Au Tambour Royal (At the Sign of the Royal Drum), run by Ramponneau. Th title of the engraving is a play on words. The suburb where Ramponneau operated was called La Courtill In French, the word for a barnyard is *basse cour*. Hence, the title, "The Phenomenon of the Basse Cou tille," to create the idea of a low, animal-like amusement of the laboring poor.

This engraving of the Pont Neuf illustrates the crowded confusion of the place in the middle of the eig eenth century. Note the women lying in the roadway, presumably having been knocked down by team of horses, also the men dueling in front of the stalls on the left. Constables are on the way to st the fighting. In the foreground, one sees a flock of sheep out of control, and a horse rearing up and stroying the buckets of a water carrier. The Pont Neuf was in fact much as it is here depicted, the co mercial and criminal center of Paris in the eighteenth century.

[3]

THE CONDITIONS

OF LIFE

⇜ I ⇝

In 1787, a disgruntled Parisian wrote:

Ever since Paris has been in the process of becoming a new city, it is proper that the public should know that there are distinguished districts, and others that are ignoble, streets for duchesses, others for bourgeoisies, and still others, haunts for persons unknown and people in hiding.[1]

Lavallée was speaking against the then current modishness of the Palais Royal, but, more important, he was pointing to a change in the habits of Parisians in regard to their choice of dwelling places.

With the exception of a large part of the nobility of both robe and sword, which had tended to congregate in select areas like the Marais and the faubourg Saint Germain at least as early as the seventeenth century, residential segregation by class or estate was relatively undeveloped and its patterns flexible. It was only at the beginning of the nineteenth century that first individual buildings and then entire quarters became homogeneous in population, and where they remained heterogeneous, the social distance between the several types of tenants tended to diminish greatly.[2] Before the Revolution, the same house might provide lodgings for a wide variety of individuals, from the rich bourgeois on the first floor to the worker eking out a living in his tiny attic room. Once the practice of renting out sections of houses in bits and pieces—a single tenant occupying several rooms on different floors—had given

way, in the seventeenth century, to leasing by floors,[3] social distinctions came to be measured vertically rather than horizontally:
the higher the story, the lower the class.

The high cost of land, in comparison to that of building materials and labor (although the latter were increasing steadily in our
period), caused proprietors to raise their houses as high as possible
so as to secure greater income.[4] Whatever may have been the architect's original plan, matters were so arranged that the commodious
apartment on the first floor, the so-called *étage noble*, gave way,
by stages of subdivision, to the miserable mansard of the sixth or
seventh. The most common arrangement was to have floor plans
that were essentially similar from the first to the fifth floor, topped
off by one in which rooms were individually let. But the intermediary floors might be subdivided into two or more apartments
and, even when this was not so, sub-subleasing was so common
that a great many people could be crowded into a very small
space indeed.[5] Many of these buildings were in the hands of relatively modest proprietors recruited from the ranks of the master
artisans. Ownership of a house in the city, like ownership of land
in the country, was an investment that brought stability and pres-
tige, so much so that it was common for four or five people to join
together to buy a building on credit. And the desire to protect their
investment (or, in the case of a principal tenant, not to fall heir
to another man's debts) tended to make them hard in driving a
bargain and quick to enforce a contract against a delinquent tenant.[6]

Built of plaster over slats and rubble or even of freestone from
the quarries on the southern edge of the city, rental houses intended for the mass of the people were far from architectural
masterpieces. Most observers found them quite ordinary, not to
say dirty and unattractive, especially in contrast to the beautiful
monumental buildings scattered around the capital.[7] In the most
densely populated central districts, the houses tended to be narrow
and deep, perhaps 18 feet wide and 50 to 90 feet long. The typical
house rose three or four stories in addition to an attic floor. The
frontage on the street was made up of a shop and a passageway
leading to the staircase. Often, two buildings were built one behind the other, separated by a small courtyard. In that case, the
building in the back was apt to be slightly smaller and lower than the
one facing the street.[8]

Rooms in these buildings were only just beginning to be planned
for specialized functions at this time. Normally they were distinguished only by the words "chamber" and "antichamber,"
which indicated more their relationship to one another than what

one was supposed to do in them. Kitchens and dining rooms, specifically designed as such, were rarely found anywhere but on the ground floor, where they were intended to serve the needs of the tenant on the *étage noble* immediately above.[9] The laboring poor lived, ate, slept, and sometimes worked in one or two adjoining rooms, meagerly furnished and devoid of all comfort.[10] Toilets, which proprietors were sometimes obliged to install, were an integral part of lodgings intended for the prosperous but were placed on the landings when intended for use in common by the poor. Lack of ventilation caused a continual stench in the rooms and corridors adjoining.[11]

Insofar as the poor experienced difficulty in obtaining housing, it was a matter of price more than of shortage of space. Rents of all classes of accommodation rose continuously after 1760,[12] and often the only way the poor had of coping with the situation was to abandon their lodgings when the rent fell due, leaving their few miserable bits of furniture behind in lieu of payment.[13] Mercier estimated the number of families who did this as a regular practice at from 3,000 to 4,000, moving every three months.[14]

It is probable that the poor paid proportionately more for their housing than did the rich. But it is difficult to find figures or rental values other than for entire houses. The proprietors' ordinary practice was to lease the house to a principal tenant, who would sublease apartments and rooms as he chose. He alone was responsible to the proprietor and the tax collector. Occasionally, we do find statistics that confirm our initial impressions about the heterogeneity of tenancies. Take, for example, a house on the rue d'Argenteuil, Saint Roch parish, in which the choice apartment rented for 700 livres a year in 1786, but a single room on the sixth floor fetched only 40 livres. A journeyman joiner paid 130 livres a year for two rooms on the third floor. In 1777, a workingman might rent a room on the rue du Roule for 68 livres a year, or one in the faubourg Saint Honoré for 90 livres. One hundred livres would get him two rooms on the third or fourth floor on the rue de la Tixanderie (now the rue de Rivoli) in 1780. Or if he were really hard pressed, a room on the fifth floor in the rue des Grands Degrés would cost only 36 livres.[15] In almost every quarter of the city, and particularly in those of the Louvre (Saint Germain l'Auxerrois), the Halles, the Grève and the faubourg Saint Antoine most frequented by the *menu peuple*, lodging was available at one to four sous a night.[16]

None of what has been said thus far is to be taken to mean that Paris was just a mass of streets undifferentiated as to population and activity. On the contrary, each quarter and sometimes a street or groups of streets within it had, as we have seen in chapter 1, definite characteristics, both social and professional. But while it is possible to classify each of them as more or less aristocratic, more or less bourgeois, it is equally, if not more, necessary to note their inner diversity. Today, when one identifies a person as living in the sixteenth arrondissement, one means that he is bourgeois, and in the twentieth, that he is a blue-collar or low-ranking white-collar worker. It was precisely this kind of identification that could not be made, at least not with the same degree of assurance, in the eighteenth century. It may have been the mixing of classes at close quarters that gave support to the established system of authority and deference in the period up to the Revolution, when the change in the political situation allowed social antagonisms to come out into the open. But such contact as there was between residents of different classes was most likely limited to brief encounters on the stairs, where the man of the people would perhaps acknowledge the passage of his socially superior neighbor. He was not even obliged to take his hat off as a sign of recognition, a lack of humility which some foreign observers found astonishing and unfortunate.[17] Nevertheless, to imagine some kind of interclass camaraderie as a result of propinquity is a delusion. People living in the same building often hardly knew each other, much less fraternized across class lines. Hardy tells the story of a man who had died in his lodgings in the Cité in May, 1777. For 10 months, no one had noted his disappearance nor entered his flat, despite the very bad odor emanating from it.[18] The anonymity of urban apartment living was already a well-established fact.[19]

Ariès has suggested that the crowding of Parisians into the city center protected them from developing a sense of isolation in the urban setting. Conversely, the subsequent development of residential segregation by district was felt by them as a deprivation.[20] Old patterns of community did break down as the nineteenth century went on, and nowhere was this more evident than in the increasing contrasts between the *beaux quartiers* and the working-class ghettoes of eastern and northeastern Paris. The miserable conditions of life fostered by these changes were not, however, caused by an increase in population density or the unmixing of the classes. Life in the working-class districts, both old and new, changed because the working class itself changed in both personnel and function. The setting reflected, even re-enforced, but did not create the social reality. The workingmen's semiarticulate feelings of loss and/or isolation sometimes focused on

his living quarters or his neighborhood as a symbol of the aliena-
tion consequent on the transformation of wage-earning Parisians
from artisans to industrial workers.

◄§ II §►

In a recent article, Robert Philippe has argued that Parisians were
a well-fed lot in 1789. Taking Lavoisier's figures on food consumption as his point of departure, he calculates that a population of
700,000 had a daily ration of 1,669 calories per person, of which
208 came from 52 grams of proteins. The theoretical ration set by
physiologists is 30 grams of protein per day, and the optimal ration
fixed by dieticians is one gram per kilo of weight. It would appear,
then, that a proper balance was maintained. In addition, 50 percent
of the total calories were made up of carbohydrates and one-third
of fats. In terms of food consumed, 50 percent of the calories came
from grains (mainly bread), 13 percent from meat, fish, and eggs,
11 percent from fats, 3 percent from sugar, 1.3 percent from dairy
products, and 10.5 percent from alcohol. On the whole, it was not
an unbalanced diet.[21]

The trouble is that these ingenious calculations are unacceptable,
both because of the information on which they are based and the
method used. First of all, Lavoisier's figures were taken from tax
registers of food brought into Paris. There is no way of knowing
whether all this food was in fact consumed in the city. Some of it
no doubt rotted, and some was re-exported, either in its original
form or, more likely, after having been processed. A part was
eaten by strangers passing only briefly through the city, and taking the figure of 700,000 as the total population does not make
sufficient allowance for their presence. It is Philippe's method,
however, that is particularly worrisome. Nowhere does he intro-
duce the concept of differential consumption by the several classes
or attempt to suggest how patterns of diet differed from the aristocracy down the ladder to the laboring poor. The only hint he
gives that such differences must have existed is in the table he
constructs of expenditure needed to buy 1,000 calories of various
foods. Taking 100 as the index number for bread, he shows that
the figure for meat of all kinds was 1,101, for fresh fish, 6,536,
for fresh cheese, 3,694, and for eggs, 600. Can it still be imagined
that the laboring poor ate as many proteins as the earlier calculation would lead us to believe? I think not. Furthermore, it should
be noted that 1,669 calories is a very moderate ration in any case,

enough perhaps for a sedentary (and not very hard) worker. Are we to suppose that it represented a true average ration, and that the protein segment was replaced, in the case of the laboring poor, by other nutrients? This is not impossible, but, even so, the total consumed can hardly be characterized as generous.[22] If it is yet to be shown that the Parisian workingman suffered from chronic malnutrition, we cannot be very sanguine about the healthfulness or sufficiency of his diet.

Bread was the basis of the Parisian diet, providing 50 percent of all the calories. In the eighteenth century, it was thought that three pounds were necessary for the daily ration of an adult worker, two pounds for a person who did no manual labor, and one and one-half pounds for a child.[23] There were several sorts of bread, varying in quality according to the type of grain used, the fineness of the milling and the proportion of bran or grits in the mixture. *Pain de ménage* was the name given the better sort of loaf, and *pain de boulanger* was a slightly inferior kind, but still of good quality.[24] The *menu peuple* insisted on pure wheat bread in preference to rye or mixed grains. As in the case of eastern European peasants, white flour was to them the symbol of a proper and nourishing diet. When hard pressed, they would eat bread made of other grains and cereals—rye, barley, oats, rice, potatoes, even turnips—but the scarcity of wheat always disturbed them profoundly.[25]

In the city proper there were between 200 and 250 bakers, most of whom sold their wares in their shops directly to a prosperous clientele, among whom the custom of having bread baked at home was on the decline. The bakers of the faubourgs, about 300 in number, were in the main small entrepreneurs who sold their goods both in their shops and in the open-air markets. But the bulk of bread consumed by the laboring poor was supplied to them by 850 to 1,000 bakers who came into the city regularly, several times a week, from the suburbs. Their centers of activity were Versailles, Saint Germain-en-Laye, Nanterre, and, above all, the village of Gonesse. Bread from Gonesse, the grain for which was grown on very rich arable land, had a particularly excellent reputation, even though it was at least 12 hours old when offered for sale in Paris. It was sold exclusively in the markets, for Parisian bakers would not stock it, and regulations forbade direct delivery to the purchaser.

The largest and most important market was held twice weekly, on Wednesdays and Saturdays, at the Halles. About 300 bakers, mainly from the faubourgs, frequented it in the 1720s. There were subsidiary markets throughout the city, notably at the Palais Royal and the Cour des Boucheries in the central area, at Saint Paul and the cemetery of Saint Jean in the east, at the Marché Neuf of the Cité, and at Saint Germain and the Place Maubert on the Left Bank. Most bakers brought no more than one hundred kilos of bread with them, and they normally traded in one market only. They were in general not permitted to take home with them any bread that had been offered for sale, with the result that when the supply was abundant, prices fell as the day went on. In order to profit from this circumstance, the poor waited until late in the day to buy their provisions.[26] It appears that Parisians did not care very much about the freshness of the bread, for they would buy a four- or five-day supply at a time. The important thing was not to be caught short.

Despite the action taken by the royal and municipal authorities to hold prices down and the availability of credit from bakers, there were some members of the laboring poor who could not afford to purchase a whole loaf of bread. They were reduced quite literally to eating crumbs, a practice which never failed to attract the attention of foreign visitors. The German, Friedrich Schulz, wrote about his visit to Paris in 1789:

I must admit that in Paris people pay great attention to bread and that scarcely a crumb is allowed to go unused. . . . Here leftovers that elsewhere are given to domestic animals are still used by people. In the eating houses bread that stays on the table in pieces one day is used the next in soup . . . and in large households it is collected by the servants or kitchen workers and—sold. It seems strange that crumbs, crusts and sliced pieces of bread should be sold here, but it is true: since in the poorer quarters of the city I have seen whole stalls full of it. These bread sellers work with a few large houses in which the servants sell them leftovers. Pieces of black, white, fine and coarse bread, some baked with water, others with milk, stand in big baskets, are neatly sorted out by the merchants and sold according to type. It is only half as expensive as fresh baked whole loaf bread. Bread crumbs are also collected and sold to even poorer people for a quarter of the price, to be used in soup.[27]

In the same way, the poor bought cooked leftovers from the tables of large houses, even from the king's table. Much of this food was moldy and inedible by the time it reached them, but they ate it anyway for lack of a better alternative. The fried dough cooked, as Mercier said, in something resembling axlegrease and hawked in the streets was not very attractive, less so than the food sold in the *gargotes* of the faubourgs, where for three sous one could dunk the bread bought elsewhere in a common soup kettle.[28]

The concern of the royal authorities was to provide an adequate supply of bread, for they knew that a shortage of this fundamental item of the workingman's diet might lead to protest and riot. Hence their numerous measures regulating the sale and purchase of grain, the composition, baking, and price of bread, and the conduct of merchants, millers, and bakers.[29] Hence also their attempts to keep the city well supplied, even when this meant a policy of importation and subsidy. All these activities were inadequate, however, inasmuch as the low technical level of agriculture, the poor transportation system, the patterns of land tenure, and local particularism, and, above all, the thousand exploitative burdens that weighed upon the peasantry made it impossible to create a truly national market capable of responding to changes in demand. Bakers sometimes made a minor contribution to the difficulties by cheating on the weight of merchandise, a short weight of five or six ounces in the ordinary four-pound loaf being not unusual.[30] The worker and the *bas peuple* were the chief victims of this practice because they hadn't the time to spend in making complaints. As a contemporary put it, "They will not sacrifice a day's work in order to complain [to the police] about two or three farthings stolen from them."[31]

But the laboring poor did complain when threatened with shortages or a decline in the quality of bread. On the first point, so much has been written about eighteenth-century bread riots that we need scarcely pause to go over familiar ground. The loss of this vital foodstuff was the only calamity for which the king himself could be held personally responsible, in consequence of his failure, as father to his people, to be a good provider.[32] To take only one example: the fact that the difficult year 1768, when the price of bread went as high as 16 sous for a four-pound loaf, saw no important riot, was something of a minor miracle. As the price rose steadily from the month of July onwards, petitions were sent to the government and to leading political figures, but without result. By September, the *menu peuple* had become angry, and signs sprang up all over Paris threatening the king and his ministers, the Duc de Choiseul and Laverdy. Threats to burn down the city unless prices decreased were probably idle, but it is nonetheless a measure of popular discontent that the following statement could have been written by Parisians, who were justly renowned as being *plus royalistes que le roi*:

. . . under Henri IV, there was an increase in the price of bread brought on by the wars, but . . . in those days, we had a king. . . .

Under Louis XIV, there were also several instances of a rise in the price of bread, caused now by war, now by a real shortage due to bad weather, but . . . we had a king. . . . Nowadays, the high cost of bread could not be attributed either to wars or a real shortage of grain but . . . we have no king, because the king is a grain merchant.[33]

Paris seems to have been adequately supplied with meat animals —steers, cows, calves, sheep and pigs—in the eighteenth century. Estimates of the number of animals entering the city annually vary in the extreme. Figures from several sources in the 1760s and 1770s put the annual importation of sheep at about 450,000 and of pigs at 35,000, in addition to an unknown quantity of meat already slaughtered and dressed when offered for sale in the city.[34] Beef cattle came from the Pays d'Auge and the Pays de Bray in Normandy and from the districts to the east and south of the Loire. Sheep and lambs were brought in from the calcareous area of the Parisian basin, Normandy, Berry, Bourbonnais, Sologne, and the Beauce. Foreign imports from the Hapsburg lands supplemented domestic production, especially in the early autumn of each year.[35] The animals were sold to Parisian butchers, some 230 in number, on Mondays and Thursdays in the markets of Sceaux and Poissy, where the government had established an administration whose purpose it was to collect a tax levied on each animal and to advance money to butchers, so that they might make their purchases. Calves were offered for sale in Paris every Friday, and the 260 pork butchers of the city bought their pigs on Wednesdays and Saturdays near the Gobelins in the faubourg Saint Marcel. They slaughtered and prepared the meat and then retailed it in their shops scattered throughout the city.[36]

Some meat was sold at retail in the *guinguettes* on the outskirts of the city, but the great majority of available animals actually entered Paris and therefore had to pay taxes to the General Farm. This inevitably pushed the price upward, out of reach of the laboring poor, except on special occasions several times a year. Lenoir noted in 1801 that one of the greatest changes of the previous 25 years was that the *menu peuple* now included meat in their diet on a regular basis.[37] A pound of butcher's meat sold at 7 sous in 1750 and rarely went above 7/6 before 1770. It then remained in the range of 8 to 8/6 from 1770 to 1785, after which date it reached 10 sous. There were, as might be expected, fluctuations in price, but these were not great in comparison with the movement of the price of bread. Still, this represents a rise of nearly 50 percent in a 40-year period. Pork products like ham and bacon were even more expensive, the price rising after 1767 from a low of 8/6 to 12 to 14 sous per pound.[38] The only meat that the laboring poor could afford, and then only in small quantities, was the *abats* (tripes and other innards, either as such or ground up into sausages), for even the mediocre cuts of the so-called *basse boucherie*, which needed heavy seasoning with salt, pepper, vinegar, garlic and shallots "to enhance their insipid taste," were not cheap.[39] Butchers took advantage of their poor customers by the use of false weights and by giving them the *réjouissances* (bones and other inedible matter), secure in the knowledge that, should they complain, they were unlikely to get a sympathetic hearing from police officials. It also seems that butchers were able to charge the same price for better and poorer cuts of meat but reserved the former for prosperous artisans, bourgeois, and "gens qui tiennent bonne table."[40] It included sweetbreads, tongue, kidneys and various cuts of steak, which is a measure of the distance that separated the bourgeois from the laborer and his classic diet of bread and cheese. No doubt the distinctions were further emphasized by the way meals were arranged in well-to-do households. Rather than the practice, which has become quasi-universal since the mid-nineteenth century, of serving each person the same foods, one after the other in this order: hors d'oeuvres, soup, fish, meat, vegetables, cheese, and dessert, the eighteenth century divided the dinner into services. Thus, twelve guests would be typically served in the following manner:

FIRST SERVICE:

    Two Soups
    A Roast Beef (in the middle of the table)
    Two Hors d'Oeuvres

SECOND SERVICE:

    Veal Roast with Truffles, *Bonne Femme*
    Lamb Chops with Basil
    Duck
    Poularde
    The Roast Beef remains

THIRD SERVICE:

    Two Roasts
    Three Sweets
    Two Salads

FOURTH SERVICE:

    A Bowl of Fresh Fruit
    A Compote of Apples

A Compote of Pears
A Plate of Biscuits
A Plate of Chestnuts
A Plate of Gooseberry Jam
A Plate of Apricot Marmalade[41]

Even if each person ate no more than he would have if served individually and with little choice of dishes, the ordering of the meal in this way created (and was intended to create) a sense of opulence and well-being. It also served to sharpen the image of the greedy, gluttonous, gout-ridden, and corrupt rich and may have contributed, in the end, to the sharpening of social antagonisms and to the development of political consciousness among the laboring poor.

With the exception of the domestic worker in a large household who ate well on the leftovers of his master's table, there were, in the opinion of contemporaries, no people in the world "more badly nourished than the people of Paris"—soup and bread afternoon and evening, with a bit of bad meat on Sunday and occasionally during the week; some cheese and a little butter from time to time; almost no fish; and no green vegetables "because the preparation is always expensive."[42] And the poor paid more than others for poorer quality food because they could not afford to buy in any but the smallest quantities. As Mercier wrote: "As he never has more cash on hand than is sufficient for his daily expenditures, he buys even cloves one at a time, in the morning only for his lunch, in the evening only for his supper."[43] The *menu peuple* were supplied by *regrattiers* and especially *regrattières*, merchants who purchased small quantities of goods in the central markets to sell at retail and who, consequently, were middlemen contributing to the rise in price of commodities of the first necessity. This was all the more true as they themselves were most often so poor that they had to borrow from usurers (at twenty percent a week) in order to replenish their stocks.[44] They did business in the central and district markets and also as pedlars in the streets. They (and other small tradesmen, like shoemakers, public letter writers, and dealers in used clothing) sometimes had little stalls set up against the walls of churches and other public buildings so they could display their goods. The authorities considered them a public nuisance and tried to limit their activity more than once. Closely watched over by the police and despite the high prices they were forced to charge, these petty merchants performed a useful service for their fellows among the laboring poor, who could not afford to go running off to a market (perhaps as far as a mile away) several times a day.[45]

At the beginning of the Revolution, there were 73 public fountains in Paris.[46] Their number was grossly inadequate for the needs of the population, and the water they provided was none too pure. It could be fetched from the fountains but was also offered for sale by water carriers at a penny or less a bucket.[47] A privileged few had wells on their own premises, and running water was for all intents and purposes unknown. The first steps to remedy this state of affairs were taken only in the 1780s with the construction of the great Samaritaine pump near the Pont Neuf. Still, only the tiny minority who could afford the price of a private subscription were directly helped by this innovation, and real change had to await the inauguration of the Canal de l'Ourcq under the Empire. Water was nonetheless the habitual, sometimes the only, drink of the laboring poor—men, women and children. Over time they developed a certain resistance to its ill effects, but strangers often fell violently sick from drinking it.[48]

It is reported that toward the end of the old regime the poor took up the habit of drinking *café au lait* in the mornings in place of wine or brandy. The coffee must have been very weak indeed, for it cost 22 to 28 sous a pound, and sugar to sweeten it cost 15 to 20 sous a pound. The only way the laboring poor could afford it was to buy it by the cup from street vendors.[49]

Beer and cider were drunk by the *menu peuple* only occasionally, and the consumption of beer in particular seems to have declined considerably from the third quarter of the century. In 1750, 40 brewers produced 75,000 *muids* of beer each year, but there remained only 23 brewers in 1782, and their total production did not exceed 26,000 *muids*.[50] Wine was more common but generally of poor quality even when it was not cut with vinegar and dyestuffs. The abolition in September, 1759 of the privilege accorded the bourgeois of Paris, which allowed them to sell wine produced from grapes grown on their own estates without paying taxes, was a considerable misfortune for their poorer clients. Henceforth, excise taxes were imposed on all wine sold in Paris by the General Farm, and it was consequently too expensive for the poor. Some smuggling went on, enough for the agents of the tax farmers to complain loudly about the lack of cooperation given them by the police in apprehending the offenders, but hardly sufficient to slake the thirst of the working classes.[51] On Sundays, they could get ferociously drunk at the *guinguettes* in the suburbs of the Right and Left Banks, where a bottle of poor quality wine cost only a penny and a half as compared with four or five sous in town. On workdays they were sober because, as an English visitor noted, wine upon entering the city "changes into *aurum potabile.* A small measure sells for more at Paris than a Barrel in the Country . . . [and the vintners] are almost all Saints, for the Virtue they have of increasing this Liquor, by changing Water into Wine, that is, by making Bacchus an Adulterer."[52] The construction of the new barriers around Paris in 1786 did not affect the taverns of the Left Bank, located as they were in Gentilly, Ivry, Montrouge and Vaugirard. On the other hand, those located on the Right Bank in Clichy, La Villette, La Petite Pologne and Les Porcherons were severely threatened by a price rise and consequent loss of business. Wine merchants, tavern keepers, grape growers and consumers worked together to keep the now contraband drinks flowing. This they did in the most ingenious ways—by laying pipelines under the barriers and sometimes catapulting sacks filled with wine over them. Both the General Farm and the city guard were power-less to stop them. In July, 1789, the attacks against the barriers were led by persons known to be engaged in the contraband trade, and disturbances of one sort or another continued to take place until the National Assembly repealed the excise taxes in 1791, about a year after it had implicitly recognized the attacks on tax collectors as revolutionary acts by ordering the suspension of prosecutions arising therefrom.[53]

⋙ III ⋘

The materials for a study of the demography of the Parisian laboring poor are all but nonexistent. If common sense leads us to suppose that the rich were better protected against illness and death than were the poor, that is about as far as we can go, sta-tistically at least. We do not have the figures by parish, but even if we did, they would not necessarily be of great use to us—first, because of the mixed nature of the population in each locality and second, because we would have no warrant to assume that everyone died in their home parish. The figures in Table 3–1 indi-cate that births and deaths very nearly balanced one another during the greater part of the eighteenth century. There are now fewer "mortal crises," years in which there was a sharp rise in the number of deaths and a sharp fall in the number of conceptions, than there had been in the seventeenth century. They had been replaced by years of "latent crises," which Meuvret has defined for a peasant

TABLE 3-1

Marriages, Births, and Deaths in Paris, 1709–1785

YEARS	MARRIAGES	BAPTISMS	DEATHS
1709–18	4,118	16,988	17,393
1710–29	4,246	17,948	17,674
1730–49	4,167	18,692	19,115
1749–71	——	19,082	19,104
1750–69	——	19,549	19,118
1764–75	4,766	19,287	19,003
1752–61	4,208	19,221	19,225
1750	4,619	19,035	17,853
1755	4,501	19,412	19,831
1760	3,787	17,991	18,332
1765	4,782	19,439	18,934
1770	4,775	19,549	18,719
1775	5,016	19,650	18,662
1780	——	19,617	21,094
1785	——	19,855	20,147

SOURCES: *Recherches statistiques sur la ville de Paris et le Département de la Seine*, 4 vols. (Paris, 1824–1829), I, Table 55.
Ville et Faubourgs de Paris—Etat de baptêmes etc. Copy may be found in Lk⁷ 6097, Bibliothèque Nationale.
Ms. N.A. fr. 3240, Bibliothèque Nationale.
Messance, *Recherches sur la population des généralités d'Auvergne, de Lyon, de Rouen etc.* (Paris, 1768).
J. Auffray, "Etat raisonné des populations de Londres et de Paris," *Journal économique* (March, 1772): 111–116.
A. Chevallier and G. Lagneau, "Quelques remarques sur le mouvement de la population de Paris à un et, deux siècles d'intervalle," *Annales d'hygiène publique et de médecine légale,* 2nd series, XXXIX (1873).

society as a "complex of endemic unemployment and growing indebtedness . . . it did not kill immediately, nor everyone at the same time. It slowly wore people out."[54] The same might be said of Paris, where so many came to try their hand at survival, only to die before their time, used up by malnutrition, exhaustion, and the diseases to which this state exposed them. This was particularly true of the floating population and the indigent, categories which tended to overlap. If anything, we may suspect that the figures presented here err on the side of optimism, precisely because they probably do not fully take into consideration all of the floaters who died while staying in the capital. The proportion of deaths to admissions in the Hôtel-Dieu, where most of the sick belonged to the laboring poor, is a truer reflection of the situation. In the years 1724 to 1763, this figure was, on an average 1:4½, which is some measure of the difference between the general death rate and that prevailing among the *menu peuple*.[55] The former was variously estimated at 1:30 to 1:35 (28.6 to 33.3 per thousand) by con-

temporary demographers.[56] Clearly, the rate among workingmen
and women was not seven times as great, but we do have some
figures for the parish of Saint Etienne du Mont in 1766–1783 that
work out to a rate of 1:8.75 (114 per thousand), or almost four
times as great.[57] Saint Etienne was a densely populated and extremely popular district on the fringes of the faubourg Saint
Marcel.

On the basis of figures for 1764–1775, it has been calculated that
for every 10,000 births, there were 9,853 deaths in Paris.[58] This
was hardly a significant growth ratio, the more so as the calculation ignores the mortality of infant children sent out of the city
to be nursed—and to die. Despite a birth rate variously estimated
at 1:29.5 to 1:35 (28.6 to 33.8 per thousand), Paris would probably have lost population in the eighteenth century had it not been
for a steady flow of immigrants from the provinces. They were
mainly workingmen, and they came from every part of France,
but particularly from the Parisian region, Normandy and the east.
At certain times of the year, the seasonal migrants from the Massif
Central and other provinces arrived to work in the building trades
or to add to the extraordinary number of petty street workers
who crowded the hotels and lodging houses. Many of those who
came with no intention of settling eventually became permanent
residents, but usually only after several journeys back to their
homes in the country or some time spent wandering in the environs
of Paris searching for work.[59]

The population of late eighteenth-century France was a young
one. About 1775, for every thousand persons, 426 were under 20
years of age, 503 were between 20 and 49, 83 between 50 and 59,
and only 71 over 60.[60] The population of Paris was probably even
younger, with the greatest portion in the 20- to 40-year age group.
It was an age pyramid that resulted from the twin effects of infant
mortality and internal migration. The great majority of migrants
were young adult males, as the survey of the hotel population
carried out in the summer of 1791, shows. In the section de
l'Oratoire, 70.5 percent of this category were aged 20 to 40, while
the figure for the section of la place Vendôme was 66 percent.[61]
Although there were perhaps 104 males born for every 100 females
in the middle of the century, the male death rate was also high,
115 men for every 100 women. Various explanations of this phenomenon have been proposed, of which two ought to be kept in
mind. First, men were exposed to more risks than were women,
in the form of military service, quarrels, accidents of work, and
travel. Second, bad working conditions and bad hygiene combined

to make men more susceptible to the effects of epidemics and famine. In any case, it is clear that after the age of 14, women out-numbered men in the domiciled population to a considerable extent.[62] The migration of young men from the provinces was thus a social and sexual necessity as well as an economic one.

It was commonly agreed in the first half of the century that one-quarter of all children born in a given year would die before they reached 1 year of age. In consequence, any statistic of the average life span is misleading. Except insofar as they may be compared with one another, figures of this sort bear very little relation to reality. When Deparcieux tells us that a survey of 3,700 children born in Paris showed an average life span of 23.6 years, as compared to 37 years in the Laón region and 41 years in the Cévennes and Bas Languedoc, we may legitimately inquire as to what made the capital so insalubrious, but we cannot assume that each child had at birth a life expectancy of 23.6 years.[63]

Life expectancy is quite another problem. Clearly, once the great hecatombs of early childhood were past, the survivors had a better chance of living to a relatively substantial age than they had had before. According to Duvillard's calculations, published in 1806 but based on information concerning the period *circa* 1770, 1,000 children at birth had a life expectancy of 28.8 years, but the 767 survivors at the end of the first year might expect to live an additional 36.3 years. The 672 who passed the barrier of their second birthday increased their expectancy to 40.4 years and so on, with the number of years to live increasing each year and peaking at 43.4 for 583 survivors, at age 5. The figure then de-creased gradually to 40.8 years at age 10, 37.3 at age 15, 34.3 at age 20 with only one-half of the original group still living.[64] The figures in Table 3-2 obtained by Dupré de St. Maur and published

TABLE 3-2

Number of Deaths Before Age Five per One Hundred Deaths, Paris

PARISH	AGE 0–1	1–2	2–3	3–4	4–5	TOTAL
St. André des Arts	11.7	7.0	5.4	4.7	2.0	31.5
St. Hippolyte	30.0	14.4	5.0	2.5	2.4	54.3
St. Nicolas	19.7	10.4	4.6	3.3	2.6	41.6
Paris	20.7	10.7	4.8	3.4	2.5	42.1
Rural parishes	34.5	8.9	3.2	2.4	1.6	50.6
St. Sulpice	21.3	(24.8 for ages 1–5)				

SOURCE: Roger Mols, *Introduction à la démographie historique des villes d'Europe du XIV au XVIIIe siècle*, 3 vols. (Gem'bloux, 1955–1956), II: 315 and III: 146, 213.

by Buffon coincide with Duvillard's results as to infant mortality and life expectancy, the overall differences of a minor sort being attributable to the normal variations over a short period of time. But there are differences among the parishes which are suggestive. Whereas the parish of Saint Nicolas follows the Paris average very closely in each of the five years studied, this is not so either for Saint André des Arts or Saint Hippolyte. The former had a large number of robe and intellectual families who probably sent their children to be nursed outside the city—hence the relatively low mortality rate for the first two years of life. The latter seems to be the reverse side of the coin. In a sector where the laboring poor were numerous, it is possible that the women of this parish did some baby farming, with the usual disastrous results. On the other hand, the high infant mortality rate may have affected only their own children and have been due simply to the high level of misery and poor health conditions. The figures for the rural parishes, we can be sure, reflect the losses of urban, as well as rural, children.

Contemporary doctors were certain that infant mortality weighed more heavily on children born in big cities than on those born in small towns and in the country, and on the children of the poor more than on the children of the rich. The reason for this, they said, was that too many urban mothers did not nurse their own children, generally out of necessity, particularly women of the *menu peuple*, more rarely (among the aristocrats and the bourgeois) for reasons of fashion.[65] The wet nurses who replaced the natural mothers were often still poorer than their clients. Undernourished and haggard, their milk could be nothing else but bad. Furthermore, they did not pay proper attention to the children in their care, with the result that those who survived often became twisted and infirm. Meanwhile, mothers who did not nurse were likely to conceive again in too short a space of time before having properly recovered from their earlier pregnancy. Children born of these mothers would be weak and less likely to live than their immediate predecessors.[66]

There was much truth in these observations. Women who nurse are less likely to become pregnant again so quickly, and this can only improve the health of the mother and subsequent children. As for the conduct of nurses, it ought to be said in their defense that their job was an immensely difficult one. All the conditions under which they worked—having several children to deal with at once, the prevalence of disease, inadequate medical supervision, their own poverty—conspired to kill off their charges, were they the sweetest and most tender of women. We hardly need to call on their fancied cruelties to explain infant morality.[67] In the second half of the century, a campaign developed to induce mothers to breast-feed their children or, otherwise, to use animal milk.[68] But cow's or goat's milk was an expensive commodity, not so easily available to the urban poor. Their children continued to be exposed to the contagion of *muguet* (*trush*, an oral infection with a fungus [*candida albicans*] characterized by white eruptions in the mouth) carried by wet nurses, despite the efforts of the government to check on the health of women who presented themselves for these jobs.[69] To this end, a special office called a Bureau de Recommanderesses was created in 1715 and reorganized in 1769. Women wishing to hire themselves out as nurses came to its hiring hall, where their milk and general state of health was tested. They also had to present a certificate of good morals from their parish priest and to prove that they possessed both a cradle and a fire screen. If employed, they were paid eight livres a month, with the management of the Bureau acting as intermediary between the nurse and the parents. The cost was relatively high, and payments were not easy to collect. The nurses were subject to quarterly visits by surgeon-inspectors appointed by the lieutenant-general of police. In this way, Parisians sent children into some 12,000 households within a 50-league radius of the city. Despite these precautions, the curés of these villages spent a lot of time sending death certificates back to the Bureau.[70]

Children who survived their early years often developed poorly and were particularly subject to diseases caused by nutritional deficiencies, like rickets and malformations of various parts of the body. They did not grow tall. According to military records, soldiers recruited in Paris reached an average height of from 5′1″ to 5′4″, but the evidence indicates that 10 to 20 percent of otherwise eligible men were exempt from army service because they were shorter than the minimum prescribed height of 5′1″.[71] Observers constantly noted the prodigious number of "deformed women and girls."[72] If Restif de la Bretonne, an ardent feminist, defended women from the charges of deformity, it was only because of their superior resistance, for he admitted that bad diet and poor living conditions did combine to produce physical malformations of the worst sort among men:

See all those who are of the people or merchants of Paris, that is, three-quarters of the city, floundering from childhood, in the depths of the back streets, in a gutter of filth. See their pallor! They look like plants that grow in the shade and have neither force nor substance.

These misshapen beings grow through the force of their fathers' blood, fathers who are often from the provinces: but if by misfortune they are of Parisian origin, they bend backwards, become bandy-legged, hunchbacked, twisted and of a fearful deformity; or at least of such delicate health that continual attention would be needed to keep their chest well. I have been speaking of women. But how does it happen that men degenerate faster in Paris, than do women: because girls there are often big, pretty, and well-built, although there are exceptions! This is because a sedentary life is less harmful to a woman, whose fiber is softer. But there is another reason. It is that the moral education of Paris is less harmful to the second sex, than to the first. Everything is craft, trade, and home work in Paris—which is what degrades men, but is particularly suitable for women.[73]

The other great scourge of childhood was smallpox. Once again it is from army records that we learn that few young adults did not carry some pock marks on their bodies as souvenirs of the disease, if indeed they survived its visitation.[74] Although inoculation was practiced by the aristocracy and the top layer of the bourgeoisie, it was still unknown among the other classes, least of all among the laboring poor. Mercier attributed this to the Parisians' lack of good sense, to their preference for prejudices and outmoded ideas. We shall see in a moment that he was substantially correct.[75]

In the absence of a coherent germ theory of disease, eighteenth-century doctors believed, reasonably enough, that there was a very close and direct relationship between climate and illness. Each session's papers of the Société Royale de Médecine began with an extensive analysis of changes in the weather in the year just past.[76] In the last quarter of the century, a new genre of medical topographical literature came to the fore, in which the authors studied the physical features of the city—the elevation of the quarters, the slopes of the streets, the height of the buildings, the direction of the winds, the course of the river—with a view to ascertaining their combined effect on the health of the population.[77]

The climate of Paris was mild, the average temperature being 12.5 degrees centigrade. In winter, −2 or −3 degrees was normal, in spring, 9 to 14 degrees, in summer, 15 to 32 degrees, and in the fall, 10 to 22.5 degrees, none of which figures are extreme. Every few years it would get cold enough for the Seine to freeze over. Happily, the ice did not usually remain solid for more than a few weeks, for disruption of water transport over a long period of time would have been disastrous. On the other hand, only about one-third of the days could be described as fine. A covered sky, humid atmosphere, and rain and fog were most usual. Contemporaries complained of a constant patch of smog, particularly strong in the populous quarters of the city center.[78] They agreed that narrow streets and tall buildings obstructed the free circulation of air, already corrupted by the presence of overly crowded cemeteries throughout the city. The common burial pits were left open until completely filled, with only a thin covering of earth spread over each layer of bodies. The bodies decomposed rapidly enough, but the ground was reused again too soon. The odors that emanated from the 15-foot deep pits were nauseating and, whether or not we can believe, as certain doctors did, that they were the cause of maladies of the brain and central nervous system, it is sure that they were hard to take, both physically and psychologically.[79] Some idea of this discomfort can be had by noting that each year 2,000 bodies were buried in the cemetery of the Holy Innocents in the very heart of the markets until it was at last closed in 1780. Most of the other parish cemeteries were not transferred until the Revolution, in what was an attempt to improve public health rather than to persecute Catholics and desecrate graves, as has sometimes been maintained.

The stench in the air was made worse by the habit Parisians had of emptying their chamber pots from their windows into the streets. The total lack of toilet facilities (in older buildings) or their disposition in one distant corner of a five- or six-storey house rather than any inherent hatred of hygiene, explain this practice well enough, perhaps along with the incidental pleasure of victimizing the watch companies during their night patrols.[80]

The streets were filthy as well as odoriferous. The slaughter houses, located in the quarters of heaviest population density (there were no fewer than 15 on the rue Saint Martin between the rue Maire and the rue de Montmorency, a distance of 160 yards) were largely at fault. The blood that flowed from them and the waste products strewn about were sources of "dirt, infection and illness" for the inhabitants of this "corrupt atmosphere . . . from which they cannot protect themselves."[81] Despite continuously repeated police ordinances requiring proprietors and tenants to clean their courtyards and street frontage, dirt continued to pile up year after year. Mud, household garbage, animal and human excrement, together with industrial waste from laundries, tanneries, weaving establishments, and others were jointly responsible for the filth.[82]

The chief illnesses, the true *maladies populaires* to which the laboring poor fell victim were "stoppage of the bowels, dropsies, consumptions [i.e. tuberculosis], and even a tendency to scurvy

supported and favored among the class of indigent citizens by
dearness of food, pollution of the air, and filth."[83] Of the epidemic
diseases, plague had entirely disappeared, to be replaced by typhoid,
malaria, and smallpox. Typhoid was endemic because of a poor
water supply that overcrowding contaminated with fecal matter,
and an outbreak always meant a high death rate, as in Paris in 1730
and 1779. Malaria was even more common but less fatal. Known
as autumnal fever because of its frequency at that season of the
year and treated with cinchona bark, it was particularly prevalent
during the second half of the century, in 1773, 1775–1776, 1780–
1785, and 1787–1788. Smallpox was also endemic in large cities and
was particularly murderous when it led to hemorrhaging. In Paris,
there were epidemics in 1770, each year from 1781 to 1784, in
1788, and in 1791. The grippe was common throughout the century under a variety of names, the ignorance of viruses making
it impossible to identify its many manifestations as a single disease.
Seventeen fifty-eight, 1782–1783, and 1799 were years of world
pandemics, from which Paris was not spared.[84]

Among other common diseases were scurvy and erysipelas, both
of them debilitating but not usually fatal in and of themselves.
Victims of gallstones and strangled hernias were subject to a high
rate of mortality during operations to relieve those obstructions.
Puerperal fever, not yet recognized as an infectious disease, killed
many women in childbirth, while hypertrophy of the prostate was
considered a perfectly normal cause of death in old men. Pulmonary tuberculosis and other lung diseases were rampant; one
doctor attributed this to "our sedentary labor; our excesses of all
kinds, our debauchery of every sort: the abuse of coffee, the
murderous use of swaddling clothes and whalebone corsets."[85] In
reality, tuberculosis, together with fevers of all types, accompanied
by rashes and often complicated by pleurisy and peripneumonia,
were just the kind of diseases that malnutrition, poor lodgings, and
bad hygiene helped to induce by weakening resistance and providing breeding grounds for dangerous germs.[86]

The narrow circumstances of the poor also facilitated the spread
of contagious diseases, for many were obliged to sleep with several others in a single bed, regardless of their state of health.[87]
Similar conditions prevailed in the hospitals, and patients often
contracted terrible skin diseases, like the mange, which they then
spread to people they came in contact with in their homes.[88] And
it was the laboring poor, the chief clients of the hospitals, who
were most often affected by a syndrome known as *pourriture
d'hôpital*, the crippling and mutilation that resulted from the fail-

ure of the staff to clean instruments and bandages that had been applied to gangrenous wounds before reuse.

The existence of occupational disease did not escape the notice of doctors, who were particularly keen on this branch of medicine, since the Italian, Ramazzini, had shown the way in 1700. His work, *De Morbis Artificum*, remained the standard authority for more than a century.

Metal workers (engravers, boilermakers, mirror makers), painters, potters, and glaziers were subject to mercury, copper, and lead poisoning through the constant inhalation of tiny particles of these materials. Although rarely fatal, these illnesses were chronic and debilitating. They were characterized by coughing, trembling and, eventually, paralysis, and those afflicted became incapable of working at an early age.[89] Tanners, dyers, saddlers, candlemakers, and others who worked with animal products contracted anthrax and similar diseases.[90] Dock workers were known to carry 1,200-pound loads, and the porters of the Halles carried sacks of flour weighing 320 pounds up four flights of stairs. Their loads were too great, and the strain caused some to die young on account of inflammations of the internal organs and apoplectic strokes.[91] But sedentary workers fared no better. Tailors, knife-grinders, and shoemakers sat all day long in dank, unventilated workshops, hunched over their labor. This was an unnatural position and "consequently must contribute to the deterioration of health. Thus, one hears these workers complain generally of bad digestion, flatulence or wind, headaches, chest pains, etc."[92]

The number of doctors and surgeons was grossly inadequate to meet the needs of Parisians in our period.[93] Considering the state of their knowledge, however, the limited access the poor had to them may have been a blessing in disguise. In 1758, Arnault de Nobleville described bleeding and purging as the "two principal remedies in medicine, and almost the only ones that one can use among the poor." And the pharmacopeia was composed largely of potions made from roots or even stranger ingredients, like crushed snails. External treatment was equally bizarre, viz. the following remedy for pleurisy: "Take a live pigeon, cut it down the back lengthwise: place it still warm on the aching side . . . and leave it there for 18 or 20 hours until the bad odor forces you to remove it."[94]

The laboring poor were habitually recalcitrant about taking medicine internally, the more so if no results were immediately forthcoming.[95] The quest for immediate satisfaction of their felt needs was a particular characteristic of the *menu peuple*, but there was something even more basic at work here. The poor were conservative, that is, they did not wish to disturb the ordered pattern of their daily lives. They distrusted innovation, especially when it had to do with one's body. They particularly disliked the innovators, the doctors and *dames de charité* who came from outside the community and were therefore automatically suspect. The poor did not have to, and probably did not, identify them as the class enemy in order for suspicion to grow. It was sufficient that they were strangers interfering with the normal order of things, imposing their will, and demanding that the poor take medicine if they wished to be eligible for charitable aid.

Instead of following doctors' orders, the *menu peuple* clung to their own remedies, tested and approved by the experience of innumerable centuries. Fever and sore throat were fought by carrying cloves of garlic in one's pockets, which was supposed to rid the air of the infection it contained.[96] It is important to note that popular practice in these matters had already made a certain protoscientific progress beyond the use of talismans. In fact, there was often not a very great difference between the recipes of the poor and the prescriptions of the doctors, although the coincidence of method did nothing to alleviate the antagonism felt by the former toward the latter. Potions and plasters were favorites of the poor as well, the crucial difference being that they prescribed for themselves. Everyone *knew* that wine, sugar and 24 hours in bed was a sovereign remedy against influenza and that chest complaints could be resolved by living in a cow stable until perspiration had purified the blood and driven off the "malignant humors." For difficult childbirth, one placed a paste made of bay leaf and olive oil on the women's navel, and "at that very moment, no matter how difficult the position the child may be in, he will turn and present himself so happily and so promptly that there will be reason to be astonished." And so on, with bleeding for madness, salt pastes for rabies, elixirs of youth made of wine, brandy, and spices for what ails you.[97] This was all guarded in the storehouse of common wisdom, transmitted by word of mouth and finally set down in books. The authority figure represented by the doctor (or other outsider) was distinctly superfluous.

Under these conditions, it is highly unlikely that there was any significant decline in the mortality rate in eighteenth-century Paris, although there were now fewer instances of catastrophic increases in the number of deaths than ever before. On the other hand, the birth rate may have begun to fall slightly. If this is so (and we can only be very tentative for the time being), our earlier hypoth-

esis to the effect that Paris grew in population only as a result of
migration would be re-enforced.

The loss of the parish registers means that we shall never know
the exact number of marriages contracted and of births and deaths
that took place in the city. In the period 1708–1800, there were
55 years in which the number of marriages ranged between 4,000
and 5,000, 18 years between 5,000 and 6,000, only 13 years between 3,000 and 4,000, and 6 years between 6,000 and 9,000 (in
the last decade of the century). What little evidence we have
seems to verify an observation often made by historical demographers, that the number of marriages tended to increase sharply
with economic recovery after a run of depression years, a kind of
upsurge of vitality to restore the recently disturbed balance. In
the difficult years 1780–1789, there were 8.6 marriages per thousand population, but the figure increased to 10.2 (1790), 11.2
(1791), 14.9 (1794), before falling once again to 7.8 (1795, a
result of the severe crisis of the year III).[98]

According to Buffon's researches for the years 1745–1766, the
greatest number of marriages took place in February and November, the smallest number in March and December. This indicates
a persistence of Catholic practice in the population at large, for
March and December correspond to Lent and Advent, when wed-
dings were prohibited. It was a widespread custom among couples
planning to wed to have the ceremony performed just before the
interdicted period, to get under the wire so to speak.[99]

It is more difficult to explain the frequency of births by month.
The sources show a high degree of congruence at the top and
bottom of the scale. It may well be true that the low number of
births in November and December corresponds to the sexual abstinence of Lent in March and April. But what of June, for which
October is the month of conception? Might it be that part of
the male population was away from Paris at that time, looking
for work or engaged in the grain and wine harvests? As for the
many conceptions of July, May, and June (births in March, Jan-

TABLE 3–3

Months with Highest Number of Births, in Decreasing Order

Buffon (1745–66)	March Jan Feb Oct Aug May April Sept July Nov Dec June
Messance (1724–63)	March Jan Feb April May Aug Oct Sept July Nov Dec June

SOURCES: Buffon, cited in Roger Mols, *Introduction à la démographie historique des villes
d'Europe du XIV au XVIIIe siècles*, 3 vols. (Gem'bloux, 1955–1956), II: 296–299.
Messance, *Recherches et considérations sur la population de la France* (Paris, 1788), p. 179.

uary, and February), shall we consider this proof of the old adage that in the spring, young people's fancy lightly turns to thoughts of sex? So far, no one has suggested a more plausible explanation.

According to calculations made by Mols on the basis of information recapitulating the number of marriages and births over more than a century, the simple rate of fecundity (ratio of births to marriages over a given number of years) underwent a significant decline in our period. Thus, the rate fell from 5.8 (1670–1675) to 3.8 (1711–1715), then rose to 4.7 (1721–1725), remained stable until 1740, fell to 4.2 (1741–1745), varied between 4.4 and 4.1 (1746–1770), fell again to 4.0 (1771–1775), 3.9 (1776–1785), 3.5 (1786–1790), and reached the nadir of 2.7 (1791). There then followed a notable rise to 3.3 (years I–III) [1792–1795], 4.3 (years IV–VIII) [1795–1800], and 5.0 (years IX–XIII) [1800–1805].[100] It is difficult to know what to make of these figures and how closely they reflect reality. The statistics on which they are based are more than likely incomplete because there were couples living in Paris who had been married elsewhere and children whose births were not properly registered, but in what proportion one to the other we do not know. Moreover, the figures tell us nothing about variations within the city or by class, and they may hide short-term movements. The general movement up to the early years of the Revolution does, however, support what recent demographic research has shown about the widespread introduction of contraceptive techniques in France from the middle of the seventeenth century. Authorities differ in their explanations of this phenomenon, some attributing it to the needs of domestic economy and the desire to climb up the social ladder,[101] others to the new consciousness of man's ability to act upon and control his environment, still others to an increased understanding and appreciation of the value of children.[102] In my view, these explanations complement one another in the case of nobles and bourgeois, among whom the movement for family limitation got its start, but it still remains necessary, insofar as the laboring poor are concerned, to discover the reasons for so dramatic a break with an earlier cultural heritage. For the moment, we have to content ourselves with evidence that they did, in fact, follow suit sufficiently to provoke loud outcries from the populationists and *bien pensants* alike. For Turmeau de la Morandière, "It would be sufficient to consult the confessors in the city of Paris. . . . This infamous practice is spreading like an epidemic, and the confessors will confirm that all classes of society, rich and poor alike, indulge in it." He was seconded by the Abbé Jean Novi de Caveinac, who wrote: "The fear of leaving their children in poverty leads men to renounce without regret the sweet name of father . . . some master their desires, others defraud nature, but all refuse to increase the population by honest means."[103] The most common method was coitus interruptus, which the moralists labeled the sin of Onan. For Féline, "This unfortunate disposition is common to the rich and the poor: their motives are different, but their crime is the same." Nothing could justify it, not even poverty and a large number of children. After all, "It is up to Providence to furnish the means of subsistence to the children of the poor: it takes pleasure in blessing their families, while the families of the rich perish."[104]

[4]

ATTITUDES AND
INSTITUTIONS

The hospitals of Paris were of many sorts. The two principal
establishments to which the laboring poor had access were the
Hôpital Général and the Hôtel-Dieu, which cared for 10,000–
12,000 and 3,000–4,000 patients respectively at a time.[1] The Hôpital
Général was made up of several parts, of which the most important
were La Salpêtrière for women and Bicêtre for men. In the 1780s,
the former cared for 4,700 persons with a staff of 1,800, and the
latter had a population of perhaps 3,500.[2] The Salpêtrière took in
women and girls of all ages, and boys up to the age of 4. The
majority of the inmates were simply poor and/or ill, but there
were also a certain number of persons detained on account of in-
sanity, prostitution, or by royal or administrative order. Restif
called La Salpêtrière "the dead end of hell . . . the sojourn of
misfortune, sadness, and despair."[3] Bicêtre performed the same
functions for men, but the population there seems to have been
older and contained a higher percentage of criminals. The Hôpital
de La Pitié cared for about 1,200–1,400 boys between the ages of
5 and 16 who came from the foundling hospital and poor families
of Paris and its environs. When they came of age, they were sent
out into the world either as apprentices or to become agricultural
workers in the neighborhood of Melun. In the Hôpital de la
Saint Esprit on the place de Grève, approximately 100 orphans of
both sexes were taught to read and write before being sent out as
apprentices. Only those born in Paris or Versailles and whose
fathers had been master craftsmen could hope for admission to this
privileged asylum.[4]

Other hospitals, like La Trinité and the Petites Maisons, under the jurisdiction of the Grand Bureau des Pauvres, gave shelter to the young and old. The first had room for 100 Parisian boys (aged 8–12) and 36 girls (aged 8–9) of legitimate birth who had lost at least one parent. They, too, were made ready to be bound apprentices. The second, located on the rue de Sèvres, lodged 300 persons, mainly women, aged 60 or more. They were given a room and 40 sous a week, along with a few perquisites like firewood and salt, from time to time. The waiting list for admission to these institutions was very long, for the space available was grossly inadequate to the needs of the city. We can cite the case of Marie Anne Morgny, aged 73, who had been waiting for a place for 13 years. Her application had little hope of success because there were still 185 persons, all older than she, to be served before her turn came.[5]

The Hospice de Vaugirard was founded in 1780 to care for pregnant women who had venereal disease, and for their infants congenitally affected by it. It does not seem to have been a terribly successful enterprise, for in the first three and one-half years of its existence, of 598 babies admitted, 336 died of venereal disease, 140 of other maladies, and only 36 were cured. The women admitted were mainly artisans' wives "who have got this horrible malady from their husbands. These faithless men go to drink in the guinguettes with the dregs of whoredom and, all dirtied by this infamous commerce, come home to befoul the conjugal bed and to give to their faithful spouse and to their children a horrible disease, the sad fruit of their libertinage." This is not to say that the poor had a monopoly on extramarital sex but only that they, as distinct from their more prosperous neighbors, could turn for help only to the hospital and that, in consequence, their misfortunes were more likely to be made public.[6]

The Hôtel-Dieu cared for persons suffering from every sort of disease other than "tinea, the itch or venereal ills." An additional 300 patients lived in the Hôpital des Incurables, where they had the right to remain until they died. This accommodation was not, however, available to the very poor, for there was an entrance fee of 69 livres, and the right to name the occupant of each bed belonged to the person who had endowed it or his heirs. Several other institutions belonging either to lay charitable bodies or religious orders gave assistance to a few hundred diversely afflicted individuals.

The able-bodied inmates of the hospitals were made to work for their keep. At Bicêtre and La Salpêtrière, the spinning and weaving of wool and linen were the main occupations. Women were also trained to do tapestry and embroidery, while men drew water from the wells and threshed and milled grain to meet the establishments' needs.[7] In return for their work, older children and adults were paid a wage, once they had completed their training. Under certain conditions, they were even allowed to trade on their own account.

The daily ration of inmates at Bicêtre and La Salpêtrière consisted of five *quarterons* (a pound and a quarter) of bread, and a little wine. Three times a week they were given soup and a little bit of meat, on Sundays, Tuesdays and Thursdays. On the other four days they got a piece of cheese or a little salt butter or some peas.[8] At the Hôtel-Dieu, some elementary dietetic rules were followed. Patients who drank only bouillon were given a bowl every two hours, while those who could eat more solid food had soup and meat twice a day together with a daily ration of a *demi-septier* (quarter of a liter) of wine.[9] All in all, this was not a very generous diet, but it was probably no less than the amount to which the laboring poor were accustomed. The quality of the food is another matter altogether. Doctors' orders were not always observed by the nursing staff, and the use of rotten vegetables made scurvy and diseases of the mouth very prevalent.[10]

Conditions in the hospitals were scandalous. In the Hôtel-Dieu and La Salpêtrière, five or six persons slept in beds scarcely large enough for two, while single beds were reserved for those able to pay.[11] Patients were bedded down indiscriminately with no regard to the nature of their illness so that they infected one another. The sight of men dead or dying bred terror in the mildly ill as did the spectacle of the insane caged in behind iron bars and treated like animals. Both must certainly have retarded convalescence.[12] To the people, the Hôtel-Dieu was an "object of terror," feared and detested "by the lowest of men."[13] The excuses of the administrators on the grounds of lack of money and space did not carry much weight with the poor.[14] To them, the hospital was a place one went to die, a kind of Malthusian instrument before the letter.[15] For this belief they had some statistical justification. At the Hospice de la Charité, which admitted only patients whose maladies were amenable to treatment and excluded cases of old age (*caducité*) and pulmonary disease, there was a death rate of 1:8. This was a low figure in comparison to the ratio of 1:4½ prevailing in other Parisian hospitals.[16] The inadequate medical attention and unsanitary conditions that lay at the root of this extraordinary mortality were aggravated by corruption among the hospital staff. Workingmen who couldn't afford to pay for services often went without care.[17]

Towards the end of the old regime, there was a considerable movement for hospital reform and changes in the care of the indigent. We have already noted the founding of the Hospice de la Charité. In addition, some parishes opened small hospices (Saint Sulpice, Saint André des Arts, Saint Merry, Saint Jacques du Haut Pas) or arranged to employ a doctor to attend to those sick who could not afford to pay for treatment (Saint Roch, Saint Eustache). A few reformers recognized that sending the poor to large hospitals meant depriving them of family and friends and exposing them to the added risk of infection while at the same time incurring high costs. Dupont de Nemours proposed the creation of private nursing homes by the rich for the poor. If such existed, he argued, rich masters would be obliged to send their domestics there, and the "well-off persons would be solicited by their own hearts and by those surrounding them, to support artisans who had served them or were well known in their households."[18]

The concern here was with the settled, well-known, one might say honorable, poor, rather than with those whose relationships to their superiors were more tenuous, the unskilled streetworkers and merchants, the floaters who most needed help. The latter were the victims of a long-standing prejudice which denied them almost all forms of charitable aid except when they were severely ill. Beginning in the 1650s, two charity organizations had been formed in each parish of the city: La Compagnie des Dames (for the sick poor), and La Compagnie des Messieurs (for the *pauvres honteux*). The motives behind their foundation were of a narrowly confessional sort, as much to save one's own soul as to lead the poor into salvation. Only good Catholics were eligible for aid, and very careful investigations of their moral characters were made before help was given. Threats to withdraw charity were used to keep the beneficiaries pious and practicing.[19]

Morality is in the eye of the beholder, and most of the characteristics reprehended by parish charitable officers could easily be attributed to the nonincorporated poor. The parish of Saint Martin des Champs refused aid to "those persons given over to wine or debauchery, professional idlers, swearers, and in general all those who are of unrighteous conduct, and in the same way those who neglect to send their children to school, catchechism, and other religious instructions.[20] But how many drinks constituted debauchery, how many days without work constituted idleness? And "mauvaise vie et moeurs" could mean almost anything, from working in a theatre to renting a room to a prostitute.[21] It was an expression that could and did designate someone who was not a master or who did not occupy at least an equivalent place in society.

If moral character were not a sufficient standard by which to pick and choose among petitioners for charity, other rules could be invoked, all of them intended to fend off the importunities of feared and despised indigents. Eligibility was limited to persons having a fixed domicile in the parish for at least three years at the time of application, but those who lived in furnished rooms or who moved frequently, even within the parish, were excluded. No doubt this regulation was, at least in part, the result of a fear that masses of the poor would invade the city from the countryside and force the parishes to support them. But there was also the belief that, among the able-bodied indigent, only persons having some stake in society ought to be helped. Certainly they were the only ones to be trusted with money, for the others would only squander it on drink and sin.[22]

In sum, then, only the *pauvres honteux*, that is "persons worthy of consideration on account of their birth or professions"[23] could count on obtaining substantial aid from the parish companies, whose principal purpose was to help impoverished master artisans over difficult periods. Journeymen were not given assistance because they might fall into habits of idleness. Nor were they encouraged to become masters for fear of overburdening the guilds. I am not suggesting that this practice was conceived of by the donors in economic terms. Rather, it was consequent on their world view which included a belief in an organically hierarchical and static society. Each man was to remain in his place; not even the master artisan was to be helped to change his profession. And those who were so low down on the social ladder as to have no functional place in the hierarchy were not to be helped at all. Work is not, in this formulation, a primary value, and it is less important to keep people working than to keep them in order, preferably in their home districts, where they could be bound by a whole series of constraints and would therefore find it more difficult to make trouble. Is it too much to suggest that changes in the attitudes of administrators of charity at the national level, as evidenced by the founding of *ateliers de charité* and *dépôts de mendicité* (which shared the characteristics of the workhouse), is part and parcel of a developing bourgeois world view? Labor—free, unrestrained, and mobile—is now necessary to the dynamics of capitalist enterprise. It is therefore desirable to keep the laborers alive and available while inculcating into them habits of work and discipline. Even parish charity of the more enlightened sort, such as practiced in Saint Sulpice, was now extended to wider strata of the population, and its main form was the provision of work to the unemployed. Still, a certain provincialism and fear worked against helping the undomiciled poor.[24]

Other sources of charitable aid were few. The Grand Bureau des Pauvres, founded in the sixteenth century, assisted persons over 60 and young children, preferably born in Paris and in possession of a fixed address for the previous three years. The beneficiaries had to have a priest's certificate attesting that they were good Catholics, a requirement which no doubt re-enforced the need for a well-established domicile. Once again, the practice of the Grand Bureau was to help only master artisans or others of higher rank.[25] The number of persons who were to benefit from this aid was fixed annually by the *procureur général du roi*. In 1738, the number was 1,400, in 1791, 1,471. Each adult was given 10 sous a week, each child, 5 sous.[26] Between 1747 and 1771, 4,565 persons were found on the rolls of the Grand Bureau at one time or another and beween 1771 and 1791, 6,132.[27] Let us assume that the average was 1,400 a year. This means that approximately 20 percent of the total were replaced each year. Some were taken off the rolls only to be sent to the Petites Maisons. In any case, neither the practice nor the resources of the Grand Bureau were sufficient to meet the needs of even the domiciled poor.[28]

Some private organizations, like the Société Philanthropique de Paris, founded in 1780, sought to help the lesser poor, provided always that they were stable and did not wander from one dwelling place to another. The society specifically excluded master artisans from its charities, no doubt reasoning that they could find help elsewhere. But it limited its activities to certain rather special categories: (1) octogenarians (of whom it demanded a baptismal certificate), (2) persons blind from birth, (3) pregnant women, provided they were legitimately married, and (4) widows with at least six children, the eldest of whom was not over 15. It was planned to help 1,100 persons in 1787. The most instructive thing about this program is the rationale adopted for it. The philanthropists wrote:

It is certain that the earnings of a worker, however sober he may be, are too limited, so that they are sufficient, at the very most, to allow him and his family to live from day to day, and when weakness due to age no longer permits him to work, he finds himself completely deprived in the midst of the infirmities which are inseparable from old age. . . . It is nonetheless true that a worker who has no other resource than the work of his hands cannot support a large family, pay for the nursing of several infants, and provide the aid needed by his wife at the critical moment when she brings into the world a new fruit of their union; and that often the unfortunate woman, cursing her fecundity, perishes from need in the process of a difficult birth, or as a result of postpartum neglect.[29]

It was a dismal, but accurate, picture of the human condition as experienced by the laboring poor.

Failing direct charitable aid, a man or a woman desperately in need of cash might pawn some belongings at the Mont de Piété, founded in 1777 to provide an alternate source of loans to the poor and thus take them out of the clutches of usurers who charged interest at rates of 30 to 50 percent a year and often stole the mortgaged items. The cost to the borrower was two pennies per livre each month, or 10 percent per annum. In the event of the pawn being sold, the proprietor realized any surplus over and above the money originally lent him, plus costs. It was a vastly popular institution much resorted to by "the working and laboring class," whom it protected against "its former leaches . . . the odious capitalists of shadowy pawnshops," as a pamphlet of 1793 put it.[30] The proof is to be found in the list of pawns: a pair of buckles at three livres, two men's shirts and a handkerchief at six, sheets, curtains, a pair of stockings, a suit, or a silver goblet at similarly modest sums.[31]

In crisis years, the authorities were faced with the need to prevent even the able-bodied from starving to death. In 1780, Lenoir boasted that each winter the unemployed were put to work breaking up ice, cleaning the streets, and repairing the roads. "These enormous details," he wrote, "occupy in winter almost all of those who are without work: no economies are permitted on this point; and so the number of workers is sometimes excessive."[32] In reality, it does not appear that large, not to say adequate, sums were devoted to this purpose, except in moments of considerable stress. In 1775, a year of grain shortages and high bread prices, 100,000 livres were granted by the royal government to the city for relief work. This was done once more in 1788. At the same time, the municipal authorities were reluctant to spend money on *ateliers de charité*, arguing that the little they had to disburse could hardly help and would possibly worsen the situation by creating jealousy of those receiving aid among the unemployed.[33] In ordinary years,

less money was spent on providing work for the indigent than
on hunting down beggars.[34]

The poor were often reluctant to declare their poverty to the
authorities for fear that they would be imprisoned or otherwise
molested. It was not an idle worry in an era when a suspected beggar could be killed for resisting arrest.[35] And when workingmen
accepted charity, it was not always with the humility and meek-
ness expected of them. They seemed to have identified the dis-
tributors of charity, especially the clergy, with the causes of their
ills. In 1718, the Lieutenant-general of Police Machault had to
threaten to throw into prison those poor who "instead of receiving
aid with gentleness, gratitude, and modesty, not only protest and
complain but go so far in their ingratitude and insolence that they
desire to insult, threaten, even to strike and mistreat" the Sisters
of Charity concerned. At the other end of our period, we read
of "la populace" insulting priests when fear of bread shortages
arose, as in the parish of Saint Séverin in 1784.[36]

To argue that the clergy became the targets of the poor because
of a long-standing anti-clericalism and the fact that priests were
well fed is essentially to beg the question. The hatred shown by
the *menu peuple* for their social betters, however limited in scope,
proceeded from an elemental form of consciousness to which we
may not even attach the prefix "class," the kind that is capable
of identifying only the differences between "us" and "them," the
ins and the outs, or what Baehrel has called the *minores* and the
gros.[37] The wish to avoid the hospital and the refusal to accept
charity were both aspects of a withdrawal by workingmen from
the cadres of a society which they despised. It was a withdrawal
motivated by equal parts of hatred and fear of a society that did
them harm (psychologically, at the very least) even in the guise
of giving them help.

Restif wrote once of "our laws, made by the rich, who can
pardon nothing to the poor."[38] The scorn and contempt in which
the poor were held by both the upper classes and government
agents shows up time and again in our sources and made it possible
for them to speak of the "poor and idlers" in the same breath and
to chase the undomiciled poor from the city in time of famine and
crisis, as in 1740 and 1789.[39] Contempt was institutionalized in
the way hospitals were run, charity given, the army recruited, and
the law executed.[40] But it was perhaps most evident in dealings
between individuals. In 1784, Hardy reported the case of an "elegant *petit maître*" who collided with a mason's helper in the
gardens of the Palais Royal. The worker was carrying two buckets

of water and spilled some on the fop. An altercation ensued, during which the young man ran the worker through with his sword. The assassin was immediately arrested, but, as Hardy said, no one really expected that he would be punished. Instead, a way would be found to blame the whole affair on the dead man.[41]

Was this an isolated incident, of no particular value as historical evidence? Or was it a manifestation of the kind of violence peculiar to the eighteenth century, which found its classic expression in the duel over matters of personal honor? Violence towards the lower classes required no challenge, no elaborate organization, but because it might be spontaneous, it was not necessarily insignificant. Nor was it contradicted by the paternalistic attitude that men of property of all classes were supposed to display toward the laboring poor.[42] The question that presents itself is: Would the *petit maître* have acted in the same way to a man of his own class? And the answer is a definite no.

If we look again at the institutional level, the view of laborers as objects for manipulation comes through clearly.

Educational opportunities for the children of the *menu peuple* were limited but improving in the last century of the old regime. As a result of the work of seventeenth-century clerics inspired by the example of Saint Vincent de Paul, charity schools for the indigent were founded in every parish, beginning with the 1640s. By 1765, there were 45 such schools for boys and 29 for girls, and the number continued to grow until the Revolution. In addition, there were several hundred *petites écoles* run by religious organizations, like the Frères des Écoles Chrétiennes in the faubourg Saint Antoine and by individual schoolmasters, for which tuition was paid.[43] The charity schools were free of charge, and books were provided for those who could not afford to buy them. Children normally spent two years in the schools, attending the year-round for about five hours a day, morning and afternoon. They were taught to read and to write both French and Latin, a little arithmetic, and a great deal of religion. In fact, all instruction was considered subordinate to the training of good Christians. The books used were all religious in nature, with the exception of the necessary grammars and treatises on pronunciation.[44]

"The principal aim of charity schools is to instruct children in the truths of religion and to inspire in them the love of piety. . . ." It was to this end and to enable them to achieve salvation that the children were taught at parish expense, for it was all too regrettably true that ordinarily the children of the poor "live without having the fear of God, and without knowing the first elements of Christianity."[45] The stated motive implied an attempt to control the morality of the poor, to mold the children into docile and therefore socially acceptable beings or, in current jargon, to socialize them to the dominant values of their society. Parents were required to send their children to school if they wished to benefit from parish charities. The children were watched over carefully for any sign of mischief in word or deed. While it was recommended that reason be used as much as possible, it would nonetheless be wrong to spare the rod. Warnings, the imposition of penitence, and blows across the hands were all to be exhausted before the application of the whip, whose moderate use only was allowed. Good children were rewarded with praise and the gift of pious literature, and the most worthy pupils were placed by the parish as apprentices when they finished school.

The children were taught very much the same doctrine to which their parents were exposed in countless sermons. There was no salvation outside the Church. Be good, clean, attentive, wise, modest; neither swear, lie, fight, nor steal; obey both parents and superiors, respect the clergy; eschew familiarity; learn the catechism and attend mass regularly.[46] Upon the fulfillment of these duties depended one's happiness in this life and the life to come.

The teaching of obedience to the children of the laboring poor took on a special significance in addition to its general virtues if they were later to be used as cannon fodder in the king's armies. Recruitment for the armies was carried out, in theory at least, on a voluntary basis. In fact, abuses were rampant, despite a series of ordinances (in 1701, 1716, 1737, 1760, and 1778) forbidding the use of the press gang. The last of these edicts forbade recruiting officers to enter the Hôtel-Dieu, which appears to have been one of their favorite haunts. They were not allowed to force anyone into service, nor might they wear disguises to conceal their identity. Tavern keepers were ordered not to tolerate them on their premises, and a police officer was to verify the good faith of all enlistments within 24 hours after they had taken place.[47]

The hospital and the tavern were the two places where poor artisans and day laborers were to be found in abundance and not in a fit state to resist the blandishments of unscrupulous recruiters, not to mention the physical force they might employ. All orders to the contrary notwithstanding, men were continuously drafted in this way and made to serve average terms of twelve years in the forces despite the fact that the official period of enlistment was first six, then eight years. An incident was recorded in 1788 of a man joining the army in the mistaken belief that he was being engaged as a domestic.[48] Recruiters picked up 15-year-old children as they came out of school, and they were even known to run along in back of carriages hitting at the legs of the postillions in order to make them fall off so that they could be pressed into service. Persons who refused to volunteer were on occasion killed by an overzealous recruiter.[49] Given these conditions of enlistment, it is no wonder that desertions were so extraordinarily frequent.[50]

The laboring poor were abused in yet another way, this time institutionalized by the law concerning militia service. By an order of October 30, 1742, the militia established in 1688 and recruited since that time in all rural parishes was extended to include the cities of the realm. This was done at least in part because so many peasants chose to leave their homes rather than take part in the annual drawing of lots. The ordinance of 1742 required all unmarried men who were "artisans, or sons of artisans, small merchants, and workingmen" between the ages of 16 and 40 and over five feet tall to be available to bear arms. If there were not enough bachelors to fill the quota, married men were to be taken. The "gens de condition" and bourgeois (including the merchants of the Six Corps), their children, and at least some of their domestics were exempt. Master artisans were granted exemptions for their sons, employees, and domestics in proportion to the amount of capitation tax they paid. And those who did not qualify for exemption on this basis could hire someone to serve in their stead. The result was that the major burden fell on the *menu peuple*, even on those who had previously done voluntary service. For the poor man chosen to serve, the only means of escape was to turn over to the authorities someone who had failed to register for the draft, who would then be forced to take his place. This he was not altogether loath to do, as shown by the (often unjustified) denunciation and arrest of some 650 draft dodgers in 1743. On the other hand, there is evidence that men who gave others away were looked upon with contempt by their neighbors.[51]

It was not simply "the common people" who served in the militia but that portion of them least protected by their jobs or associations in the city. The first to go were the new arrivals, who were assumed to have left their homes precisely in order to avoid the militia. In general, the pattern of exemptions for master and, on occasion, lesser artisans and for domestics left the unskilled, nonguild workers holding the bag. They might protest, but they were least able to make their protests effective. And so, by a technique of divide and conquer, the monarchy filled its military quota and at the same time removed from Paris some of the unstable elements of which it was most anxious to be rid. Whether this was conscious policy or not, it is impossible to say. The government's actions might be explained just as well by its desire to fill the ranks with a minimum of upset on the domestic scene. In any case, the results were the same.

Behind all this lay a set of assumptions the laboring poor could not fail to notice. They were inferior and condemned to remain so, not because they individually lacked character or personal qualities that would enable them to adapt to and advance within any given situations, as the later theorists of social Darwinism had it, but because they had been born as a group to play a specific role or set of roles from which there was no escape. When, on a rare occasion, a laborer sought to establish himself in a role for which he was thought unsuited, the barriers were set up in a more explicit manner. In 1781, the Parlement of Paris, following its usual practice of excluding anyone who paid less than a total of 12 livres in direct taxes or who exercised a "mechanical art," annulled the election of an agricultural day laborer as a vestryman in the parish church of suburban Chaillot. It gave as its reason that "persons of a vile profession, or day laborers, who earn their living by means which are the proof of their indigence" were clearly unfit.[52]

Even death did not put an end to the indignities to which the *menu peuple* were subject. A funeral, of whatever class, appears to have been a costly affair, for the assistance of the clergy was in principle necessary.[53] Attempts to raise the price provoked the poor to anger as did the refusal of the clergy and the pallbearers to do their duty unless properly rewarded.[54] In June, 1781, a poor parishioner of Saint Sulpice, having somehow come up with enough money to buy a coffin for his late wife, still lacked funds to pay the pallbearers. Service was refused him, and he finally had to solicit the aid of six neighbor women to transport the body from his home to the church. This was the kind of thing to which the poor were particularly sensitive, as Christians concerned with the welfare of their immortal souls. They showed their annoyance by treating the parish clergy, whom they held responsible for the pallbearers' loutish behavior, to a steady stream of abuse when they dared to appear on the streets at the head of another, presumably well-paid, procession.[55] The poor, who left little or no trace of their existence behind them, could not even be buried properly. If relatives or friends did not pay for the burial, their bodies were thrown into the common pits of the Cemetery of the Holy Innocents near the Halles or at suburban Clamart, and not much care was taken to record their names. Until a police order put an end to the custom in 1775, the death certificate of a person buried at public expense could not be signed by his relatives or friends, and information for the parish registers was taken from the grave-diggers only. This was the ultimate indignity, a kind of final deprivation of identity.[56]

The Parisian poor lived surrounded by violence. It was the so-cially approved violence of a society based on principles of in-equality, whose every institution worked to deprive the laborer of any sense of his personal worth. The Dickensian image of the driver who ran down those who dared to get in the way of his coach-and-four is a kind of materialization of an endemic, deeply rooted but less tangible kind of violence used as a means of keep-ing the *menu peuple* in their place, examples of which form the substance of this chapter. There was also the socially disapproved violence of the professional criminal, with whom the poor lived at close quarters. The laboring poor might be cruel, but the vio-lence in which they engaged was limited. When they dabbled, amateurishly, in crime, it rarely involved physical harm to the victim. Quarrels were often loud and boisterous, but they do not seem to have usually led even to fist fights, much less to significant injuries. Evidence to the contrary is truly exceptional and is asso-ciated either with defense of hearth and home (a young woman threw her landlord out of a window when he came with a police officer to complain of her conduct) or with psychopathology (the case of three young men, two the sons of petty mercers and one the son of a watchmaker, who murdered the whore they had been visiting by cutting off her breasts and putting out her eyes).[57]

Nor were the laboring poor very anxious to escape the miseries of this life by resorting to suicide. True, Hardy spoke of it as "a crime become so common since, in the last several years, it has been committed almost daily and in cold blood in this immense capital," and he attributed this penchant to the effect of evil books and the lack of religious instruction.[58] Mercier, too, was convinced that the number of suicides among the lower classes had increased in the quarter century before the Revolution because of the high taxes and bread prices which made life so difficult. His reasons for suicide being in fashion were more plausible than those offered by Hardy or Laliman, but his figure of 150 a year is not very high for a population of well over 600,000.[59]

So, far from trying to escape from their life of misery, the labor-ing poor accepted their condition and tried to make the best of it. They were disciplined in the most fundamental sense, although they did not always obey the orders issued by their bosses or the public authorities. They got roaring drunk in the guinguettes of La Courtille and Les Porcherons on Sundays, where they were among their own class, unobserved by outsiders who frequented the more fashionable cafés in the city or on the northern boulevards. Like their English contemporaries, they often honored Saint Monday by continuing their libations.[60] Although these habits would have made it difficult to integrate them into a modern factory system of production, they were neither lazy nor dissipated. On the contrary, they enjoyed a reputation for assiduity in the performance of their tasks when they chose to work.[61] Not labor but the regularity of the six-day week and the factory whistle was alien to them.

As laboring men worked hard, so they played hard. The amusements they sought in their taverns or elsewhere were of a rough-and-ready sort.[62] They pushed one another about, took offense at minor insults, and fought and made up before returning home, when their money ran out. Their motto was: *Vive hodie, eras incertum*.[63] This kind of instant gratification was a great safety valve for the daily frustrations to which they were subject. So long as they obtained satisfaction from fighting among themselves, they were less likely to turn their anger against authority, whether in the form of their employers or the agents of government. This fact did not, however, stop bourgeois observers from deploring what they considered to be the degraded practices of the lower orders. Words like "license" and "orgies" constantly recur in their descriptions, but one may wonder if at least part of their genuine shock did not arise out of their envy of people who, however downtrodden, were able to let themselves go completely and unself-consciously.[64]

Their language, which was both violent and extremely pungent, also set the *menu peuple* off from the rest of the population. Peysonnel called it "a disgusting monster made up of all the barbarisms and solecisms that it is possible to commit in the French language."[65] Leaving aside the host of migrant workers who spoke French only as a second language, he must no doubt have had reference to their inelegant habits, which still persist, of replacing *de* with *à* as a possessive, or of saying *ben* for *bien*, or *ça* for *cela*. Worse yet was the tendency to place *z* sounds in unwanted places, as in *Menez moi-z-y* or *donnez-moi-z-en*, a custom more recently associated with North African speakers of French.[66]

Our chief source of knowledge of these speech patterns is found in the literature of the *genre poissard*, which flourished in the mid-

eighteenth century. Authors like Vadé and Cailleau, who themselves were of common origin, used colloquial language to write
about the laboring poor in a realistic, albeit burlesque, fashion.[67]
The term *poissard* is the equivalent of the English *billingsgate*,
the jargon of the marketwomen. The most common characteristic of this language, aside from the grammatical errors, is its
pungency. Its speakers would call each other everything and anything. A whole range of insults were available for men, from
espion de culs mal torchés to *échappé de Bicêtre*. A woman was
better classified as a *paillasse de corps-de-garde* or a *chiffon ramassé
dans les latrines*. Or, to sum it up, the following stanza of invective:

> . . . T'es t'un poltron
> Tu n'vaux seul'ment pas t'un étron.
> Moisy, trouvé dans de la paille;
> Tu faraud's avec ta ferraille
> Qui t'pend z'au cul: ça t'rend glorieux;
> D' la merde à ton nez t'siéroit mieux.[68]*

The poor did not, of course, normally speak in rhyming couplets,
but the vocabulary was the same. It shows an extraordinary pre-
occupation with sex and still more with the excremental functions,
almost as if an entire section of the population was anally fixated.
Unfortunately, it is not likely that we shall ever be able to understand the full significance of these expressions.

Perhaps more important is the social content of the insults.
Apparently the worst thing one could say was an intimation that
the adversary had fallen, or would fall, afoul of the law or the
Church. Expressions like *reste de carcan, modèle de fripon,
étendard de pilori, carcasse d'excommunié* or *espion de Lucifer*
were most common, to the point that we may wonder whether
their use, even in a bantering way, did not betray a fundamental
respect for law and order. Curiously, it appears that popular
speech and *argot*, the language of the criminals, although they
influenced one another, remained essentially separate until the
end of the eighteenth century.[69]

Preoccupations of a scatological and sexual nature show up once
again in the humor favored by the laboring poor, much of which
took the form of practical jokes, and is evidence of a well-established strain of cruelty in their character. They liked to scare

---

* You're chicken hearted. You're not worth a mouldy piece of shit. You swash
about with that sword hanging down from your ass: it makes you a big deal.
But shit on your nose would suit you better.

old ladies by putting pieces of white metal resembling rats on their coats as they walked down the street on the way to church. Or they nailed a coin to the pavement next to a hot iron so that the person who stooped to gather in easy money was burned.[70] But perhaps their favorite amusement was the *charivari*, or what Middle Western Americans call chiveree. It was "a confused noise made by lower-class persons with pots, pans, cauldrons and other pieces of furniture . . . with hoots and cries, so as to insult some-one who is getting married, and who marries a person of a greatly disproportionate age; and especially when it is a second marriage." The victim par excellence was the journeyman who married a master's widow, and the verbal humor that accompanied the noise was always in questionable taste even if there was no intent to be vicious. If one had asked a laborer why he enjoyed this activity, he would probably have replied that it was fun, wholly un-aware that he was, after a fashion, asserting his masculinity or escaping the impotence of his daily life in this moment of fantasy.[71]

Epiphany, the days of Saint Martin and Saint Jean, the Eve of Saint Louis, and the feast of the kings of France, were moments of great popular rejoicing, but Mardi Gras, the end of carnival, was their principal holiday. The poor (but not only they) went around masquerading, parading, drinking, and, in general, having an excellent time, the more so as it was preface to the deprivations of the Lenten season. The reaction of the solid citizens was the same as always when laboring men appeared to be enjoying them-selves. It was shocking that this low life, these "extravagants," these *chianlis* (200 years before General De Gaulle) should be able to hold the streets with an utter lack of consideration for decency and good morals. Hardy was convinced, as he noted each year in his diary, that the people of the faubourg Saint Antoine, where the bulk of the festivities took place, were either employed by the police or clandestinely given money to spend, in order that their minds be taken off any causes of current dis-satisfaction, whether it be the absence of the Parlement in 1772 or the bread shortage in 1787.[72]

In the evenings after work, the laboring poor lived in the streets and the parks of the capital—the Tuileries, the Luxembourg, and the Palais Royal. Their homes were too small to serve as anything other than places to sleep. They could not go to the theatre or permit themselves the luxury of a meal in one of the newly estab-lished restaurants, for those pastimes were too expensive. The cheapest seats at a play cost twelve sous, at least one-third of a day's wages, and a meal cost three livres.[73] I do not mean to suggest that the poor necessarily missed the things of which they were ignorant but only the limits of their horizons. On the other hand, there is no warrant to assume, as contemporary authors were wont to do, that because a poor man did not know what one did at the opera, he did not mind being excluded from doing it.[74]

Be that as it may, frustrations of a personal nature rarely, if ever, gave rise to action for the redress of grievances. To the outside observer, one of the most striking characteristics of the Parisian laboring poor was their "native cheerfulness."[75] Arthur Young thought that "nothing contributes more to make them a happy people than the cheerful and facile pliancy of disposition with which they adapt themselves to the circumstances of life. . . ."[76] But it was Mrs. Piozzi who got to the heart of the matter when she wrote:

The French are really a contented race of mortals;—precluded almost from the possibility of adventure, the low Parisian leads a gentle, humble life, nor envies the greatness he can never obtain; but either wonders delightedly, or diverts himself philosophically with the sight of splendours which seldom fail to excite serious envy in an Englishman, and sometimes occasion even suicide from disappointed hopes, which never could take root in the heart of these unaspiring people. . . . Emulation, ambition, avarice, however, must in all arbitrary governments be confined to the great; the other set of mortals, for there are none there of middling rank, live, as it should seem, like eunuchs in a seraglio; feel themselves irrevocably doomed to promote the pleasures of their superiors, nor even dream of fighting for enjoyments from which an irremediable boundary divides them. They see at the beginning of their lives how that life must necessarily end, and trot with a quiet, contented and unaltered pace down their long, straight and shaded avenue. . . .[77]

Her rather cavalier dismissal of the bourgeoisie ought not to prejudice us against Mrs. Piozzi's powers of observation. The avenue that led the *menu peuple* through life to an obscure grave was neither so long nor so shaded as she indicates, but her statements are nonetheless substantially true. Like the many bourgeois who aspired only to be noble,[78] the laboring poor accepted the basic justice of the society in which they lived and never thought of offering it any essential challenge. Consequently, contemporaries thought of them as "gentle, honest, polite, easy to lead" or "soft, pale, small, stunted," lacking "the nerve and the insolence" which were the guarantee of "their frankness, their probity, their devotion." On the one hand, they were pleasant enough and easy to handle; on the other, they had not the stuff of which true republicans were made.[79] They were simple and childlike and, in the reformers' eyes, contemptible, because they represented no danger to the status quo. A vicious and circular dialectic of economic misery and psychological subjection was at work here to imprison the laboring poor who were its victims. They would have the greatest trouble in breaking their bonds, and it may be argued that if left to themselves, they would never have done so. The sans-culottes were, in large measure, born of the laboring poor, but they were nurtured by the bourgeoisie. At the height of their action in the year II (1792–1793), they were no longer the same men they had been in 1789. The force of revolution itself (in the first instance, someone else's revolution) had changed them. It was the failure to conceive of revolution as a process of psychological liberation, among other things, that, in 1801, still caused Lenoir to wonder at the extent of the change that had taken place:

The same people, in other words, the populace . . . had simple and coarse habits, but which seemed rather to lead them to act humanely than ferociously; despite the flightiness commonly attributed to the French and especially to the Parisians, a kind of constancy and fidelity in its customs had for centuries secured to the people of Paris, more than to any other people of France, a title which it would have been impossible to believe they would lose some day.[80]

⌐5⌐

PATTERNS OF BELIEF

⊷§ I §⊷

The religiosity of the laboring poor in eighteenth-century Paris was notorious. The earnestness of their devotion stood in sharp contrast to the practice, or lack of it, of other social classes, among whom scepticism had already made considerable inroads. For the man of the people, the very idea of religious freedom, that is, dis-association from the Catholic Church, was impossible, something of which he was unable to conceive.[1] Unlike the bourgeois, for whom uncritical acceptance of orthodox doctrine would under-mine the development of class consciousness, the *menu peuple* be-longed to a community whose distinctive mark was its corporate capacity to believe. As Groethuysen has shown, "the simple church-goer was a believer; without always knowing what he believed, he lived in a world which was that of the Church, and he could not abandon it to live elsewhere."[2] Even when popular Catholicism went beyond the cadres of the Church, when it denied the notion of obedience to the hierarchy, as it often did, its adherents remained firmly rooted in the ecclesiastical tradition.

Foreign travelers were quick to note the difference of religious practice that existed between one class and another. An English-man writing in 1706, after a residence of 10 years in Paris, affirmed:

I never saw *People* more devout, *Priests* more sober, *Clergy* more orderly, and *Those under Vows* give a better example. . . . The People resort to churches with Piety, the Marchands pray to God to prosper their Trade; it is only the Nobles and Great Ones who go thither to divert themselves, to talk and to make Love.[3]

He was closer to the mark than his countrymen of the latter part of the century, who often let their cultural chauvinism get the better of their judgment. The Earl of Clarendon thought in 1789 that the French concept of devotion was "of so portable and so accommodating a nature, that it may with equal ease, and at any time, be laid down or resumed," which explained their failure to keep Sunday in the proper English manner.[4] And Mrs. Piozzi, friend to Dr. Johnson and a lady raised in the best Sabbatarian tradition, complained:

And surely I never knew till now, that so little religion could exist in any Christian country as in this, where they drive their carts and keep their little shops open on a Sunday, forbearing neither pleasure nor business, as I see, on account of observing that day upon which their Redeemer rose again. They have a Tradition among the meaner people, that when Christ was crucified, he turned his head towards France, over which he pronounced his last blessing; but we must accuse them, if so, of being very ungrateful favourites.[5]

How Protestant! How rational, as she must have thought! But the Parisian *menu peuple* were neither Protestant nor rational in matters of religion. They went to church not to dispute the merits of high versus low church, or to hear abstruse reasoning on the efficacy of grace. They went, rather, to seek comfort and solace against the misery of life outside. They went for the ceremony that was the visible manifestation of the hope for salvation and for the sacraments which were its guarantee. Sunday was of less special significance to them because many heard mass, or at least stopped in for a prayer, every day.[6] Ceremonies were available to them in profusion at almost any hour. To cite only one example, plenary indulgences might be had by praying before the seven altars of the monasteries of the Minimes and the Jacobins of the rue Saint Honoré or at the parish church of Saint Sulpice.[7]

There were 53 parish churches in Paris in the second half of the century, whose congregations ranged in size from several hundred (La Madeleine in la Cité, Saint Croix in la Cité, Saints Innocents) to many thousands (24,000 at Saint Gervais, 26,000 at Saint Paul, 25,000 at Saint Merry—all in the Marais, 32,000 at Saint Germain L'Auxerrois, 36,000 at Sainte Marguerite in the faubourg Saint Antoine, 40,000 at Saint Laurent, and 90,000 at Saint Sulpice).[8] There were, in addition, 47 monasteries and 60 convents, in many of which the laity could attend mass or receive the ministrations of a priest. According to Expilly, the total clerical population of Paris in 1768 was approximately 8,000, including 3,156 secular priests, 2,023 regulars, 2,128 nuns and 720 nursing sisters.[9] The parish priests, about 950 in number in 1789, were recruited from every region in France, so that on the eve of the Revolution, only one-third came from Paris and its immediate environs, 15 percent from Normandy, and 5 percent each from the provinces of Picardy, Burgundy, Provence, and the Franche Comte. The laboring poor, even those from the most distant provinces, were likely, when they felt the need for religious consolation, to find a cleric who understood their needs, at least insofar as common origin and knowledge of their way of life might make this possible.[10]

The availability of religion does not explain devotion but does contribute to its continuance. The calendar was marked by a series of feast and holy days whose observance was general throughout the population, not least of all among the laboring poor. Whether a majority took communion at Easter, the act which the Church set down as the *sine qua non* of membership in the Catholic community, we do not know.[11] Parisians of this class defined religious duties for themselves instead of following the formal precepts of the hierarchy. Assiduousness at Sunday mass is not necessarily proof of anything except outward conformity. Conversely, the intensity of belief cannot be questioned because of failure to go to church or to send one's child to catechism classes in preparation for first communion.[12] It is further clear that fasting in general and during Lent in particular (that is, the taking of only one meal a day and abstinence from meat, imposed on all persons over the age of 21) lost currency toward the end of the old regime. Archbishop Le Clerc de Juigné implicitly admitted as much in 1786 when he exhorted the people to participate in one way or another—through prayer, contributions, or privations of another sort—in the general contrition of the faithful appropriate to that season.[13] But while some duties were abandoned, others were held onto more firmly than ever. The more intensely religion is felt, the more idiosyncratic are likely to be its manifestations, especially among the illiterate or uneducated.

Every indication is that the *menu peuple* believed in the cult of the saints and eagerly participated in honoring those with whom they especially identified because of a historical or mythical association between those saints and either the city as a whole or a particular parish. Of the 29 obligatory feast days, the most popular was the Feast of Sainte Geneviève, the patron of the city, celebrated on January 3. No work was done on that day. All Saints Day, November 2, was the occasion each year of a "great gathering of people in the cemeteries of Clamart and of the Innocents," in whose mass graves so many of the friends and relatives of the laboring poor had been buried. The feast day of the patron saint of each parish was celebrated locally, while the Feast of Saint John the Baptist on June 21 called for a bonfire and much uproar in the place de Grève. (In the unenlightened past, this had been the occasion, on Midsummer's Night, when witches were exorcised by scattering herbs over, and throwing live cats into, the fire. But, a properly pious eighteenth-century lawyer noted, "our more enlightened century is well cured of these popular errors."[14] It is not altogether certain that he was right.)

For more private devotions, seven-day retreats for male workers were held twice a year, at Easter and All Saints Day, in the populous parishes of Saint Merry, Saint Sauveur and Saint Médard, as well as in Saint Roch, Saint Benoît and at the Congregation of Foreign Missions. Female artisans were welcomed four times a year at the convent of the Filles de Sainte Geneviève if they came from Paris, twice a year if they came from the country.[15] In 1735, special catechism classes and retreats were organized for the Savoyards and other street workers of Paris. Times were chosen outside working hours, and presently the organizing priest's efforts were rewarded by the regular attendance of several thousand students. As one of the founders put it, "Everywhere we found these poor people disposed to do everything we wished." The classes and retreats at Easter and All Saints Day soon spread from the parish of Saint Benoît in the faubourg Saint Marcel to at least five other parishes (Saint Merry, Saint Sulpice, Saint Médard, Saint Sauveur, Sainte Marguerite). In 1739, 800 street workers were confirmed in a single ceremony at Saint Sulpice and thus presumably set upon the road to salvation. The priest responsible congratulated himself on the achievement and reflected:

By instructing them, and by making it easier for them to acquire the means of saving themselves, we shall save ourselves; and from this moment on, we shall have the consolation of seeing the Lord glorified by an infinite number of poor people who, however vile and contemptible they may appear in our eyes, are no less agreeable to Him.[16]

Each saint had a special field of intercession, in which he or she was held to be most effective. Saint Apoline of Saint Merry cured illnesses that attacked the breasts because hers had been cut off in her martyrdom. Pregnant women implored the aid of Saint John the Baptist, reasoning that as he had had his head cut off, their children would be born in the proper position, head first. Other saints had their names, rather than their experiences, to recommend them. Thus one appealed to Saint Clair to cure one's eyes, to Saint Cloud to relieve one's *cloux* (boils), to Saint Mande to mend (*amender*) the ways of errant children. And, to stretch a point, women and girls called on Saint James because the popular saying had it that he could refuse "ni fille ni femme."[17]

The same principle applied to the choice of patron saints for the *confréries* or religious associations, most of which were organized as adjuncts to the guilds.[18] Verbal analogy made the Holy Ghost the patron of the spirit makers (Saint Esprit), and Saint Clair the patron of the lanternmakers. Saint Joseph shared a profession with the carpenters as did Saint Côme with the surgeons. Saint Laurent was roasted on a grill and thereby became associated with the *rotisseurs*, and Saint Barthélemy, having been skinned alive, was destined for the tanners. Saint Nicolas protected pilgrims in a storm and so was chosen for the devotions of the wood and coal merchants, whose goods reached Paris by water. Those *confréries* not limited to members of a single profession were generally placed under the invocation of the Virgin or the Sacred Heart of Jesus. All of them sponsored masses, retreats, and various charitable works.[19]

The great emphasis placed by the masses on the cult of the saints offended the ecclesiastical authorities, who considered it to be tinged with heterodoxy. No doubt the bishops were right, for these special forms of worship bore the stamp of all popular religion, the tendency to combine into a single entity spiritual aspirations and profane concerns, adoration of the mysteries and an affirmation of life.[20] Such a religion always tends to overflow the boundaries of the established church, can easily become anticlerical and antihierarchical and, given the right circumstances, may even turn into a vehicle for the development of political consciousness. Fears of this kind of development may have lain behind the action taken by both ecclesiastical and secular authorities. The new Parisian liturgy adopted by Archbishop François Harley de Champvallon in 1680, in the midst of the struggle over the Gallican Church, restricted worship of the saints and even put less stress than previously on the cult of the Virgin, a particular object of adoration of the Parisian masses, which was associated with Jesuit ultramontanism.[21] More than 40 legends concerning saints were dropped for lack of proof.[22] In 1760, it was ordered that no further *confréries* should be created, but all this seems to have had little effect on the patterns of popular religious belief. The adoration of the saints continued to flourish, even when other seams of the church fabric had been almost completely rent. In 1792, an English observer noted:

Another absurdity . . . is, that most of the almanacks, even that which is prefixed to Mr. Rabaut's [de Saint Etienne] Account of the Revolution, contains against every day in the year, the name of some saint of other, male or female, some of them martyrs, and others not, others archangels, angels, arch-bishops, bishops, popes, virgins, to the number of twenty four, and of these, four were martyrs into the bargain; and this at a time when churches are selling by auction and pulling down, when the convents are turned into barracks, when there is neither monk nor nun to be seen in the kingdom, nor yet any *Abbé*, and when no priest dares appear in any sacerdotal garment, or even with anything which might mark him as an ecclesiastic.[23]

Almanacs being one of the most extensively distributed forms of mass literature,[24] it is perhaps not going too far to argue that we have here evidence of the remarkable tenacity of popular faith. So deeply were these patterns of belief implanted in the minds of the laboring poor that they continued to serve as a framework for worship, even when they lost their specifically Christian content. The de-Christianization policies of the Revolutionary Government may temporarily and partially have won sans-culottes and peasants away from the Church, but the need and will to believe were not even touched upon.[25]

ᴥ§ II §ᴥ

Popular, syncretic Catholicism set its own norms of religious behavior, much to the horror of Protestants and other outsiders. The German traveler Neimitz described the midnight mass at Christmas as

remarkable. . . . All the churches, all the convents are invaded by crowds, and people run from one place to another. It is not precisely religious music that is played then in the temples; one hears minuets and other profane tunes. Many sacrileges and impieties are committed. The populace stays out all night, and from mass they go to the cabaret, where they revel until dawn. A fine preparation for so great and holy a day![26]

But the fact remains that the poor did go to church, and when they did so, they demanded that the ceremonies be well ordered and unvarying. It was the only way that their sense of security could be preserved.[27] No priest ought to be allowed to shorten or otherwise change established practice. If he tried to do so, he was sure to cause trouble. Hardy cites several occasions on which the municipal guard had to be called in to quell disturbances of this sort. In the Parish of Saint Merry on June 19, 1783, the Corpus Christie procession had just begun when it started to rain, and the vicar ordered a return to the church. Popular reaction was so great that he was "forced to go out, to continue the procession, and was thus scandalously made to obey the law laid down by the *menu peuple* of his parish who cried out loudly that he was not much to be pitied, since he had a whole year in which to get dry."[28] On Easter Tuesday, 1786, the parish church of Saint Nicolas des Champs was the scene of a similar incident, when the clergy decided, for the first time, to dispense with the chanting of the Stabat Mater and the benediction of the host. "This people . . . of rather bad composition" was so upset by this that they had to be put out of the church by violence, and Hardy was moved to wonder whether it would not have been more politic to let them have their own way.[29]

The sermon was an integral part of the mass, and a useful means of propagandizing the faithful. Although the practice of lay preaching never developed in France in any way comparable to that of Protestant England,[30] the hierarchy seems to have been fearful of unauthorized tampering with the word of God. As early as 1673, the statutes of the synod of the diocese of Paris forbade anyone to preach who had attained the grade of deacon and did not have the authorization of the vicar-general of the diocese. In the following year, all laymen were formally forbidden, under penalty of excommunication, "to meddle in pronouncing the word of God, and in preaching at crossroads and in the streets." The clergy was enjoined to prevent irreverent behavior on these occasions and to call upon the civil authorities to stamp out "these disorders."[31] The danger was that someone might cast protests against the temporal order in religious terms, the only frame of reference that had any significant meaning for the laboring poor, and thereby inflame them into violence and revolt.

Clearly, the sermons preached to captive congregations were intended to have the opposite effect. On this matter, official church doctrine seems never to have varied.[32] The chief emphasis was laid on man's offensiveness in the sight of God, his sinfulness, the need for Christian humility, the efficacy of regular church attendance and prayer, and the cult of the Virgin and the saints.[33] The elements of traditional Catholic teaching were all there: trust in the Lord rather than in one's self, make good use of your spiritual and physical powers, and pray and hope that the grace of God will descend upon you.[34] But beyond these generalities, it was also agreed that one did not preach to everyone in the same way.

Sermons and counsel ought to be appropriate not only to the occasion but also to the social position of the parishioner. Joseph Lambert, who held his doctorate in theology from the Sorbonne, cited no less an authority than the Council of Aix la Chapelle in the year 816 to argue that it was

a bad way of instructing the poor to speak of things not usual among them. . . . When one teaches the poor, one must choose one's subject with greater care. The truths of the Gospel presented clearly, simply, and in a paternal manner are heeded. They please and nourish [the listeners' souls]. Declamation that is strong but prudent and charitable in denouncing impurity, revenge, intemperance, drunkenness, complaining, indecency, quarrels, injustices, theft, dancing, late-night parties, and laziness in fulfilling the duties of a Christian; that is the morality of the countryside.[35]

And of the city, too, if we read further in his homilies. Above all, the poor must be told to be happy with their poverty. They owed God an immense debt for having put them in a situation that made it easier to be saved than if they had been rich. "Not only does the true believer not complain, but he blesses God in his poverty. . . . How unhappy are those who are so preoccupied by their poverty that they do not think of God. They are unhappy, not because they are poor, but because they forget God."[36] To do otherwise than to accept one's fate with resignation and thanks was to be guilty of "criminal revolt," the implication being that damnation would be too generous a punishment. The man who was truly poor, in spirit as well as in pocket, was an uncomplaining cog in a very great wheel. As an artisan, he offered and dedicated his work to God. As a parent, he raised his children in the fear of God. As a domestic ("for holiness is communicated to all"), he remembered that Christ himself had served the apostles and so was faithful to his masters. As a man . . . the category did not exist.[37]

◁§ I I I §▷

Superstition was a strong element in the syncretic Catholicism of the laboring poor. That they believed in miracles is not surprising and does not set them apart, although they were no doubt more willing to recognize a miracle than were their more sophisticated contemporaries or the official doctrine of the Church. But they also believed in the ubiquity of the supernatural, and they carried this belief, not totally unsupported by the theologians, to extremes.[38] There was no doubt in their minds that ghosts existed, so it was normal for crowds to gather whenever one's presence was reported.[39] More unusual but still possible for the *menu peuple* to credit was the report that the wife of de Barentin, *premier président* of the Cour des Aides, had given birth to "a bush recognized as a gooseberry bush, although without gooseberries, but bearing . . . cherries. This monster of an entirely new species had nothing of human shape about it and was absolutely inanimate. This singular birth could not fail to cause much chagrin to the entire family."[40] After all, God in His infinite wisdom could do anything.

Neither the poor nor the maintenance of public order were threatened by these aberrant beliefs. But the effect of rumor mongering and credulity was not always so benign. In a society like that of Paris in the eighteenth century, where the majority of people were functionally illiterate and the means of communication underdeveloped, it was extremely difficult to control the flow of information. There was no mass media to counteract the spread of news and speculation by word of mouth. Government publications were either not read or disregarded, while rather more attention was paid to "mauvais propos" and clandestine pamphlets.[41] Given proper conditions of stress, the propensity to believe might have dangerous effects indeed, as witness the incidents of May, 1750, when a roundup of stray children by the police caused a riot and several deaths because it was thought that their blood was to be used to bathe a princess stricken with a disease for which it was the only cure.[42] Lenoir reported that 50 years later the memory of the events had not yet faded among the people of Paris.[43]

This was not an isolated incident. In the summer of 1777, a rumor spread that sun spots recently observed were the biblical signs foretelling the end of the world, and it was necessary to invoke the authority of the astronomer Lalande in order to calm nerves.[44] Two years later, there was the case of the self-styled prophet Dame Sainte-Catherine who, finding herself pregnant, preached that she was about to give birth to the Messiah. She lived in the rue Louisine of the faubourg Saint Marcel, where her landlord, a master carpenter named Jamel, gave her space in which to hold prayer meetings. She had converted some 300 persons to her sect and asked of them principally that they no longer attend mass. Worse still, she was accused of keeping a great number of parishioners of Saint Hyppolite from performing their paschal duties.[45]

The extent to which rumor can play upon the fears of the *menu peuple* is again illustrated by the case of Lavallée d'Arancy, who was imprisoned by order of the lieutenant-general of police in July, 1778. He had for some time been telling his neighbors—"40 locataires du bas peuple"—in great detail of a plot to kill the royal family and seize control of the state apparatus. Far from thinking of him as insane, they were inclined to take his warnings seriously. Hence, his tales "might give rise to ferment and trouble public order" and he had, as a preventive measure, to be put away.[46] Each time the government or municipal officials reacted harshly to the spread of gossip, it was less on account of the specific content of the story told than because uncensored speculation might have the unfortunate effect of bringing into question the authority of the constituted bodies, both of church and state.

We have the word of no less an authority than Restif de la Bretonne that the *gens du peuple* were superstitious.[47] And among them, the *poissardes* or marketwomen stood in the first rank. They were

to the utmost extent pious and superstitious, pray to Sainte Geneviève, the Patron of Paris, have an unconditional confidence in the splendid chest in which her relics are preserved, love the clergy so long as they buy and pay for their fish, but execrate the atheistic Abbés who eat meat on Friday, and doubly so, because it is a sin, and still more because their principles might harm the fish trade. . . .[48]

As they were further in the habit of talking politics and philosophy, the authorities might well worry about their effect on their equally credulous listeners.

Marville put the matter perfectly in 1745 when he spoke of being "threatened" by two new saints. In these years, when a vulgarized kind of Jansenism was still very popular among the *menu peuple*, it was not unusual to hear of rioting at the death of a particularly beloved priest or deacon. For example the hair and nails were cut off and the clothes stripped from the corpse of the Abbé Maurice Tissart before it was buried. After the funeral, large numbers of people came to pray at his grave and to fill their mouths and pockets with this holy earth.[49] A generation later, in 1772, a faith healer attracted gatherings of as many as 30,000 persons in a single day by his miraculous cures. The crippled were said to walk, the blind to see, and the deaf to hear once they declared their belief in God. A guard had to be set up around his house and the prophet himself finally disposed of, for fear of the "fanaticism of the people, who believe in God."[50]

The trouble was less that the people believed in God than that they chose to identify Him with certain individuals and movements here on earth. The case in point is the Jansenism with which they were repeatedly associated between the 1720s and 1750s. Now, I think we may take it as given that the laboring poor knew little and cared less about the abstruse problems of the debased nature of man, the sufficiency of grace, and predestination. Augustine, like Aquinas, was an intellectual's saint, lacking the attributes that attract popular reverence. If the poor distrusted reason, it was not because they thought it to be the product of a corrupt nature but because it was a tool with which they were unfamiliar. Never did they dream of retiring from the world in the fashion of a Duvergier de Hauranne or a Pascal. It was a luxury they could not afford. Similarly, the many values—individualism, democracy, and national independence—to whose development Jansenism is supposed to have contributed—were empty concepts to them.[51] If by the early eighteenth century Jansenism had become a political movement, it was not as such that it appealed to them either, although it may be said that their affinity for it was manipulated by others, notably the Parlement of Paris, for political ends. Indeed, it may be argued that the *menu peuple* were not attracted to Jansenism as much as they happened to cross paths with it at a propitious moment. As I have already noted, the laboring poor were constantly searching for consolation and assurance of salvation, and the Church was not, some of them felt (no doubt, obscurely), giving it to them. Their dissent, or better still their dissatisfaction, was not doctrinal but visceral. They displayed no reforming zeal, did not believe, in the manner of the Calvinists, that the Church had unfrocked itself, and proclaimed no holy war against the Beast, despite the example of the Abbé Etemare.[52] Even to call them enthusiasts is perhaps to abuse the word insofar as it has come to be associated with ultrapersonal, mystical religion.[53] They were not mystics, for mysticism presupposes the kind of individualism that is at the opposite pole from the communal patterns of belief so characteristic of them. But they were dissatisfied with the dreariness of the usual Catholic practice and the vagueness of its promises. They were thus available for another experience within the confines of the Catholic community, an experience to which they would bring their usual enthusiasm and excitation. The Jansenist movement, just then fighting for its life against the pressures of pope and king, symbolized by the Bull Unigenitus, was much present and talked about. Certain Jansenists had acquired remarkable personal reputations for holiness and charity among the poor, which could not help but facilitate its liaison with popular religion. What was needed was some catalytic agent, and that came in the form of a series of miracles associated with the person of the Diacre Pâris and other Jansenist worthies.

The first of these miracles took place in June, 1725 in the faubourg Saint Antoine. The wife of the woodworker Lafosse had been paralyzed for a long time when she attended the parish procession for Corpus Christi. She prayed for a cure, using the words of the paralytic in the Gospel, "Lord, You can cure me, if You will," and she walked. The initial phase of incredulity past, she became the object of political-ecclesiastical covetousness, with both the Molinists and the Jansenists trying to get her to say that she was in their respective camps. She protested her ignorance of such matters, with the result that the credit for her cure went to the Jansenists, since the vicar of her parish was an appellant against the Bull.[54]

This miracle remained, however, an isolated incident until about two years later and the death of the Diacre Pâris. Pâris was the son of a counselor of the Parlement who had been led by the intensity of a mystical experience to abandon his worldly concerns in favor of a simple life of exemplary piety on the Jansenist model among the poor of the faubourg Saint Marcel. The veneration and awe in which he was held by the people testify to the force of his personality. On the day of his burial, a certain Madeleine Biegney, another 20-year paralytic, claimed to have been cured by kissing the feet of the corpse. She was followed by Mademoiselle Thibault, who was cured of what may have been arthritic or rheumatic pains by praying at the tomb.[55] It will be noted that in the miracles that followed, the great majority of the beneficiaries were women and mainly, with few exceptions, of the laboring poor. By October, 1728, the Diacre's reputation was so secure and his sect so popular among the people that they looked upon the Cardinal de Noailles' break with Jansenism as reprehensible and little short of treason. Anyone who dared to question the authenticity of the miracles put his life in jeopardy. Orders emanating from the Archbishop forbidding worship at the tomb were completely ignored and, in fact, had the effect of re-enforcing the practice. As Barbier wrote, "The people will make him a saint without the Court of Rome if this continues."[56] In order that this might not happen, the royal administration thought it best to close the cemetery of Saint Médard on Januuary 27, 1732, an action which gave rise to an immortal piece of graffiti found the next day posted on the gates:

De par le roi
Défenses à Dieu
De faire miracle
En ce lieu.*

Popular affection for Jansenism was circumstantial rather than profound. When the *menu peuple* worshipped (it is the only appropriate word) Pâris, they were also attracted to the memory of Dourdan, a monk of the Abbey of Saint Victor, who died in 1729. He, too, had a reputation as a great friend of the poor, and he died without the sacraments because he had refused to take them from the hand of his superior, a Jansenist. Yet by 1731 his cult had waned into nothingness for reasons far removed from his practice of the Donatist heresy. There was no one ready to exploit this popular infatuation as there was in the case of Pâris. Whereas robe and other well-placed Jansenists were not averse to mobilizing the *menu peuple* for their own ends, essentially to scare the royal authorities, the Molinists were in power and consequently thought they could dispense with this popular support.[57]

The movement built around Jansenism might have become the central element in the development of political consciousness among the poor. As we have seen, it was far from lacking in ideas useful for challenging the distribution of power and its institutional forms. Yet it became neither a radical sect, like the Anabaptists of sixteenth-century Germany, nor a training ground for future militants, like some of the Methodist communions in late eighteenth- and early nineteenth-century England. The old bourgeoisie and nobility of the robe, who were its chief adherents, were *frondeurs*, not revolutionaries. They were fundamentally attached to the maintenance of the old regime, as their actions in 1732 (observation of the law of silence**) and in 1754 (end of the affair of the refusal of sacraments) show. The new, enterprising bourgeoisie might be attracted by its potential for liberalism, individualism, and its morality of conscience but was repelled by its unfriendliness toward the bourgeois values of capital accumulation and worldly success.[58] The laboring poor were as yet incapable, without leadership from another class, of creating their own ideology. They began the long and arduous process of doing so during the revo-

---

* The King's order
 Forbids God
 To make a miracle
 In this place.
** The law of silence was the expression used to refer to the royal order forbidding discussion of all matters pertaining to the Jansenist controversy.

lutionary period and afterward, while being transformed into a proletariat. At this stage, the Church, as an instrument of reaction, had been so discredited that no system of ideas in any way related to traditional Christianity could appeal to them. And by then, the revolutionary experience and the consequent transformation of the mode of social existence had made alternatives available.

In the meantime, popular Jansenism rapidly degenerated into personal hysteria. As early as July, 1731, there were reports of violent seizures among the women who came to pray and be cured at Pâris's grave. These were generally considered by the believers to be part of the cure. But very shortly after the closing of the cemetery of Saint Médard, these convulsions seem to have taken on a life of their own, to have become, strictly speaking, a form of religious witness. Various mysteries of the life of Christ, especially his sufferings, were acted out. The participants spoke in tongues, preached against Molinism, and prophesied on the apostasy of the Gentiles, the conversion of the Jews, and other matters of great moment. They also demanded and received what came to be called *secours*, or beatings, a practice which alienated some of the more *bien-pensants* among the Jansenists. As one who was favorable to these activities wrote:

The beatings that these girls call for with alacrity are administered to them by men in preference to women, and often in preference to other men; their choice does not waver, and falls commonly upon priests and men: the women sit on their laps so as to allow their convulsions to pass; they demand that the men lift them into the air, like children; they sit astride their necks, as they would on a horse, their legs hanging over the stomach, and are thus carried around the rooms; they have marked predilections for certain men, whose hands, they say, bring them greater comfort than others, and all these charitable kindnesses are rewarded by airs and graces, sweet words, lewd gestures, little slaps.[59]

Others were less indulgent, scandalized by the physical pain inflicted on the young ladies, albeit at their own request and without their experiencing any apparent harm as a result. They were stomped upon, choked, and crucified in order to make manifest "the omnipotence of God in the state of invulnerability in which He places them."[60] Adversaries of these procedures sniggeringly suggested that the assemblies of convulsionaries were nothing more than free-wheeling orgies, an assertion for which there is no proof. But the sexual symbolism of the constant piercing of all parts of the women's bodies with knives and pins, as well as in the pressing

and pulling of their breasts by male accomplices is unmistakable.[61]
The acting out of libidinous fantasies found its religious justification in that current of Jansenist doctrine which called for
a rejection of this-worldly standards and a total dedication to the
will of God. Like the Cathari and a hundred other sects, the convulsionaries were seeking to purify themselves so that they might
play the role God intended to confer on them in His plan for
the transformation of the universe.

The poverty of the convulsionaries was the sign of their election.
Once in a while, a member of the sect made a more explicit connection between poverty and goodness, on the one hand, and
wealth, power, and evil, on the other. In August, 1770, a certain
Mademoiselle Maillard, identified only as a worker but probably,
from the internal evidence, a *chambrelan*, wrote a letter to the
king, in which she pleaded for the release of a fellow Jansenist.
This woman, Mademoiselle Mote, had been captured by the parish
clergy of Saint André des Arts, a group of furious Jesuits, and
was being held against her will somewhere in Paris. Four persons
had fallen on her "like poverty upon the world" and had attempted
to kill her. Because the petitioner had come to her aid, she, too,
was in danger. There was a giant conspiracy afoot by the Jesuits
to foment civil war. They were in league with atheists who poison
people's minds with vicious books. The atheists were "more vile
than the atoms that fly in the air" and the Jesuits were an "evil
sect that likes to play ball, but hasn't enough skittles." Satan was at
work in their machinations, and it was by magic "that they cause
cupidity to reign in this world. It is at a high point, and they do so
in order to give the world over to the devil." She outlined the
king's duty:

Vous nous donnerez de bons pasteurs pour epurez nos ames et nous fair
approchez sil est possible tous les jours de la sainte communion. . . .
dieu createur du ciel et de la terre a bien voulu morire pour nous sur
larbre de la crois et rependre tous son sang pour le faire ruiseler dans
les veine de tous les du genrumain et il ruiselle encore tous les jour
sur nos autelle pour nous en nourire dune maniere invisible pour le
salue de nos ame et nous accordez tout les grace que nous lui demandont
pour la necesite de la vie. . . . O mon dieu . . . delivre encore les pauvre
qu'il ni ai plus darchez de gaux [archers de gueux] car qui persecute
le pauvre persecute Jesus Christ [deux mots illisibles] ete par la mani-
gance de tous ces vilains gens que le peuple a tant soufert par la fain
la soif la nudite il avoit trop de monde il falloit les faire morire et
jetez des cantite de ble dans la riviere et cela pour les exceder et les
reduire par la grand misere a une guere civile il ni a pas jusqu'au

religieuse qui font des envoy [de grains?] Cest pour parvenir a leur but il posede lor et largent ils en donne au roy il lui font leur cour mais cest pour parvenir a leur but et par consequan se rendre maitre. . . .

You will give us good pastors to purify our souls and bring us to the communion table every day if possible. . . . God the creator of heaven and earth, condescended to die for us on the tree of the cross and to spill all His blood so as to make it run in the veins of all the human race, and it still runs every day on our altars to nourish us in an invisible manner for the salvation of our souls and to give us all the grace we ask of it for the necessities of life. . . . O my God . . . deliver us, the poor. May there be no more policemen [*archers de gueux*] for whosoever persecutes the poor persecutes Jesus Christ [two illegible words] was by the machination of all these evil men that the people have suffered so greatly from hunger, thirst, and lack of clothing. The population was too large. It was necessary that some should be caused to die, and quantities of grain be thrown in the river so as to harass them and reduce them through great misery to a civil war. Even the nuns make shipments [of grain]. To reach their goal, they possess gold and silver. They give to the king and pay him their court, but it is in order to reach their goal and consequently to become the masters. . . .[62]

The accusation contains all of the common themes: fear of starvation, the existence of a *pacte de famine*, the oppression of the poor by magic and secret machinations, Jesuitical omnipotence, the fear of the devil, the distrust of intellectuals and atheists (often taken to be synonymous terms), trust in the king but not of those around him, and belief in the virtues of poverty. Its formulation in the phonetic spelling of a semiliterate workingwoman is testimony to the fact that popular Jansenism had at least some potential as a vehicle of political protest. But that potential was never developed any further. Unlike some of the primitive rebels studied by Eric Hobsbawm,[63] the Jansenists remained socially passive and their movement left no heritage on which to build a new politics.

[6]

BEGGARS AND
CRIMINALS

The number of persons arrested as beggars was very considerable. In 1763, Sir William Mildmay described "the swarms of beggars, which infest the streets of Paris . . . for as their hospital can hold only a certain number, it is suspected, that as fast as the magistrates send a crowd of vagrants to be admitted at one door, the administrators let out as many at another."[1] Despite the difficulties of execution to which the repetition of antibegging ordinances calls our attention, Bicêtre, La Pitié and the Salpêtrière counted 2,158 entries of sturdy beggars and 1,985 of sick beggars in 1751.[2] The still more rigorous practice of the Royal Declaration of 1764 produced a total of 18,523 prisoners in the *dépôts de mendicité* of the Generality of Paris by the end of 1773. (Of these, 11,895 were eventually allowed to go free, while 88 entered the army, 3,158 died in captivity, and 1,963 escaped.)[3] The number of arrests continued to be high in the last years of the old regime. Between July, 1784 and June, 1785, the commissaires of the Châtelet had arrested and imprisoned 1,762 beggars. In 1788, 2,650 persons were arrested, of whom 2,219 were jailed.[4] In 1784, Necker estimated that there were 7,000 to 8,000 beggars in 33 *dépôts* at any given time.[5]

When arrested, beggars rarely admitted their fault, or, if they did, sought to invoke extenuating circumstances, as for example the journeyman leather worker who told the police that "it is only when he has no work that he begs in order to survive"[6] and the case of Edme Gardy, a street messenger condemned in June, 1775 to stand in the pillory for two hours, to pay a fine of three livres, and to be banished from Paris for three years. His tale is familiar: age 27, born near Auxerre, he had been coming to Paris regularly over a period of three years before having settled there six months earlier. He worked when he could find employment. He had recently sustained an injury while doing some farm work in the Brie and so had to beg to tide himself over.[7]

The police may have been suspicious of these professions of innocence, but they rarely took the trouble to press their investigations. If the accused said he was not guilty, he was generally given his freedom within a few days. If he pleaded guilty with an explanation, as in the examples cited above, he got a light sentence and was sent away from Paris. Only if he were suspected of fraud (faking an illness, pretending to be at death's door) or of having bad morals (that a suspect was living adulterously with a married woman was a point urged against him) did the judges take stronger action, usually branding and commitment to the galleys. These signs appear to have been the means employed by the authorities to distinguish "simple, nondangerous beggars" from "beggars suspected of maintaining relations with the thieves of Paris." In 1780, the police began to hire the former to spy on the latter but with what results we do not know.[8]

In 1764, this somewhat pragmatic way of distinguishing between good and bad beggars was sytematized by a royal declaration. The simple beggars were already covered by the legislation of 1724, which provided for their return to the home parish. The point of the new law was to punish the "vagabonds et gens sans aveu" who, it was felt, constituted the real danger to social peace. They were defined as those who "for six full months have not exercised either profession or trade, and who, having neither status nor place to live, cannot secure testimony to their good morals from persons worthy of belief." Men between the ages of 16 and 70 were to be sentenced to three years on the galleys for a first offense, nine years for a second. The time was the same for women, children, and men over seventy, but it was to be served in a hospital. After 1767, the specially created *dépôts de mendicité* took the place of the hospitals and sometimes the galleys. They also served as temporary detention centers for beggars being sent home.[9] The Paris Generality counted five *dépôts* at Saint Denis, Pontoise, Sens, Meaux and Melun. Two others, at Dreux and Senlis, were closed in 1773. At Saint Denis, a factory of woolen cloth and blankets was established, while the administrators of both Meaux and Pontoise put their inmates to work spinning cotton. In return for their work, the prisoners were paid a token sum, given daily rations of one and a half pounds of mixed grain bread, some vegetables, and a bit of meat three times a week, and were allowed to sleep only two to a bed. It was a regime calculated to be "better than prison, worse than the army."[10]

The provisions of this legislation corresponded to an illusion nourished by contemporaries as to the great number of habitual or professional beggars supposed to be infesting the realm. They were, in this formulation, persons "whose profession it is to do nothing and to live at the expense of others, who have given up work and residence completely, who know neither rule, nor yoke, nor superior, who are not only independent, but know how to inspire fear and obedience in others."[11] Another commentator called them "born beggars" and found many of them living as couples in Paris, Picardy, and Champagne. "These households," he wrote, "are recruited among weak laborers whom women debauch by promising to support them. . . . They then hide in the guise of small mercers, repairers of buckles, founders of spoons, sellers of Saint Hubert's rings, etc."[12] And Turmeau de La Morandière claimed to know in Paris "among other idlers, four families who have lazily indulged in begging since 1740, and whose male and female children and grandchildren are big and strong, just like their fathers and mothers, who were tall. In the hay harvest season, these rogues have a scythe; in the grain harvest time, they have a sickle; at the time of the grape harvest, they have sacks and pails, so as to persuade people that they have found no work, and that they are ready to work; but these misfits are not really looking for any."[13]

This was a happy breed, or would have been, had it existed in truly significant numbers. There were, of course, beggars on the model of Peachum and company, indistinguishable from the fraternity of professional criminals. They covered themselves with disguises to simulate infirmities in order to attract the pity of the public. To this end, women hired sick children to hang onto their apron strings so as to demonstrate how difficult life really was. The more miserable and downtrodden the children looked, the more they were likely to fetch in this odd market place. A German observer reported a fight between two beggar women in the faubourg Saint Antoine over who was to have the right to the use of one such child.[14] And in the evening, in a "cabaret hidden off in some faubourg," they drank and rejoiced over their frauds.[15] The great Cour des Miracles off the rue Saint Denis had been cleared by La Reynie, the first lieutenant-general of police, in 1667, and there were no longer any great national/regional associations of beggars as in the sixteenth century and earlier.[16] The unemployed and the

uprooted wandered all over Paris and appear to have had their
favored meeting places. They were not necessarily *gens sans aveu*
or vagabonds in the legal sense of the words, but it is clearly to
them that the various ordinances against popular assemblies refer.
Just as in 1789 the Great Fear of brigands was to hold all France
in its grip, the last years of the old regime saw the ruling classes
develop their old fears into a paranoid dread of crowds. In 1784,
not only vagabonds and *gens sans aveu* but also water-carriers, porters, and other laborers were forbidden to enter, assemble, or pass
through the place Royale. In 1781, the seigneurial court of the
Chapter of Saint Médard, in the midst of the most populous quarter of Paris, complained about and forbade

the almost continual gatherings of vagabonds, and vagrants who play
all sorts of games, do not respect the hours of divine service . . . often
quarrels take place among them which give rise to curses, blasphemies,
which are heard in the Churches . . . they throw stones which fall into
the choir or the Churches of St. Marcel and St. Martin, which troubles
and disturbs divine service . . .

It may be argued that esthetic or religious considerations sufficiently explain this diligence, but it is also possible to see in it an
avowal of a deteriorating social situation and of the authorities' inability to exercise control.[17]

In this era of the Enlightenment, when advanced thinkers
prided themselves on having at last found that the long sought
after philosopher's stone was, in the words of the Abbé Malvaux,
nothing else but *work*, the *menu peuple*, who did not mainly define themselves as producers, were out of step with the cause of
progress.[18] Beggars who did not work were assumed to be running
away from productive activity. They were evil because they were
not useful but rather a burden to society. By refusing to do their
share, they made it necessary for others to work harder and at
the same time to pay great taxes in order to support them. Their
unsettled habits—and first of all, their irregular family life—
caused an increase in debauchery and a loss of population, without
which society could not expand and develop.[19] The indictment
reads like a list of bourgeois values—work, thrift, sobriety—which
perhaps explains why it could not be shared by the laboring poor.
This is just another way of saying that workingmen and women
were conscious of belonging to the same social group as the beggars into whose ranks they might fall at any moment. They often
took action to prevent the capture of a beggar by the police.

Soldiers and domestics were known to claim that the person about to be arrested was in fact no beggar but a member of their regiment or household and, if that did not work, to force his surrender by violence. For the Parisian people, whether a person worked or not was of secondary consideration in comparison to his quality as a poor man and therefore a possessor of Christian virtues.[20]

Laws against beggary were an absurdity in a country where one-fifth of the population was always "because of circumstances about to ask for charity."[21] Leclerc de Montlinot went on to say that it was calumny to denounce workingmen for drinking or their failure to save money for their old age. They had no money to begin with, and they drank only for the lack of anything else to do. In what is perhaps the most eloquent defense of the laboring poor published during the old regime, he wrote:

Society devours the poor man like a bit of food. . . . If the remedy were not contained within the evil itself, if nineteen-twentieths of the people without property did not die before their time, the weight of these unfortunates could not even be borne by the Administration; it is a sophism to say that those who exercise the arts [i.e., who work] live as long as those who enjoy them. One meets walking skeletons only in the city. All that is weak dies an early death, especially in the country. Most of those who write about the people are not sufficiently aware of this frightful truth, and they slander them almost always.[22]

But before they died their premature deaths, beggars dragged their misery about for all to see. The legislation against them, while annoying and without any hope of helping them to resolve their difficulties, was intended not so much to punish them as to render them less visible. There is no evidence to indicate that any systematic attempt was ever made to control the flow of labor on the model of the English laws of settlement. What mattered above all was that the unemployed be kept away from the turbulent atmosphere of the great cities, where their presence could only add another explosive element to a situation already difficult to control.

I have already indicated that this policy was, in general, an extraordinary failure. Paris was the great magnet for the laboring poor from all over the kingdom, although some areas were more privileged in this regard than others. Of 421 male beggars sent to Bicêtre in 1750, 35 came from Paris, 58 from the Parisian region (Ile de France, Beauce, and the dioceses of Sens and Auxerre), 38 from Normandy, 39 from the north, and 47 from eastern France

(Champagne, Lorraine, and Alsace). Burgundians numbered 30, and there were 20 Lyonnais. The center furnished 79 recruits, of whom 46 were Auvergnats. On the other hand, only 26 persons came from the west between Blois and the sea, together with 13 from Brittany. The southeast sent 11 representatives. Provence and the southwest were least well represented, there being only 9 from the entire region. There were, in addition, 15 foreigners.[23] To be sure, the figures may be slightly misleading in regard to the patterns of migration of the laboring poor as a whole. First, the sample comes from one year and one establishment only. Second, certain groups of migrants, like the Savoyards, were so well organized that they got into trouble with the police less frequently than others. On the other hand, the statistics do coincide rather well with other samples taken from the police records of Versailles and Saint Denis, to the effect that the Parisian region, Normandy, the north and the east, the areas of easiest access to the capital, accounted for 50 percent of all migrants in the city at a given time. Burgundy and the Massif Central constituted a secondary area of recruitment. This pattern also held true for the street merchants discussed above.[24]

The median age of the beggar in this sample was 51 to 55, which meant that a large proportion were likely to be ill or otherwise not in a position to exercise their trades. Their qualifications read like a list of the occupations of the laboring poor. The largest group consisted of 109 agricultural laborers. Of this number, 56 were unskilled: *manoeuvres* (unskilled workers in general), *journaliers* (agricultural day laborers or any unskilled worker hired at a daily wage), *batteurs en grange* (threshers), *jardiniers* (gardeners). There were 30 vine-growers, 10 *laboureurs*, 3 horse and cattle dealers, 2 millers, and 2 blacksmiths. Sixty-nine persons were unskilled urban workers: *gagne-deniers* (workers at menial jobs), *commissionnaires* (errand boys), and water carriers. Forty-six made or sold clothes; 16 worked in food industries and 27 in construction. There were also lesser quantities of innkeepers, boilermakers, pedlars, schoolmasters, and public letter writers. Lastly, there were 13 domestics, 17 who had no profession, and a single noble. The figures indicate that the unskilled, both in town and country, were somewhat more likely to become beggars than skilled artisans, but the latter, especially when unsupported by capital and a master's title, were often constrained to ask for charity with increasing frequency as they grew older and lost their health.

Samples taken from the archives of the *dépôts de mendicité* tend to confirm initial impressions. The beggars were recruited from the ranks of the unskilled workers and, to a lesser extent, of journeymen artisans. Rarely is a master artisan accused. Some of those picked up were aged and infirm and were, indeed, captured only a short time after leaving the Hôtel-Dieu.[25] Others had been ruined by imprisonment on suspicion of crimes they had not committed. There were also army deserters, thieves, imbeciles, and *filles libertines*. None of these descriptions were incompatible with membership in the laboring poor. As the certificate of good character given to Jacques Verdier, who had been detained at Meaux, by his fellow townsmen of Compans and Briom near Besse in the Auvergne put it:

For several years he has been in the habit of leaving the province during every [off] season and of going into foreign provinces to earn his living there by his labor and industry and to bring some help to Marie Auzany, his wife, and to their six children, of whom the eldest is with him helping to sweep chimneys, and the youngest is still being breastfed. . . . The said Jacques Verdier goes home every spring to plow his small piece of land and to busy himself, as best he can, with the work of the land. We believe him to be an upstanding man [honnête homme], we have never heard nor known him to practice the trade of beggar. . . .[26]

"The trade of beggar . . ." It is a phrase which marginally respects the truth. Verdier would have no doubt maintained that there was a vast difference between beggary as a profession and his practice of asking for an occasional handout. At least that was the common defense of his fellows, as for example François Bernard of Bressac who admitted to having begged off and on over a period of three years but asked nothing better than to return to his hometown, where he might find work as an apprentice waterman. Rare were those who, like Catherine Bouillat, the wife of a navvy of Molonpied (Election of Saint Flour), legitimated their importunings as being part of their chosen profession—in her case, to make pilgrimages on others' behalf.[27]

Of the provincials arrested in Paris, a large number had been in the city only a few months, further proof of their mobility but also of how difficult it was to find work once in the capital. Brought to Paris by the search for employment or in consequence of work they had been doing, like Hervé Peron, *ouvrier en bois flotté* (a worker who accompanied wood floated down to Paris) of the Generality of Rennes, few expressed the desire to settle there permanently. Time and again the notation recurs of a stay of two, four, or eight months, usually in one of the most populous quarters like Saint Jacques de la Boucherie, Saint Jean de Grève, or les Halles, and of a wish to return home.[28] Miserable, ill, sometimes crippled, often illiterate,[29] what choice had they but to throw themselves on the mercy of the arresting officers? Shoeshine boy, street cleaner, shepherd, apprentice artisan, these were men and women who had reached what they took to be the nadir of their fight for survival only to find that there was still another level of misery below. Under the circumstances, one had to learn to live by one's wits, and honesty was hard put to remain whole. A perspicacious observer like Caillard d'Allières, president of the Bureau du District of Mamers (Sarthe), may have been rather too fatalistic in his analysis of the inevitable progression from beggary to crime, but he expressed both his own fears and those of his class when he wrote in March, 1789:

Beggary is the apprenticeship of crime; it begins by creating a love of idleness, which will always and everywhere be the greatest political and moral evil: in this state the beggar, having no principles or at least no habit of honesty, does not resist the temptation to steal very long. Soon, there is no other brake on his ideas of plunder than the fear of punishments due wrongdoers, and as soon as he has acquired enough skill to persuade himself that he will always escape from police investigations, he becomes a thief at the very least on a daily basis and often a professional thief. Among brigands, there are very few who did not become so through this fatal progression, of which begging is the first stop and indigence the first cause.[30]

We may be permited to doubt that idleness is the devil's workshop in so simple a manner as is here stated. But what is important to note is that society, unable to deal with beggars as such, was ever waiting for them to cross the line into criminality. In this expectation, it was rarely disappointed. The occasional beggar of today became the amateur criminal of tomorrow.

⋘ II ⋙

The next day . . . I was present at the execution of a person who was broke on the wheel, as 'tis commonly called; and as several mistaken notions are entertained of this ceremony, the following account may be depended on as accurate. The unhappy criminal was convicted for shooting at a person with an intent to kill him; he wounded him terribly in the face, 'tis true, but the man survived; sentence of death, however, was notwithstanding pronounced against him. . . . The execution was performed in the place de Grève, which is a sort of square, where stands the townhouse or maison de ville. In the middle of this square was erected a scaffold; and at half an hour after four, the prisoner was brought in a cart to the place of execution, attended by the city guards, walking in procession two by two. A priest, or father confessor, accompanied the dying man. On the scaffold was erected a large cross, exactly in the form of that commonly represented for St. Andrew's. The executioner and his assistants then placed the prisoner on it, in such a manner, that his arms and legs were extended exactly agreeable to the form of the cross, and strongly tied down; under each arm, leg, etc. was cut a notch in the wood, as a mark where the executioner might strike, and break the bone with the greater facility. He held in his hand a large iron bar, not unlike one of our laborer's iron crows, and in the first place broke his arms, then in a moment after both his thighs: it was a melancholy, shocking sight, to see him heave his body up and down in his extreme agony, and hideous to behold the terrible distortions of his face: it was a considerable time before he expired, and it would have been longer, had not the executioner given him what they call here the coup de grâce, or finishing stroke, on his stomach, which puts an end to the poor wretch's inexpressible misery: when he was dead, they took him from the cross, and put his dead body on a wheel, fixed to the end of a pole, and there he was exposed for some time; and this part of the ceremony occasions the common expression of a person's being broke upon the wheel, whereas 'tis on a cross, as above described.[31]

The ceremony described by an English traveler in 1738 was a regular feature of Parisian life in the eighteenth century. On occasion the execution was carried out on the spot where the crime had been committed, but the location ordinarily chosen was the place de Grève, on the right bank of the Seine in the center of the city, in the midst of the poorest and most populous quarters. This choice of site was sanctioned by the tradition of centuries, and it also presented a certain administrative convenience. The Conciergerie prison, the death row where condemned men awaited their fate and were subjected to preliminary tortures, lay just across the river on the left bank, and the Hôtel de Ville, to which those who were about to die were brought if they indicated a last-minute desire to betray their accomplices and/or to receive the final ministrations of religion, stood on the place itself. There was thus no need to parade the criminals through the streets and thereby face the difficulties of controlling an unruly crowd.

The tactical reasons for choosing the place de Grève were, however, of secondary importance. The authorities' choice had been made with malice aforethought, so to speak, the better to demonstrate to the "lower orders" on their own home ground that crime did not pay. The theory was that law and order could be preserved by repeated examples of terrible retribution visited upon the guilty. Crime was considered to arise from the vicious nature of the criminal rather than to be socially conditioned. Cause and effect were radically confused and, accordingly, more attention was paid to the control of vice than to the removal of the conditions that bred it. Precisely for this reason all efforts to extirpate crime were doomed to failure. Far from throwing the fear of God into those who witnessed them, public executions only increased their contempt for the law and the society they were meant to defend. The contempt the audience felt and the frustration they experienced in not being able to do anything to stop the law from taking its inexorable course were thoroughly apolitical sentiments. By themselves, they led nowhere. Yet one may wonder if they did not contribute in some way to loosening the ties that bound workingmen to the larger community, thus creating the possibility for them to respond one day to a revolutionary situation not of their own making. The powerful called upon death as their ultimate weapon in the struggle against both individual and social disorders. The laboring poor, fearful and superstitious though they were, would not yield to this kind of blackmail. The paradox of their behavior is that they were consciously afraid of death and of the torments and punishments of purgatory and hell, but at the level of the subconscious its terrors had no hold over them. There is no Catholic equivalent—at least not in this milieu—of a Jonathan Edwards reaching into the innermost recesses of his sinners' hearts to make them writhe with guilt and pain.[32] Is this because the poor Catholic believer had been too often told of his fundamental goodness in the eyes of God and the Church?[33] Or perhaps was death conceived of as just another episode in a life that was a constant struggle for survival? In fact, both the material situation and a particular religious spirit were so intertwined as to make the most common response to the threat of death, whether from disease or the law, a desire to strike out for immediate gratification before it was too late.

Executions did attract large crowds. When the victim was well known, all the windows of buildings facing the place de Grève were rented well in advance, as in the case of Cartouche in November, 1721.[34] But executions became so common that they soon ceased to disturb the rhythm of work and commerce in the surrounding neighborhood. Business went on as usual except, perhaps, for the few minutes men spent casting a curious glance at the condemned. Hanging days were not public holidays, contrary to

English practice. One Englishman was so astonished by what he saw in Paris in 1777 that he wrote:

An execution in France is attended with all imaginable solemnity: no giving the unhappy object of punishment drink—no crying out, *"Die like a cock"*—nor those kind of expressions too commonly used among the vulgar in England—nor any of those comments which we hear after our Tyburn executions of *"He died hard,"* and was *"as bold as brass."*[35]

This behavior may well have been the means by which the laboring poor refused to be made accomplices in the maintenance of an unjust legal system. How, after all, could they feel indignant about theft when they were surrounded on all sides by "the extravagance and dissipation of luxury"?[36] The feeling that "there but for the grace of God go I" created a certain solidarity between the condemned man and the spectators. The crowd would not allow itself to be intimidated. It was not they, but their social betters, the pillars of the community who drew the moral lesson from the proceedings. The workingman did not despise the criminal but tended rather to celebrate his daring in life and his courage in the face of death. The difference in attitude between property holders, fearful of losing what they possessed, and laborers, who had nothing to lose, is a measure of the social conflict latent in Paris at this time.

On occasion, the crowd manifested its discontent more concretely. In 1721, a coachman in the employ of a renter of carriages in the rue des Grands Augustins stole an iron bar worth 30 sous from his employer. He was sentenced to be whipped and branded before the door of the establishment. When his employer's wife cried out that he should be whipped more soundly, the 4,000 assembled spectators went out of control, entered the house, broke the windows, set some carriages ablaze, and dragged them burning around the corner into the rue Saint André des Arts. In the following November, an even more serious outbreak occurred. A domestic was condemned to stand several hours in the pillory for having made some disobliging remarks about his mistress. The 5,000 to 6,000 people present broke the pillory and the windows of the employer's house. Called to the scene, the police opened fire and killed four or five of the participants. In the words of the lawyer Barbier, it was no longer possible to sentence offenders to the pillory for this was the third time in a single year that violence (he called it "sedition") had erupted as a result. Nor did it stop then. In 1726, "le peuple" took similar action against an employer whose servant had been sentenced to hang for having attempted to extort money from him. Barbier thought the measure was harsh but necessary in order to set an example. But those to whom the lesson was given do not seem to have been listening.[37]

The stubborn refusal of laboring men to adopt the values of the establishment was additional proof (to nobles and bourgeois) that there was something inherently wrong with them from the outset. As one reads their commentaries, one can fairly hear the tongue clicking sounds of disapproval. What the commentators did not understand was that crime, or, more often, vicarious participation in crime, was one of the few means available to the poor, short of an unthought-of revolution, for exhibiting their discontents.

This participation took various forms, some of them rather bizarre. We are told that when Antoine François Desrues was broken on the wheel and burned in 1777, "scarcely had the body of this scoundrel been reduced to ashes than a crowd of day laborers combed through them to find bones that they sold to the highest bidder."[38] The bones were believed to have magic power and to enable the possessor to win the lottery. It ought to be added that Desrues, who was executed for the murder of Madame La Motte and her son whom he had previously cheated in a business transaction, was widely believed to be not guilty. Was it his humble origins that gained him popular sympathy? (He was the son of a petty merchant from Chartres.) Or was it merely his constantly reiterated professions of innocence? In any case, the Lieutenant-general of Police Lenoir found it necessary to commission pamphleteers to write the official version of the case. Not only was it desirable to establish proofs of the act of murder against Desrues but also to demonstrate, in line with the official ideology, that he was a monster, evil from birth.[39]

Macabre incidents like this one were, however, uncommon. Ordinarily the great deeds of evildoers were celebrated in words only. Let us take the example of Louis Dominique Cartouche, who more than any other criminal captured the imagination of his contemporaries. Portraits of and poems about him were sold everywhere. A play purporting to chronicle his career was presented at the Comédie Française while he lay in prison awaiting execution (he is rumored to have tempted the fates by going to a performance during his short-lived escape from jail). The story of his life published in the Bibliothèque Bleue and other mass-consumption media went through innumerable editions until well into the nineteenth century. It was even translated into English by Defoe, and a Russian version also exists.[40]

The facts of Cartouche's story are easily established.[41] He was the son of a modest *tonnelier* (cooper) who spent his boyhood on the streets of Paris playing in the neighborhood of the Foire Saint Laurent. One day during his early adolescence, he stayed out too late and, fearing to go home, he took up with a band of Gypsies. After five years spent in their company, he did return home and went to work as an apprentice cooper. His life of crime was begun by stealing to provide for an exigent girlfriend. His father wanted to punish him by having him locked up in the prison of Saint Lazare, a place for prodigal sons likely to bring disrepute upon their families. But the younger Cartouche would have none of it. He made his escape and then worked for a time as a thief taker and army recruiter (a polite way of saying, a member of a press gang), and then served in the army himself. Returning to Paris, he organized his celebrated gang, over 200 in number, and went on to terrorize the city for the better part of four years, 1717–1721. His men were recruited from all strata of Parisian society, even among the "young men of family [both noble and bourgeois] taken in the seminary of Saint Lazare, where they were doing penance."[42] For the most part, they were members of the laboring poor down on their luck. They had contacts among domestics and the women known as *recommanderesses* who found employment for them in the homes of the rich, the gang's favorite target. Other ties bound Cartouche and his men to inn and tavernkeepers (whose establishments served as places of refuge), to gunsmiths, and to jewelers and goldsmiths who acted as fences for stolen goods. The *gardes françaises*, whose reputation for brutality and corruption was well earned, helped them to commit robberies on the king's highways.

Cartouche was distinguished from the ordinary criminal not only by the quantity but also by the quality of his work. His specialty was looting the houses of the rich,[43] although his gang did not disdain to do a little pickpocketing on the side. He frowned upon the unnecessary use of violence, and he enforced a strict code of honor among his subordinates. If not precisely a reincarnation of Robin Hood, Cartouche was nonetheless a man of the people, essentially benevolent and nonviolent. If he did not make massive contributions to the poor, he never, so the story goes, refused a man in need. He was gallant to the ladies and audacious in his numerous close calls and escapes from the long arm of the law. He was loyal to his peers and contemptuous of his social betters. Brave and unyielding under the worst torture, he finally denounced his accomplices at the very last moment and then only because they had failed to rescue him in accordance with promises earlier made.

In sum, Cartouche has a far from unattractive character. The

men, women, and children who thrilled to his exploits did not necessarily approve of them any more than modern audiences who
applaud Dillinger, Pretty Boy Floyd, or those currently fashionable heroes, Bonnie and Clyde, would like to have them as next-
door neighbors. It is sufficient that the criminals be seen as rebels
against the established (by definition, rotten) order of things for
crowds to identify with them. Even the moral conclusions of the
cheap pamphlets intended for the consumption of the poor but
not always in agreement with their own point of view reflected
this spirit. On the one hand, Cartouche was blamed for wishing
to abandon his station in life: "He had always had the ridiculous
ambition to distinguish himself from his peers by wearing better
clothes and by taking on certain foppish airs. That had been the
cause of his first thefts, and it also contributed to his relapse into
the abyss, from which he had so happily freed himself." He first
went astray because his father had sent him to a Jesuit school where
all the other students were, at the very least, sons of the *bourgeois
de Paris*. He had taken to crime in order to keep up with them in
dress and other items of expenditure. Young men, beware the en-
ticements of wealth, the story seems to say, and so the cause of
classic morality is served. On the other hand, these same writers,
as though knowing their audiences, are led to cast Cartouche in
the heroic mold: "[he] had in him qualities which could have made
an admirable man of him. Much wit, vivacity, and memory. A
great presence of mind, judgment, and intrepidity. But false ideas
of wealth and, by an easy extension, of the great of this world,
destroyed him.[44] Or, once again and still more complimentary, the
poem of Nicolas Ragot de Grandval described this master thief as:

> Vaillant dans les combats, sçavant dans les retraites,
> Ferme dans le malheur, sobre dans les Guinguettes,
> Fidèle à ses pareils, tranquile, modéré,
> Et des traîtres sur-tout ennemi déclaré. . . .
>
> Tout le monde admiroit sa physionomie;
> Sa douceur, son parler, son air, son doux maintien,
> Bref, chacun le prenoit pour un homme de bien.*[45]

---

* Valiant in fighting, skillful in retreats,
  Firm in misfortune, sober in the taverns,
  Loyal to his peers, calm, moderate,
  And above all the declared enemy of traitors. . . .

  Everyone admired his appearance;
  His gentleness, his way of speaking, his air, his quiet bearing,
  In short, everyone took him for a man of honor.

At once "homme de bien" and criminal challenging the injustices of wealth and, by an easy extension, of the great of this world, here was a man to celebrate. But he was not alone. The only criminals condemned out of hand by the Parisian people in the eighteenth century were the blasphemers of holy persons or things, like Damiens, executed for his attempted assassination of Louis XV in 1757, or the Chevalier de la Barre, executed for breaking a statue of the Virgin in 1766. The king was the father of his people and therefore untouchable. And the laboring poor, among whom Catholic belief was very strong, were much attached to the cult of the Virgin. Even here it was the overt act, and it alone, that merited punishment in the eyes of the masses. In September, 1758, one Mauriceau de la Motte, a *huissier des requêtes de l'hôtel*, was sentenced to death for having made a seditious speech against the king. (The *huissier* was a minor judicial officer, equivalent to the court officer today who carries out sentences handed down by judges. His duty, for instance, was to seize persons to be taken into custody or to carry out confiscation of property.) In fact, all he had done was to question the conduct of Damiens' trial. A large crowd attended his execution, but the sentiment they expressed was generally in his favor. As Barbier reported: "Some said that people aren't put to death for words or simple writings; others hoped that he would have his reprieve; but one wanted to make an example of a bourgeois of Paris, a man occupying an office, in order to suppress the license of a number of fanatics who speak too boldly of the government. . . ."[46] The impersonal *one* was ruling-class justice. Once again, the laboring poor showed that they did not share its standards.

III

Of 108 death sentences issued by the Parlement of Paris between January 1, 1775 and December 31, 1776, 69 were sanctions against thefts of one sort or another. Only 37 premeditated murders were so punished together with one rape and one case of sodomy.[47] If capital punishment, however horrible, did not succeed in controlling criminal activity, it was not the only weapon in the arsenal of repression commanded by Parisian judges on the eve of the Revolution. For lesser crimes, such as stealing a handkerchief or a loaf of bread, a man might be sentenced to imprisonment for a number of years[48] or, more likely, be sent to suffer the miseries of the galleys on the Mediterranean. Some men, like Louis Fremont, "thief, pimp, sodomist," who would ordinarily have been imprisoned at Bicêtre, were exiled "a la suite d'un régiment."[49] In all cases, the punishment was accompanied by the branding of the offender with a V (*voleur*, thief) or GAL (*galérien*, galley slave) and banishment from Paris for a period of years after the expiration of the sentence.[50] Heavy sentences upon petty offenders were made even worse by the abuses built into the judicial system. An accused person might be detained for months without trial. He was most often not represented by counsel, and there was no right to trial by jury. The appeals machinery was so cumbersome as to be, for all intents and purposes, unavailable to the great majority. On the other hand, the government prosecutor might appeal to a higher court to increase the sentence originally decreed by the trial judge (*appel à minima*). Also, imprisonment by direct order of the king without benefit of judicial process was common, especially in the case of habitual criminals. The lack of procedural and substantive safeguards was only to be expected in a society concerned not with rehabilitation but with retribution, not with justice, but with securing convictions. Where there was no promise of equal protection by the law, there could be only pity for the poor "criminals" who might fall victim to an excess of judicial zeal. One particularly horrible but by no means unusual instance suffices to make the point: on July 6, 1750, a journeyman joiner and a pork butcher, aged 18 and 25 respectively, were burned at the stake, having been caught *in flagrante delicto* in sodomy (i.e., homosexual activity). An example was made of them, for the crime, it was said, was becoming all too widespread. As Barbier noted, the fact that they were both workingmen did not do them any good: "And as these two workers had no relations with men of distinction . . . this example was made without any regard for the consequences."[51] In civil cases, too, the poor were the victims of their social situation and, more specifically, of their inability to bear the costs of trial. They could therefore be attacked with impunity by the "powerful man . . . bold enough to oppress [them] every time it was in his interest to do so."[52]

◆§ IV §◆

The criminality of old-regime Paris had many faces. Men and women, old and young, soldiers, domestic workers, apprentices and journeymen of the guilds, street merchants, unskilled laborers, persons domiciled in the city for a long while, or floaters who were only passing through, all engaged in occasional criminal activity.[53] They were the amateurs of the Parisian underworld. Professional criminals, those who depended on crime for their habitual livelihood, were another group altogether, however difficult it may be in practice to draw the fine line that separates one from the other. The laboring classes and the dangerous classes lived in constant communion with one another, and the passage of individuals between them was doubtless a gradual process more than the result of a conscious decision to lead a life of crime.

"Beggary seems to be the point of transition between the laboring classes and the criminal classes," wrote Lenoir.[54] One can easily imagine how one activity might be a prelude to the other. In principle, the administration made some attempt to distinguish between beggars who would not work out of perversity, and those who could not work for lack of a job or because of age or infirmity. The latter were cared for while the former were punished. In reality, however, these distinctions were not always maintained, and beggars were treated increasingly like criminals, especially if they were caught asking for charity more than once. A first offense was normally dealt with by assigning the beggar to the workhouse or merely sending him back to his place of origin if he could demonstrate that there was someone back home willing to vouch for his future good conduct. Poverty was so widespread and beggars so omnipresent that the administration found itself incapable of doing much more than sweeping the problem under the rug.

For the laboring poor beggary may have been a shame, but it was certainly no crime. What evil was there, after all, in asking a fellow Christian for charity, even if the clergy, in this regard no more than agents of the state, refused to bless the action? It may be that beggary led to a life of crime because the honest beggar was seduced in the course of his wanderings by his dishonest fellows, the professionals of the trade. But the moral judgments of bad nineteenth-century novels ought not to color our historical appreciation. A more satisfactory explanation of the connection between beggary and crime is that government repression of mendicity had the opposite of its desired effect by leading men to steal what they could no longer obtain by persuasion. A few contemporaries like Hardy sensed as much when he attributed the wave of robberies of the summer of 1777 in the Parisian region to the expulsion of beggars from the city by the ordinance of July 27. Some people were opposed to its execution, he wrote, because it might lead only "to peopling the forests and the highways with brigands."[55] And time and again one comes across records of beggars

engaging in the pettier sorts of crime. The stories are often melo-
dramatic in the extreme, for example, the case of a woman arrested
in December, 1767 for stealing a loaf of bread. Under questioning,
she declared that she had a husband and four children living "in
the direst poverty." A police officer escorted her home, only to
find that her husband, upon hearing of his wife's arrest, had hanged
himself in the presence of the children. The widow had better luck
than Jean Valjean, for she was immediately released, and the police
officer himself paid for the bread she had stolen.[56]

Parisians were arrested for drunk and disorderly conduct, for
libertinage, for defrauding the Farmers General at the customs
barriers, and for running out on unpaid bills.[57] Murder and arson
were far from unknown, and a treatise might be written on the
varieties of prostitution alone. Still, thefts so far dominated the
criminal scene as to make up nine-tenths of all the crimes committed. The citation of statistics to back up this impression would
be fastidious in the extreme, nor would it be certain that by using
them we would come any closer to the reality at hand. The dark
figure so well known to criminologists, that percentage of crime
that goes forever undetected by the police and which, under
eighteenth-century conditions, may have been greater than known
breaches of the law, ought to be sufficient to warn us against undue
reliance on numbers, however attractive and scientific they may
appear.[58] My statement about theft remains an assertion based on
long examination of the archives, notably the collections of the
Prefecture of Police and of the commissaires of the Châtelet in the
Archives Nationales, not proven and not, in any absolute sense,
subject to proof.[59]

The picture of Parisian crime that emerges is that of a pre-
Industrial Revolution urban center in which crimes against property far outweigh crimes against persons and where personal violence
is a means to an end but not an end in itself. I have not studied
the seventeenth-century records and so can say nothing about
changes in the nature of Parisian crime in the course of the century
before the Revolution. But the role of theft is clear, and on this
point I am in agreement with the work of Gégot and Boutelet on
the tribunals of Falaise and Pont-de-l'Arche, when they speak of
the increase in stealing in the eighteenth century. Chaunu adds that
"the criminality of the thieves of the eighteenth century is a criminality of vagabonds. It corresponds, in liaison with the demographic upsurge, to the rise of a mass of seasonal migrants, of day
laborers without ties and without land, the privileged milieu of
'passive professional criminals who refuse to work.' "[60] In Paris,

too, much of the theft was carried on by migrants and/or vagabonds—the two are not the same—and one precise distinction that
can be drawn between them is whether or not they have any
attachment to a home base. Gégot's remarks are less likely to apply
to Paris when he insists on the professional nature of his thieves,
organized into gangs and living on the margin of society. Such
groups did exist in Paris, but they were only a small part of the
whole. The difference between Gégot's observations and my own
may very well be due to the fact that he has studied a rural population and I, an urban one. Gangs may have had a greater raison
d'être (the need for protection) in open country and greater
stability (relative freedom from police surveillance) in the country
than in the city.

The motif, then, is clear: an extraordinarily high incidence of
theft carried out by amateurs, like the 35 judged by the Parlement
in February, 1732 and found to be mainly *gens de métier* and
domestics, which, as Barbier said, "was of great consequence."[61]
Not all the thefts for which laboring men were arrested can be
viewed as true offenses. One example that comes to mind is the
case of three young soldiers banished from Paris for three years
because they were found in possession of grapes "stolen from the
vineyards of Belleville for which they could not properly account."
But the lowest common denominator of amateur crime was that
the perpetrators stole out of need and whatever lay close at hand.
To take money from a church poor box or bread from a baker
was the most common method of appeasing one's hunger, but this
could not always be managed.[62] Sometimes it was necessary to con-
vert stolen goods into cash before going to the baker's shop, and
for this any kind of property would do—handkerchiefs, watches,
blankets, a sheet from the Hôtel-Dieu, lead from rooftops, coal
from a dockside, wood from a building site. One gravedigger was
arrested for selling a cadaver for dissection, and one of his col-
leagues employed in the parish cemetery of Saint Sulpice was sentenced to the galleys for stealing a shroud.[63] Gardeners stole
vegetables from suburban farms to sell at les Halles, and workers,
especially domestics who had the greatest opportunities to do so,
frequently stole the personal effects of their employers. Domestics
accused of crime, together with journeymen locksmiths found in
possession of skeleton keys, were the most despised and most severely dealt with by the law, presumably because it was difficult
to control their movements and because they constituted a direct
threat to the security of home and person.

Like the beggars held in the *dépôts de mendicité* of the Generality of Paris, accused malefactors came from all parts of France and even from foreign countries.[64] Especially numerous were natives of Normandy, the north, and the east. Paris was a center of emigration as well as of immigration,[65] and even many natives of the city and its region spent a good part of their time traveling through the provinces in search of work. It was very common for a man or woman to spend part of the year in Paris, part in home village, and another part following the harvest or other agricultural labor wherever it might lead. This was admittedly the case of Louis Prévost, an ironmonger who spent only his winters in the capital, and of Michel Albert, a native of Naples who wandered about as a "kind of pilgrim selling kinds of relics . . . begging in the evenings[,] lodging at two sous the night [and] suspect." Even a long and uninterrupted stay in Paris did not guarantee a permanent settlement. Claude Breton, a worker in the silk stocking manufacture, did nothing unusual when he left Paris after a sojourn of 34 months to spend a year in his native Nîmes.[66]

Although the typical criminal found in the police records is a man between the ages of 18 and 40, neither age nor sex was an obstacle to carrying out an occasional crime. There are numerous examples of young boys imprisoned for petty theft in one or another of the hospitals of Paris. In 1749, Nicolas Dejouatte, aged 10½, was given three years for having stolen 24 livres from a piggy bank belonging to someone else. Five years later, Charles Lebret, a 12-year-old apprentice blacksmith, suffered the same fate for pinching a few shirts. Both were soundly whipped in the bargain.

Women are also to be found in the ranks of accused thieves. Whether acting independently or as aides to their husbands and lovers, their reasons for stealing were the same as those of their male coworkers. They wanted to survive. As Angélique Jubin, a 69-year-old nurse and widow of a stocking weaver, said, she stole a hamhock "on account of need" and a bread "because it had been two days since she had eaten."[67]

≈§ V §≈

Although there is no evidence that the rate of crime, either amateur or professional, increased notably as the century progressed, fear of criminal attack became an increasingly dominant motif in the minds of the Parisian bourgeois. They constantly alluded in their diaries and letters to bands of thieves lurking in the environs, and they attacked the officers of justice for being too indulgent in dealing with those they had arrested.[68] Hardy seems almost to have been paranoid in his constant denunciations of dangerous "libertines." Rumors were always reaching him of a newly discovered den of thieves, and this allowed him to exercise his *frondeur* spirit against the administration.[69]

If the fears appear somewhat exaggerated in retrospect, they did nonetheless have a basis in fact. Gangs of professional criminals did exist, like the one led by Raffiat in the 1740s. He was himself a *crieur de listes de loterie* and recruited his personnel from among the journeymen craftsmen of the capital. The gang was called *assommeurs*, from their habit of knocking their victims on the head with clubs.[70] The existence of such gangs was a matter of common knowledge, and there were periodic outbursts of public indignation whenever they became particularly active or annoying. In 1752, Barbier reported that "one no longer dared go out in the evening" for fear of being knocked down. In 1778, one risked being attacked and robbed "by a group of libertines and bandits called *épateurs*, no doubt because they lay people flat with blows either to the back or the stomach, or by clubbing them on the head."[71] And in 1784, Poulaillier appeared on the scene, the last professional Parisian criminal to capture the public imagination before the Revolution. Like Cartouche, he was generally supposed to have been born in the faubourg Saint Antoine or Charenton, the son of a humble artisan. He was dynamic, daring and attractive as he stood at the head of his troops headquartered in the Bois de Vincennes. In the words of the somewhat scandalized but still impressed Hardy:

Each day some new story was told of this ingenious brigand who . . . took a malicious pleasure in introducing himself each time he left a place. He had a reputation for humanity. Which is why he not only did not permit any kind of killing, but also was very open-handed, zealously helping the indigent. It was claimed that once in a tavern he had paid the chit for a brigade of the *maréchaussée* [mounted constabulary] that had drunk there with him, not failing to identify himself, as was his custom, when making off.[72]

The only characteristic these gangs necessarily had in common was their professionalism. A man or a woman becomes a professional criminal at the point when he or she gives up the usual, socially approved means of making a living to become parasitic upon society. This is not easily measured by the number of times he has been arrested nor even by his skill in carrying out a job—

characteristics which, to complicate matters still further, may be inversely proportional to one another. If professionalism is equated with skill, it follows that the professional crook stands more of a chance of avoiding the attention of the police than the poor wretch who turns to crime on two or three occasions only to be caught each time. To make of the latter a hardened criminal on the basis of a long series of arrests would be a gross error.

It is commitment to a life of crime rather than success in any particular undertakings that defines the professional thief, arsonist, or murderer. Furthermore, the professional did not generally limit himself to only one kind of activity, and he did not work alone. He may have been a member of a large group or worked with one or two associates only. Cooperation of this kind was made necessary by the need for labor in carrying out plans and in disposing of stolen goods. The records are full of cases of men sentenced for having stood watch while a crime was being committed or for acting as fences. Sometimes the professional's business partners were also his relatives. There are examples of entire families—father, mother, and children—laboring together in the good cause. In 1747, Edme Godier, Anne Rabbe, his wife, and Jean, their son, were arrested near Ecouen because they appeared suspect. In their baggage was found a big skein of thread weighing three or four pounds and five tin spoons of different sorts, the whole no doubt stolen. The police report continued: "The woman admitted that the said Godier had been in prison in Meaux several times. And the child [stated] that his father had met some people near the Forest of Senlis who, he explained to the mother, were wool-combers turned thieves. He himself [the child] had in his pocket an instrument for stealing chickens which he called a *baganche*, and with which he admitted having stolen some several times." The father and mother were sentenced to three years' banishment from the Parisian region, and the boy was sent to Bicêtre "for correction."[73] In all particulars, this family was typical of one sort of professional criminal. They were floaters, long since detached from their provincial roots (in this case, Burgundy). They came and went from Paris, begging and stealing for a living, each member of the family contributing to the common fund. There are instances of criminal dynasties that extended over several generations. All were not necessarily as mobile as the Godiers, although theirs was the common pattern. There were those who remained sedentary, working only in Paris and even remaining in a single quarter, like the environs of the Pont Neuf, a notorious center of mischief. Family gangs seem also to have been rather stable arrangements, albeit men and women lived together without benefit of clergy.[74]

We have already noted the importance of the role played by women among amateur criminals. They were equally well represented in the professional milieu as, among other functions, simple thieves or false beggars—the case comes to mind of Marie Mercier from Lorraine, fined in 1779 for soliciting charity by claiming to be pregnant by a priest, no less.[75] But the crime *par excellence* of women in eighteenth-century Paris was prostitution. "Voleuse et concubine" was the usual notation set against a woman's name in the police records, and for good reason. In 1762, a police informer put the number of prostitutes at 25,000, and Restif de la Bretonne's estimate of 20,000 is of the same order of magnitude.[76] Many, it would appear, engaged in the trade only because they were "more starving than libertine" and were seeking to supplement their inadequate wages.[77] The fact that only clandestine prostitution was punished while the organized variety was allowed to go on undisturbed made it possible for women to be sold into it by their relatives, but we have no way of knowing how frequently this may have happened. Our only indication is a comment by Berenger in 1790 to the effect that the massive poverty of recent date "has prodigiously increased this revolting crime."[78]

Numerous categories of prostitutes existed (a contemporary listed 12). Their degree of professionalism, in our sense of the professional criminal, was determined not only by the frequency of their activity but by their ability to make a living from other sources. There was all the difference in the world between a woman kept as the mistress of a single noble or bourgeois and the "filles de moyenne vertu, qui ne se prostituent que par interim, dans des mortes saisons pour leurs metiers, et dans la vue de subvenir à des besoins pressants," as there was, in terms of wealth and status, between the former and the *boucaneuses, raccrocheuses* and *barboteuses* of the whorehouses and alleyways.[79] The last named were those who had fallen to the lowest depths—miserably poor, ill-fed, ill-lodged and abandoned by the keepers of houses of prostitution and exploited by small-time pimps, they were the least likely to be reintegrated into the society of the laboring poor and the most likely to turn to other sorts of antisocial works. All the evidence suggests that the milieu in which they worked and the relationships to which it gave rise had more resemblance to the degradation of a Hogarthian universe than to the modern myth of the whore with the heart of gold.

When both mother and father were thus engaged in getting

their daily bread, it was normal that some children should be born to criminal ways. The police and public opinion took youthful crime to be a sure sign of an evil nature, but in reality, it was the result of adult pressure on children to make themselves useful in the family business. Like Jean Godier, of whom I have written above, or Louis Lantier in league with Jean Baptiste Marcé and Martial Desbois "aged 11 or 12," whose specialty was to slip into the crowds that gathered around the Pont Neuf and slip out again with a pile of handkerchiefs, boys and girls were seasoned thieves by the time they reached puberty.

The existence of *classes dangereuses*, of what is today called the *milieu*, was a constant scandal to eighteenth-century administrators. A careful record was kept of relationships among criminals, and no entry in the registers was complete without a reminder of the origin of the accused, usually intended as a casual statement. When a young priest with the predestined name of Pierre *Chrisologue Toussaint* Delplane was arrested for theft in 1747, it was noted that, despite outward appearances of education and good breeding, he was the son of a beggar and a washerwoman. Similarly, any breach of the accepted moral code by the accused was used as evidence against him. In 1748, Michel Ourdet and Claudine Chenu, suspected of theft and the receipt of stolen goods, were put down as living together "as if they were married, although they were not." The fact that a woman named La Forget, called *Quarante Coups*, was "the mistress of Marlet and of the majority of the thieves of Paris" was far from immaterial to the law officers, although she was imprisoned for other reasons altogether. One may imagine the indignation provoked by Jean Baptiste DuVarry when it was discovered that "he lived with his 40-year-old mother, and although he was 22 he slept with her because they had only one bed. . . ."

Professional criminals formed a special subculture within Parisian society. They even had a language of their own, called *argot*. The word has by now lost much of its meaning and may be translated as slang, of which there are many varieties in all languages. But from the sixteenth to the eighteenth centuries, it was used to refer specifically to the *language des gueux*, criminal parlance as distinct from popular speech. In many gangs, one member was given the responsibility of teaching *argot* to new recruits and children, along with other tricks of the trade, so that they would be able to communicate with their fellows without being detected and know what to say to the police when arrested.[80] To be sure, many expressions passed from *argot* into popular speech, if only because criminals were in the main recruited from the *menu peuple* and remained in constant contact with them.[81]

For the rest, it may be said that contemporaries placed too much emphasis on the supposedly radical denial of commonly accepted standards by professional criminals. A couple lived together without being married, and a mother and son shared a single bed, but this is not to say that any of them had the intention of violating the susceptibilities of their "betters." Married or no, couples were remarkably stable, and there is nothing more than an assumption to show that the poverty that made mother and son share a single bed also caused the taboo of incest to be broken. The relationship of the criminal subculture to the dominant culture was basically a mimetic one, with only a few adjustments made either from necessity or convenience. If criminals refused to act in accordance with the legal norms of behavior of a society that they might legitimately feel had rejected them, they nonetheless shared many of the moral and ethical values of their law-abiding fellow subjects. Criminologists and literary men have been impressed by this phenomenon in a variety of settings. "When a felon's not employed in his employment or maturing his felonious little plan . . . ," he is good, honest, loyal, brave and the rest of the adjectives of the boy-scout oath, to paraphrase W. S. Gilbert. And we have all heard humorous references to the Mafioso who thinks nothing of committing murder but would consider himself criminally negligent if he failed to open a door for a lady. There is more than humor here, for what the evidence points to is the fundamental attachment of the professional criminal to the society upon which he is parasitic. He does not want to kill the goose that lays the golden eggs. More important still, he in fact approves of the way in which society is run. Far from being a radical critic of social arrangements, the professional criminal seeks to reproduce them in his own milieu. The principle of hierarchy and obedience is observed absolutely in the underworld, and its chiefs imitate in dress and bearing men of similar rank in the larger society.[82]

The real threat to the establishment, insofar as it came from criminals at all, was presented by the amateurs, by people who only occasionally and incidentally fell afoul of the law. To them crime was always a way of satisfying an immediate need when all other means had been exhausted, rather than the sole source of revenue or a way to get rich quickly. Their criminality was caused by the poverty and rootlessness[83] endemic to urban centers in the old regime and may even be seen, in part, as a protest against that poverty. It was apolitical, but it may have been a stage through which the laboring poor had to pass on the way to political consciousness. When they attained it, they put away the childish and ultimately futile thing that is individual petty crime.

It was a simple matter for counter-revolutionaries to point to the criminals in the ranks of the Parisian revolutionary crowds. Their rhetoric was not so much wrong as it was out of date. There were criminals present beyond any doubt, the professionals among them being attracted to violent action and the hope of loot. But the purpose of the crowd and of the majority of its constituent elements had become political, an entirely new state of affairs.

[7]

IN THE GUISE OF CONCLUSION: POLITICAL ACTION IN A CULTURE OF POVERTY

✌ I ☙

The laboring poor were essentially prepolitical. They never organized themselves to take power or change society at its roots. Indeed, they were absolutely incapable of doing so. Like the social bandits studied by Eric Hobsbawm, their aim, when they acted in an upsurge of fury and around a specific issue, was "fair dealing in a society of oppression," rather than the creation of a new and egalitarian social order.[1] But they could create a good deal of trouble in the short term, and the government was attentive to the rumors and rumblings to be heard among them. The police even went so far as to hire men to spread joy and good cheer in the popular districts on important occasions.[2]

Fair dealing in the old regime meant the protection of the people against death and destruction by their father, the king. The attachment of the Parisian *menu peuple* to the person of the monarch was proverbial. He could do no evil. The fault for everything that went wrong, even the high price of bread, might be attributed to the machinations of the ministers, but never to the sovereign himself, for, as two German travelers noted in 1789, "the people, especially since the assassination of Henry IV, have come to think of the king as so holy, venerable and sacrosanct, that to revile him is to blaspheme God. . . ."[3] The king was the people's talisman as well as their protector, a fact which goes a long way towards explaining why they so desired the presence of the royal family in Paris at the beginning of the Revolution and why they felt so betrayed by their flight to Varennes in 1791. On earlier occasions, a bit of good news from Versailles, like the birth of the dauphin in 1781, had been capable of turning the people's attention away from the resentment they felt at the dismissal of Necker and the increase in taxes, so much so that Hardy was moved to write that Louis XVI was surely the happiest of kings for he was the one "who could count most on the love, respect, and inviolable loyalty of his subjects."[4] It would take all of his considerable ineptitude to destroy this stock of confidence.

Allegiance to the king was never, even in the best of times, exclusive. The laboring poor were loyal also to the Parlement of Paris and generally took its side in its disputes with the government, at least on occasions when it seemed to be defending the rights of the nation against the usurpations of the royal ministers. If the action of the Parlement in protesting the reduction of the rate of interest on state obligations (April, 1720) or the collection of the *centième denier* on judicial offices (1748–1749) failed to capture the popular imagination, it was because these issues were totally foreign to the preoccupations of the laboring poor. In any case, they constitute the sole exceptions to the rule in the eighteenth century.[5]

The Parisian laborers were particularly sensitive to two questions on which the magistrates periodically took positions. The first had to do with the suppression of Jansenism, the second with the regulation of the grain trade.

A great wave of popular Jansenism swept through Paris in the late 1720s and early 1730s.[6] This was the epoch of Diacre Pâris and the convulsionaries. It was also the time when the government was doing its best to enforce religious uniformity by demanding the acceptance of the Papal Bull Unigenitus. Parliamentary remonstrances in 1730 and 1731 were to no avail. From September to November, 1732, the Parlement was exiled briefly until a compromise with the monarchy could be reached. After 20 years of relative calm, the controversy broke out once again in 1751. When a priest refused the sacraments to a dying man accused of professing Jansenist doctrines, the Parlement ordered his arrest and kept him in prison for a short time. But the magistrates were not yet willing to fight to a conclusion. The next year, more refusals of extreme unction brought the matter to a head. The Parlement fined priests guilty of such conduct and then forbade the clergy to refuse the sacraments because the person concerned had not proven his acceptance of ecclesiastical discipline. A flurry of conflicting orders now came from the King's Council and the Parlement, which ended only when the latter was exiled in April, 1753. The exile lasted until September, 1754. For three more years the struggle went on between the magistrates, on the one hand, and the Archbishop of Paris, Christophe de Beaumont, and the government, on the other. With the help of the feeling of unity and loyalty to which Damiens' attempt on the king's life gave rise, a compromise was achieved, whereby the disciplinary measures taken against members of Parlement were revoked, and the declaration of submission to Unigenitus—as a law but not as an article of faith—was registered. Hereafter, Jansenism ceased to have any major political significance, although discrimination against Jansenists could still provoke unfavorable crowd response.[7] In those years, it is clear that hatred of an untaxed clergy and the suspicion that high bread prices were the result of speculation in the grain supply played at least as conspicuous a role in determining the hold of Parlement over the people as religious principles or the love of freedom.[8] In addition, the exile of Parlement meant the absence from Paris of a great many people who normally gave employment or custom to the laboring poor. Domestics were let go and hotels remained empty. All in all, the government's order caused considerable economic harm to persons least able to afford it.[9]

The freedom of the grain trade inaugurated in 1763 was opposed by the Parlement, which was careful to appear to champion the people's interest. It was only in December, 1768 and January, 1769, in the wake of a considerable rise in the price of bread, that the magistrates petitioned the king to restrict the grain trade once again. They went so far as to issue an order implicitly abrogating freedom in this domain, but the monarchy would not let them have their way. The following March, the Parlement revised its position to ask only that the export of grain be prohibited and some protection be afforded against monopoly but that free circulation within the realm be allowed to continue. How the *menu peuple* reacted to this spirit of compromise we do not know, but if there was any feeling of resentment toward the judges, it soon vanished in the face of a more serious challenge.

The destruction of the Parlements by Maupeou in 1771 was

greeted by Parisians with marked hostility, not least of all because
the Abbé Terray, the chief promoter of an unfettered grain trade,
was intimately associated with the policy. Maupeou himself could
hardly ride about in public without being insulted. In 1772, Hardy
reported public indignation at the hanging of two burglars, a not
uncommon occurrence. But this time, the sentence had been
stiffened on appeal to the new Parlement, and people said it was
too harsh "especially on the part of judges like the *inamovibles*
(i.e., those having life tenure), who could be neither too much on
their guard nor too distrustful of their knowledge."[10] Executions,
however unpleasant, could be accepted but only when the order
came from properly constituted authority, not from usurpers.

The laboring poor were so apt to express their joy at the return
of Parlement from exile that special measures to keep order usually
had to be taken. In 1754, it was decided not to recall the Parlement
before August 15 because of the procession of the Feast of the
Assumption. If the Parlement had been in attendance, too many
of the *menu peuple* would have come along, and it was to be feared
that they might do "something indecent" to the Archbishop. When
the presiding magistrate of the Court returned on the night of
August 27, there were "demonstrations of joy with bonfires,
illuminations and fireworks until four or five in the morning."[11]
At the end of August, 1774, patrols had to be sent into the courtyard of the Palace of Justice to put an end to gatherings of a
"quantity of workers of all trades" who were exploding fireworks
and saying nasty things about the magistrates who had served
Maupeou. Forced from the courtyard, the demonstrators continued
their activity in adjacent streets until the early hours of the morning. A brigade of the guard reported that the crowd was made up
of "laborers, Savoyards, and other vagabonds, and shop boys,"
which just about accounts for all the constituent elements of the
laboring poor, a larger and more significant group than the *clercs
de procureur* (law clerks) and other *gens de palais* (subordinate
personnel of the law courts and clerical workers) to whom responsibility for this sort of rejoicing is usually attributed. They
were in attendance, but they were not alone. The situation wors-
ened, so that on September 1, Hardy thought it imperative that
means be found to calm the furious crowd. He wrote:

The so-called magistrates who since the exile of their protector
[Maupeou] have been able to administer justice only in the midst of
a great number of soldiers dared, it was said, to go to the Palace [of
Justice] only in colored dress [in contrast to the ordinary black robes,
by which they might be identified] and entered by back doors. Those

whose clothing testified that they might belong to the new magistrature were insulted in the streets.[12]

In November, the same crowds welcomed the return of the old Parlement with great joy.[13]

There can be no easy explanation of the loyalty of the laboring poor to the Parlement. It was not simply the coincidence that they found themselves on the same side of questions of religion and bread, although that certainly helped. The poor tended to appropriate any current religious idea, Jansenism no less than simple superstition, and to adjust it to their own needs. We have seen that they wished to determine their own modes of belief and did not like others to tamper with them. The magistrates, on the other hand, fought the crown on this issue less out of Catholic conscience than to determine who should rule. For the poor, the regulation of the grain trade and of market prices was a matter of life and death. For the Parlement, it was once again a matter of exercising power and of establishing a clientele.[14] A rise in grain prices would presumably have been to the benefit of the land-owning magistrates, but they were willing to sacrifice immediate pecuniary gain in the interests of power and because they believed in the obligations that power carried with it. Moreover, they were, and took care to appear, the only visible friends of the poor. They had no administrative responsibilities, so they could not really be blamed for the inadequacies of the government machinery. On the contrary, they were able to denounce every failure in the fine rhetoric of the rights of the Nation and the role of the *corps intermédiaires*. In an era when the *menu peuple* had not yet learned to look for leaders in their own ranks, he who appeared most willing to defend them from the abuses of power would gain their support. If the abusers were seen, with some truth, as men of low status (police, administrators) in comparison to the "natural superiors" of the robe nobility, the alliance became that much easier to achieve.[15] The alliance would last as long as the poor, who had no political role to play in the system, remained unconscious of their right to step outside it and of the threat they would constitute if they did so. The belief that government policy is "like the course of the sun, physically determined by an unvarying nature"[16] was basic to the acceptance by the laboring poor of their need for protection and, hence, the impossibility of independent action. It was left to the reform movement of 1787–1788 to begin to give these assumptions the lie.

In the early days of prerevolutionary agitation, there was little reason to believe that popular action would go beyond the normal bounds of the traditional bread riot or protest movement. The disturbances led by the clerks of the Palace of Justice and the apprentices and journeymen of the luxury trades of the place Dauphine after the exile of the magistrates in the early summer of 1787 were of a familiar sort, resembling in every particular those of 1771 to 1774. The withdrawal of the offending edicts on September 21 was the pretext for a further series of outbursts, but the Parlement had only to call for an end to them on October 3 for order to be restored. The working people, only a small fraction of whom were active here, were still obedient.[17]

In May, 1788, the Parlement was once again able to mobilize the support of the laboring poor on its behalf with a declaration against the tyranny of arbitrary government. The magistrates were once again exiled for their trouble, but it was not until bread prices started to rise in mid-August (from 9 to 11 sous for a four-pound loaf) that serious resistance began. This time, numerous wage-earners joined the ranks of demonstrators favorable to restoration of the Court. The dismissal of the hated Lamoignon on September 14 and the return of the Parlement a week later, so far from putting a stop to the rioting, only served to increase its scope. Journeymen, master craftsmen, and small traders and shopkeepers from the center of the city, the faubourg Saint Germain, and the northern quarters now took a hand. It soon became clear that all this agitation was adding up to an experience qualitatively different from any earlier one. If the threat to the bread supply still remained the key to the behavior of the masses, a new factor had just made its appearance on the scene: bread and politics were no longer considered in isolation from one another. A junction between them had been effected so that it was now impossible to raise the question of hunger without simultaneously questioning the viability of the regime. The next step was to cast the discussion in terms of power, and that, too, would be done in the last half of 1788, after the principle of the convocation of the Estates General had been established.

Analyzing the troubles of August and September, Charon wished to distinguish between *peuple, public, populace,* and *canaille*:

It was the *People* [he wrote] who asked for the expulsion of the two ministers, their enemies, and who applauded the justice of the Monarch who accorded it to them.

It was the *Public* who, crowded into the Château de Versailles, caused the apartments to resound with the repeated cries of *Long Live the King.*

It was the *Populace* who mustered in the Place Dauphine and lighted bonfires there.

And it was the *Rabble* (canaille) who burned the effigies of Mm. de Brienne and de Lamoignon in the place de Grève.

But he also admitted that "it is to be noted that the public encouraged the populace, and that the latter emboldened the rabble."[18] He was pointing to the effect upon the *menu peuple* of the increasing activity of the bourgeoisie. From this time onward, the laboring poor would become infused with ideas of liberty and equality and with the notion that politics was a legitimate enterprise. As George Rudé has said, "Once these ideas began to permeate the common people . . . a new direction and purpose was given to popular unrest, already nurtured on economic hardship and traditional grievances."[19] Mercier had once written that "a riot that would degenerate into sedition has become morally impossible" in Paris because of the presence of the police among other reasons.[20] He had not been entirely incorrect, but it seems that what changed matters was not any removal of the police so much as the dissolution of the consensus supporting the monarchy. What made popular revolutionary action possible was the disaffection of the bourgeoisie and a part of the *classes supérieures* in general. In a more lucid moment, Mercier had seen them as "the most powerful brake on a populace gone astray." "The populace," he had maintained, "will always look to the bourgeois classes; and so long as the bourgeois smile, the People will find it impossible to bestir themselves for more than two weeks."[21] The bourgeois were no longer smiling, and the laboring poor were ready to take their cue.

The only arena for political action available to the laboring poor was the streets, for they were still excluded from the normal or newly created channels of expression. Persons who paid less than six livres capitation tax could not take part in the assemblies that elected deputies to the Estates General, and this provision effectively barred the *menu peuple*.[22] The capitation rolls for Paris have been lost, but surviving ones for the suburban town of Saint Denis show that artisans (we may assume that they were journeymen) rarely paid more than two or three livres and that unskilled laborers and petty traders paid as little as one livre, four sous.[23] If they could not vote in the primary assemblies, it was all the more true that they could not be named electors. Of the 407 electors of Paris *intramuros*, 170 were men of the law, 137 were *négociants*, shopkeepers, merchants, and master artisans (among whom only a handful *may* have at one time, but clearly no longer, belonged to the *menu peuple*), and 95 were members of the intelligentsia (civil servants, doctors, men of letters, artists).[24] In the words of the anonymous author of the *Pétition de cent cinquante mille ouvriers et artisans de Paris*, who wrote in May, 1789:

Scarcely can we distinguish, among 400 electors, 4 or 5 persons who, knowing our needs, our way of life and our misfortunes, can take a reasonable interest in them. . . .

Where then are there among you those men accustomed to guiding our steps, to directing our labor? Did you think that the disciple of Demosthenes or the emulator of Plato would suddenly transform themselves into founders, engravers, locksmiths, carpenters, stone-cutters, roofers, plumbers, etc., etc., limeburners, porters, etc., etc.; all of us who, like you, have difficulties and troubles peculiar to our various stations in life? Why do we not see among your commissioners and your representatives, our masters and your brothers? Will the scholar and the man of letters be able to appreciate or interpret our needs before this august tribunal, where all just demands ought to be discussed and welcomed?[25]

It is curious to note that the persons attacked are all intellectuals, the disciples of Demosthenes and the emulators of Plato, rather than the bankers, merchants, and big businessmen who were present in almost equal number. This was no doubt the result of the outstanding vociferous role played by the former in the deliberations, but it is also evidence that the laboring poor—or their spokesman of whatever class—still believed in a necessary union between master and worker and had not yet begun to think of oppression in terms of economic exploitation, that is to say, they had as yet no class consciousness.

The citizens who participated in the electoral process were occasionally aware of their isolation from the *menu peuple* but seem to have relied on a theory of virtual representation in the manner of English counter-revolutionaries a decade earlier. Thus they spoke of "the class of citizens . . . who have confided us their interests, like agricultural workers and urban laborers," who had done nothing of the kind. Once in a while, but not very often, a district cahier would allude to the special problems of the poor, asking that they be exempt from taxation and that they be allowed to ply their trades or peddle their wares without official hindrance.[26] Normally, the poverty of workingmen and women was mentioned only in connection with the *crise de subsistances*. Insofar as this was accompanied by declarations to the effect that "poverty ought not to be the lot of workingmen," it may be seen as an expression of the generosity of the revolutionary bourgeoisie. At least the poor were not to be held responsible for their own misery, which was attributed instead to the high price of bread.[27] Alternately, the blame was laid in more radical fashion on a "shameless luxury" that allowed nothing to stand in its way. The interests of the rich and poor were "common and inseparable," but too often insufficient provision was made for the protection of the poor. The arbitrary power of the government had to be limited, and the abuse of property and freedom by some individuals corrected. Hand in hand, proprietors and nonproprietors, the only two "truly distinct classes of citizens," would carry the day. In these words of Lambert, as in Sieyès, there is some attempt to create a nation out of the disparate elements of the Third Estate, but whereas the latter preached the triumph of the bourgeois world order, the former spoke in the accents of radical Jacobinism:

The unanimous wish of all France is that a constitution be drawn up which, in all areas of public order, may deliver us forever from arbitrary power. Property, liberty, that is what all the *cahiers* come down to in the last analysis. But, if only the State is taken care of; if private persons continue to be able to abuse both property and liberty, everything will have been done for the rich man, but nothing, absolutely nothing for oneself, as a man. . . . The Constitution would, in this hypothesis, have delivered up the poor to the entire discretion of the rich.

It is no doubt necessary that the rich should never cease to be the masters of their purse strings, but it is no less necessary that it not be in their power to be unjust and inhuman towards the hardworking and useful man who carries for them the burden of the day and of the heat, that they may no longer lightheartedly sacrifice to their ever-renewed and never satisfied whims of an insatiable and destructive luxury those very men who have with such great difficulty acquired definite rights to their unlimited gratitude.[28]

While the primary assemblies and the Estates General were preparing their several varieties of revolution from above, the *menu peuple* descended into the streets but not all at once and not always in support of revolutionary goals. Insurrection became their method while reform was still their madness. Not quite three months would pass after the beginnings of insurrectionary action until the unity of form and content was achieved.

The winter of 1788–1789 was one of the most severe in human memory, comparable to the furies of 1709, of which three generations had already been accustomed to speak. The price of bread went up to 14 sous on February 1 and remained at that level until the following July. Thousands of people poured into the city in search of subsistence and the work that was denied them in the country. It was under these conditions that the agitation of Orléanist and other politicians could gain ground. The shortage of bread and the benevolence of the bourgeoisie, the twin conditions of popular revolutionary action, were like germs maturing in an ever more favorable culture.

The first really insurrectionary action was the attack on Réveillon's wallpaper factory in the faubourg Saint Antoine on April 27. A few days before, Réveillon had spoken in the electoral assembly of the Sainte Marguerite district and had made a claim that it was no longer possible to pay a worker 15 sous a day. Whether this was a prelude to an attempt to reduce wages or not, we do not know. In any case, the issue raised went far beyond the fate of the manufacturer's 350 workers. His remarks stirred indignation among the wage earners of the faubourg, and they took up arms against him. The insurrectionaries were mainly journeymen artisans, and what they sought was a decrease in the price of bread. Necker and the third estate would give them the bread they needed, so they shouted their support even as they were being massacred by the *gardes françaises* under the orders of the Duc du Châtelet. What made this movement insurrectionary was not only the fact that arms were taken up but that a political meaning was conferred on the slogans used. As Rudé has pointed out, *Vive le Tiers Etat* in the mouths of workingmen was a "rallying cry of the poor against the rich rather than of the nation as a whole against a handful of privileged persons."[29] In this sense, the bourgeois Réveillon was outside the third estate. There is one point, however, on which I find myself in disagreement, perhaps only in a matter of emphasis, with Rudé. He writes that the Réveillon riots were unique in the history of the Revolution because they represented an insurrectionary movement of wage earners, the only occasion on which an appeal was made to them as a social group.[30] But bread still remained the point of reference among the Réveillon rioters even though it now was one of two terms in an equation that related wages to purchasing power. It seems to me that the appeal to wage earners was a matter of circumstance only (Réveillon was an employer of labor) and not indicative of the existence of a self-conscious group in contradistinction to the sans-culottes or the laboring poor as a whole.

Anonymous appeals to respectability notwithstanding,[31] it was indeed the artisans of the faubourg Saint Antoine who made life difficult for Réveillon. They were not joined in any substantial measure by persons from outside the immediate vicinity nor by other elements of the laboring poor. The participation of petty traders, laborers, water carriers, building workers, and the unemployed of the *ateliers de charité* came later in the revolutionary days of July 12–14. Even then, there seems to have been a kind of division of labor between the journeymen, on the one hand, who were notably absent from the attacks on the barriers and the grain stores of the Saint Lazare Monastery, and the rest of the *menu peuple*, on the other, which points to a more highly developed political consciousness on the part of the artisans. The latter were already capable of striking for power, albeit not independently, while other wage earners and petty traders, both domiciled and the floaters among them, could still concern themselves only with the food supply. (To be sure, their willingness now to take part in an insurrection and no longer to content themselves with moaning and small-scale riots is a sign of their evolution.) That this should be so is not surprising for a variety of reasons. First, the artisans worked and lived in a stable environment, in which they had been able in some small degree to cultivate a tradition of defense of their corporate interests. This was the "insubordination" of which Mercier complained when he wrote that journeymen no longer cared for whom they worked, thinking themselves the equal of their masters and being tied to them only by the consideration of wages.[32] Second, and paradoxically, the *compagnons* still worked side by side with their masters, who were thus able to act as their political as well as their professional cadres. Just as a revolution without the bourgeoisie to set the process in motion was unthinkable, so was the formation of the sans-culottes without the participation of the master artisans impossible. The sans-culottes as an entity were not synonymous with the laboring poor of the old regime. They were rather one of the provisional forms, in this case primarily a political one, that grew out of the disintegration of that regime as carried on by the Revolution. It is even possible that what has so often been spoken of as the basic identity of interests among the sans-culottes around questions of bread supply and the establishment of a Jacobin style of society may be more a specific revolutionary phenomenon than a legacy of the old regime, although it no doubt had roots in the earlier period. If, as I have argued throughout this book, the laboring poor is a useful category of social analysis in a precapitalist society, then there was a real cleavage between the master artisans, on the one hand, and the journeymen and the rest of the lower-status groups on the other, a cleavage that must have been all the more felt as mobility across the line was restricted in the years before the Revolution. At the same time, relations between masters and journeymen in the work process may be viewed as the coming into contact of two distinct, if related, cultures. The contact may have permitted the journeymen to make some progress towards liberating themselves from the debilitating culture of poverty in which they lived and thus to prepare themselves for revolutionary action.

The concept of the laboring poor loses all validity as soon as modern industrial capitalism starts to become the dominant mode of production. The paradox is that political consciousness begins to penetrate the ranks of the *menu peuple* at the very time they lose their integrity as a social group. Not only must the popular movement in the Revolution be seen as a struggle between bourgeois and sans-culottes, but the contradictions among the sans-culottes must be conceived of as a result of the political alliance between the master artisans and independent shopkeepers (proprietors), on the one hand, and the laboring poor (wage earners, or more generally, nonproprietors) on the other. Furthermore, within the disintegrating ranks of the laboring poor, the conditions of life and the ideological options were many and varied. In France, the transition to modern capitalist society was long and hard, and the social struggles were numerous before its embodiment was achieved in the bourgeois state of the Third Republic. For the workingman, these struggles began with his progressive liberation from the repression of the old regime and from the culture it had imposed on him. They ended, temporarily, in a new form of exploitation but one in which a *working-class* culture could grow and lay the foundation for a new tradition of revolutionary struggle.

⋖§ II §⋗

For a long time historians tended to regard the initiatives of the laboring poor, both before and during the Revolution, as the result of manipulation by their "social betters." It is only in relatively recent years that we have, by stages, come to recognize the often autonomous nature of their action. We have even tried to explain that action as a set of simple responses to the stimuli of bread shortages and high prices, exclusively. This is not enough. While I have no doubt that the laboring poor believed with Brecht that one ought "first feed the face and then tell right from wrong," bread alone—or the lack of it—will not explain what makes a man obedient or what turns him into a revolutionary. The entire experience of the eighteenth-century bread riots bears witness to the fact. Contemporaries were consistently astonished at the inactivity of the common people in the midst of wanton poverty. The best they could do was to attribute it to the "natural tendency" in man to do nothing. As Leclerc de Montlinot wrote:

Il y a peu d'hommes qui ne fassent entrer comme élément dans leur spéculations de bonheur, une oisiveté, sinon absolue, au moins relative. Le Sauvage qui reste les bras croisés plutôt que de se donner une sensation de plus, et l'homme policé qui se contente, de peu, plutôt que de s'agiter se ressemblent plus qu'on ne pense. Cette apathie, cette indolence imprimée par la nature, est peut-être la plus grande sauve-garde des propriétés. . . . Il n'est guère arrivé de révolutions, que quand toute une Nation occupée de la même idée, l'a suivie avec fureur.[33]

There are few men who do not include in their speculations on happiness a certain sum of idleness, relative if not absolute. The savage who keeps his arms crossed rather than give himself one additional sensation and the civilized man who contents himself with little rather than take action resembles one another more than one might think. This apathy, this indolence created by nature, is perhaps the greatest safeguard of property. . . . Revolutions have happened mainly when an entire nation has shared a single idea and pursued it with fury.

Even when great ideas were abroad in the land, they were not always accepted. In 1789, we hear an unemployed and starving *découpeuse en gaze* (textile worker) say: "The king is good; if he knew how unfortunate we are, he would not allow us to suffer . . ."[34] She had six children, and her husband made 18 sous a day, earning an annual wage of about 252 livres, assuming that he could find work on at least 280 out of 365 days a year. (Rudé estimates that on 111 days per year there was no work because of Sundays and holidays, in which case the total wage would come to 228 livres.) In 1790, a year of more or less normal prices, the Comité de Mendicité of the Constituent Assembly estimated that a family of five needed a strict minimum of 435 livres a year in order to survive.[35] In other words and making full allowance for the wages received by the woman in question and perhaps several of her children, we have here a case of absolute indigence accompanied by protestations of loyalty to the monarchy and, by inference, the established order. Despite her misery, this woman was unlikely to join her next-door neighbors in storming the Bastille. Why this should be so, why it took so long for political consciousness to mature among the *menu peuple* are the questions this book has attempted to answer. If, at the end, I can still agree with Mercier that the lack of bread was a necessary condition for the upheaval, I must also conclude that it was not a sufficient one.[36]

I am convinced that a culture of poverty did in fact exist in eighteenth-century Paris and that it consisted of a great deal more than getting drunk on gin or cheap wine. If this culture of poverty and the conditions in which it grew were not the same as those brought to our attention by contemporary social scientists,[37] the results they had were often similar. Like the residents of present-day ghettos, individuals raised in the slums of Paris had strong feelings of fatalism, helplessness, dependence, and inferiority. The strong orientation toward living for the present, coupled with a disinclination to defer gratification of desires and to plan for the future, the gregariousness of the community, the distrust, not to say hatred, of the institutions of the ruling classes—all characteristics cited by Lewis—are to be found in prerevolutionary Paris as much as in present-day Spanish Harlem.

For the laboring poor there was no way out and no place to hide. The channels of mobility were narrow and becoming more so as the century went on. A properly trained journeyman had less hope than ever before of becoming a master, while the unskilled new arrival from the country, come to make his fortune in the great city, was lucky to get even the lowest sort of menial work and as often as not was forced to rely on public charity or to resort to beggary. In addition, death was a constant personal threat at a time when fewer than one-third of the population reached the age of fifty. There can be no wonder that workingmen developed a sense of futility, that they lost whatever dynamism they may once have had—and I am thinking here in individual, as well as collective, terms of the young men who set out to make their way in the world only to be ground down by defeat into despair. Their attitude toward death itself is characterized mainly by acceptance. "Mourning and consternation" were indeed present, but death was implacable, and there was nothing to be done but to take the cold comfort offered by the maxim *Mort saisit sans exception.* Because they had never been able to control their destinies, the very thought of someday exercising control was foreign to the *menu peuple* at this time. Babies kept coming and children kept dying, prices went up, real wages went down. It was the way of the world, not to be questioned.

In a society characterized by hereditary legal inequality, there are what may be called the ordinary discriminations, privileges having to do with taxation, justice, access to careers, precedence, etc., which, in theory at least, affect equally all non-noble persons. In reality, however, to be rich was a good thing, no less then than now. Money, if it could not buy honor—and it sometimes could and did just that—made the lack of it tolerable. The poor man lacked this resource. He lived with his family in a miserably furnished narrow little room devoid of material comfort. The single room and lone bed that often constituted his total patrimony meant that he was totally deprived of privacy, and even sex became a public activity. It is possible that he did not feel this deprivation, for privacy is very much a bourgeois value, and there is no evidence to say that the poor had accepted it. But this was not a state of affairs calculated to give the poor a sense of self-esteem.

The *menu peuple* saw just enough of another kind of life to know that they were excluded from it. When they ventured forth from their hovels, they came into contact with people outside their own class and could measure the gulf that separated them from others. Their clothing was generally secondhand and therefore out of fashion. (Even when new, the cut and cloth of the costume readily pointed to the wearer's status.)[38] The food they ate was as limited in variety as it was in quantity. They walked while others rode. They went to taverns in the Halles and to *guinguettes* in the suburbs but not to the new restaurants.[39] They could take no hand in politics or administration, and they could often not get a proper funeral. In a word, the laboring poor had neither the right nor the means to conform to the socially dominant patterns of behavior.

Under these circumstances, the poor had no alternative but to accept their situation and to make the best of it. They turned inward upon themselves to form a community with its own values and norms of behavior. The community was at once a cushion against the harsh realities of their daily lives and a barrier against full participation in the world at large. Although feelings of frustration no doubt remained quite strong at the individual level, the culture as a whole was characterized by the growth of a psychology of acceptance. As that psychology was passed down the generations from parents to children, it made it impossible for the group to develop self-esteem and class-consciousness and thereby to engage in political action.

Acceptance had its rewards. Although thoroughly despised by the men of power, "le bon peuple de Paris" enjoyed a tacit freedom to get drunk and to engage in other amusements deemed worthy of the *canaille*, to let off steam in ways not dangerous to society.

But let them engage, as they occasionally did, in the smallest strike, demand for bread or similar protest movements, then all tolerance fell by the wayside.

The turning inward of the poor may be characterized as a continuous process of sublimation. Unconsciously, they repressed the hatred they felt for the hospitals, the charities, the police, and the courts—all of them vaguely perceived as agencies of control over their lives—until it became almost impossible for them to react to oppression at all, at least on a sustained basis. Only the Church escaped their disaffection, but the precise function of that institution was to re-enforce their sense of futility, their inability to act. Similarly, concern for personal and family honor, very strong among the poor, was a surrogate not only for material goods but also for political consciousness. An errant son brought to book or a disobedient wife punished might satisfy an ego weakened by the permanent frustrations to which it was exposed. The litigiousness of the poor, particularly evident in their constant demand for reparation of verbal insults, had the same function.

In the culture of poverty as it exists today, slum dwellers are aware of the socially dominant values, although they reject them as a code of behavior. This is what social workers, in their somewhat condescending vocabulary, call characterological difficulties. Was this equally true in eighteenth-century Paris, where communication was still in a primitive state and where there were no mass media to be used for the purpose of manipulating public opinion?

On the one hand, the laboring poor did meet representatives of other classes in the course of their work and in the streets. The gossip mill may have—and no doubt did—keep them abreast of what was going on in a limited portion of the outside world, the rest of the city, and, just possibly, the rest of France. On the other hand, insofar as there was a special community of which the domiciled poor were a part (and the floating poor as well, but only if they carried their community with them by living and/or traveling in regional or local groups), they were guaranteed a certain set of roots, a place in the shadow, if not in the sun. The community protected its members by keeping them out of constant and direct contact with the pressures of the dominant culture and by giving them an alternative milieu in which to function. The poor man may thus have been spared some part of the personality conflict he would otherwise have experienced had he known the full meaning of his inability to conform.

The poor were set off from the rest of society by so many differences of work, life, and culture that they could not fail to develop some sense of themselves as belonging to a separate group, that of the bottom dogs. They knew they were different from, and less fortunate than, the nobles and bourgeois, whom they no doubt joined together in their minds in the single category of men called Monsieur. This sense of difference, which takes into account only the most obvious phenomena of social life, is perfectly compatible with a sense of inferiority, a psychology of acceptance, and deferential behavior in general, although it may serve as well to create feelings of suspicion and even contempt towards those outside the group. It is very different from class consciousness which, by definition, involves an identification of the individual with an entity having positive attributes. Corollary to class consciousness (as it develops among those deprived of power in a society) are ideas of oppression and the need for change. The bourgeois of 1789 were class conscious and were therefore able to make a revolution. The laboring poor, by contrast, had not yet developed to the same point, hence they could, in the first instance, serve only as a *force d'appoint*. In a very real way, this group consciousness corresponded to the social situation in which they found themselves. The laboring poor did not constitute a single class but rather a melange of producers and merchants, skilled and unskilled, sedentary and nomadic. The positive identifications open to them—with a craft, a province, or an occupational group—were always within the larger category of the laboring poor, never encompassing the whole. They were divisive, rather than unifying. Only later, with the development of capitalist industry, were the conditions for the development of a unitary class consciousness created.

This said, it should be remembered that the laboring poor were neither foolish nor blind. They were capable of resentment and anger, even of identifying the representatives of authority as the agents of their ills. In the main, they blamed the king's ministers for their misfortunes, but they could be driven to curse the monarch himself. At the death of Louis XV, a popular jingle was heard all over Paris:

> Cy gist Louis le fainéant
> Qui donna papier en naissant
> La guerre en grandissant
> La famine en viellissant
> Et la peste en mourant.*40

---

* Here lies Louis the Do-Nothing
  Who gave us paper [money] at his birth
  War as he grew up
  Famine as he grew old
  And the plague when he died.

But this remained a personal criticism, rather than a call for the destruction of the monarchy. When Louis XVI ascended the throne, he was immediately acclaimed a worthy successor to Henri IV of glorious memory, although one wit wrote:

> D'Henri ressucité j'adopte le bon mot
> Mais pour me décider, j'attends la poule au pot.*[41]

The poor were not capable of sustaining their anger because they did not—could not—place it in a larger context.

I submit that they were incapable of thinking in larger terms, incapable of transforming their dislike for a man or a set of men into a critique of society, not only because they were poor, over-worked, badly nourished, and uneducated but because all of their disabilities, which were the result of bitter exploitation, had led them into the blind alley of the culture of poverty. Once there, they came to feel themselves helpless, dependent, and inferior. They were caught in a vicious circle, and they could not break out until someone showed them the way. As Professor Lewis has remarked, "Any movement . . . that organizes and gives hope to the poor and effectively promotes a sense of solidarity with larger groups must effectively destroy the psychological and social core of the culture of poverty."[42] The revolutionary bourgeoisie began to do just that by putting forth the idea that it was possible, not to say legitimate, to challenge the established order. The bour-geois used the laboring poor as their shock troops, and the laboring poor, or at least some of its constituent elements, was in part shaken out of its lethargy and soon began to pursue a program of its own. At last they had a chance to prove what Marivaux had said of them 40 years earlier, that they were "much more people and much less rabble" than was generally believed.

---

* To say that Henri lives again, I agree
  But to be certain, I await the chicken in the pot.

NOTES

Chapter [1]

1. J. J. Expilly, *Dictionnaire géographique, historique et politique des Gaules et de la France*, 5 vols. Amsterdam, (1762–1770), V: 399.
2. J. J. Rousseau, *Les Confessions*, ed. Michel Launay (Paris, 1968), pp. 146–147.
3. Nikolai Karamzine, *Voyages en France, 1789–1790*, ed. A. Legrelle (Paris, 1885), p. 76.
4. A. J. P. Paucton, *Métrologie, ou traité des mesures, poids et monnaies des anciens peuples et des modernes* (Paris, 1780), pp. 195–196; Beguillet, *Description historique de Paris*, 3 vols. (Paris, 1779), I: 35–36; Armand Husson, *Les Consommations de Paris* (Paris, 1856), p. 5. Paris today covers 10,402 hectares or 28,085 acres.
5. Charles René de Fourcroy, *Essai d'une table poléométrique* (Paris, 1782), cited by François de Danville, "Grandeur et population des villes au XVIIIe siècle," *Population*, XIII (1958): 459–480.
6. After 1775, 20 permanently installed shops were allowed to open in their place.
7. For this and much of what follows, see Lesage, *Le Géographe parisien*, 2 vols. (Paris, 1769); and M. F. Hoffbauer, *Paris à travers les âges*, 2nd ed., 3 vols. (Paris, 1885), I: pt. IV, p. 16.
8. See the description in Anon., *Entretiens de la truche, ou les amours de Jean Barnabas et de la Mère Roquinard (1745)*, cited by L. Sainéan, *Les Sources de l'argot ancien*, 2 vols. (Paris, 1912), I: 66:

   > Que l'on nous regarde [les gueux] pour la plupart, sans prévention; nous sommes des objets dignes de compassion; nous tirons des larmes de ceux qui nous voyent. L'un, moyennant quelques vessies de cochon, qu'il ajuste devant lui, se fait passer pour hydropique. L'autre, avec ses deux béquilles sur lesquelles il semble se soutenir avec peine, se serviroit de ses jambes mieux qu'un dératé, s'il entendoit claquer un fouet derrière lui. . . .

9. The luxury trades were the only ones that had as yet developed an export (i.e., extra-urban) market of any significance. The lawyer B. C. Gournay explained the fact in this way:

   > Considéré comme ville de fabrique, Paris ne peut soutenir aucune comparison avec Lyon, Rouen [etc.]: la cherté de la main d'oeuvre s'oppose

à ce qu'il s'y établisse des manufactures, hors celles dont les matières premières sont précieuses ou dont la fabrication demande beaucoup de perfection et le concours immédiat des arts.

See his *Tableau general du commerce . . . années 1789 et 1790* (Paris, 1789), p. 550.

10. N. E. Restif de la Bretonne, *Les Nuits de Paris*, 16 pts. (Paris, 1788–1794), III: 635–636, called the rue Saint Honoré and the surrounding area "la quintessence de l'urbanité française" and described it (II: 470) as

superbe rue! Assemblage du luxe, du commerce, de l'éclat, de la boue, de l'opéra, des filles, de l'impudence, de l'urbanité, de la débauche, de la politesse, de l'escroquerie, de tous les avantages et de tous les abus de la sociabilité. Je voudrais qu'on y concentre tous les vices dans un espèce de bazar, afin qu'ils ne scandalisassent pas le reste de la Ville: Il faut des vices dans une Capitale; mais il faut les traiter comme le feu, auquel on abandonne une maison, en coupant toutes les communications.

11. Louis Courajod, ed., *Livre journal de Lazare Duvaux, Marchand bijoutier ordinaire du Roy, 1748–1758*, 2 vols. (Paris, 1873); Pierre Verlet, "Le Commerce des objets d'art et les marchands merciers à Paris au XVIIIe siècle," *Annales: Economies, Sociétés, Civilisations*, XIII (1958): 10–29. See also André Delcourt, "La Finance parisienne et le commerce negrier au milieu du XVIIIe siècle," *Bulletin de la Société d'Etudes historiques, géographiques et scientifiques de la région parisienne*, no. 58 (1948): 21–28.

12. H. Depors, *Recherches sur l'état de l'industrie des cuirs en France pendant le XVIIIe siècle et le début du XIXe siècle* (Paris, 1932).

13. Marcel Brongniat, *La Paroisse Saint Médard au faubourg Saint Marceau* (Paris, 1951), p. 106.

14. Louis Sébastien Mercier, *Tableau de Paris*, 12 vols. (Amsterdam, 1783), II: 254f:

C'est le quartier où habite la populace de Paris la plus pauvre, la plus remuante et la plus indisciplinable. Il y a plus d'argent dans une seule maison du fauxbourg Saint-Honoré, que dans tout le fauxbourg Saint-Marcel . . . pris collectivement . . . [les habitants sont] un peuple qui n'a aucun rapport avec les Parisiens, habitans polis des bords de la Seine. [See also I: 258.]

15. Maurice Tourneux, ed., *Les Promenades à la mode* (Paris, 1888), pp. 30–31, 46.

16. A. Parmentier, "Les Boulevards de Paris au XVIIIe siècle," *Revue du XVIIIe siècle*, I (1913): 121–137.

17. A. Babeau, "Le Faubourg Saint-Honoré sous Louis XV," *Bulletin de la Société de l'histoire de Paris et de l'Ile de France*, XXXIV (1907): 182–188; J. Bonnardot, "La Formation du faubourg poissonnière et son développement à la fin du XVIIIe siècle," *Bulletin de la Société d'Etudes historiques, géographiques et scientifiques de la région parisienne*, no. 29 (1934): I–II; also "Etat du Gros Caillou," 1725, Collection Joly de Fleury 1332, Bibliothèque Nationale, Paris.

18. The move to the west tended to make the center of the city both relatively poorer and more homogeneous. The parish of Saint Gervais

in the Marais, once the haunt of aristocrats, was described in 1768 by its pastor as follows:

> Tout le monde sçait au'aujourd'huy on abandonne la ville pour bâtir et habiter les faubourgs; ainsi les faubourgs qui n'étaient peuplés que de Pauvres et d'Artisans commencent et continueront de l'être par la première noblesse, et le centre est abandonné aux malheureux. Ce sont des faits qui se vérifient plus sur ma paroisse que sur aucune autre. Ce qui est certain, c'est qu'en 1725 on comptoit trois mille cinq cents pauvres sur Saint Gervais et on en compte aujourd'hui plus de treize mille . . . [S 7493, Archives Nationales, Paris, cited by Louis Brochard, *Saint Gervais, Histoire de la paroisse* (Paris, 1950), p. 52].

19. Me. Lescuyer, *Memoire curieux, historique et intéressant sur la fondation, le patronage et le droit de nomination à la cure de l'église paroissiale de Sainte Marguerite au faubourg Saint Antoine de Paris* (Paris, 1738). See also Jean H. Prat, *Histoire du faubourg Saint Antoine* (Paris, n.d.).

20. Michel Phlipponneau, *La Vie rurale de la banlieue parisienne* (Paris, 1956), pp. 49–58.

21. Jean Louchitsky, "Regime agraire et populations agricoles dans les environs de Paris à la veille de la Révolution," *Revue d'Histoire Moderne*, VIII (1933): 97–142. See also Jean Bastié, *La Croissance de la banlieue parisienne* (Paris, 1964), pp. 69ff., 82–84.

22. Bastié, *La Croissance*, p. 71; Philippe Dally, *Belleville, Histoire d'une localité parisienne pendant la révolution* (Paris, 1912), pp. 4–5, 72; Lucien Lambeau, *Histoire des communes annexées à Paris en 1859*, 6 vols. (Paris, 1910–1926); René Sordes, *Histoire de Suresnes* (Suresnes, 1965). The taille rolls may be found in 3 AZ 24 (Bagnolet, 1777), DC² 1 (Ivry, 1778), DC² 2 (Passy, 1779), Archives de la Seine, Paris; and in Z^{1g} 443 (Asnières, Boulogne, Gennevilliers, Suresnes, 1789), Archives Nationales.

23. J. B. Darigrand, *Mémoire pour les habitants de la banlieue de Paris* (Paris, 1789).

24. Nicolas de Lamare, *Traité de la police*, 4 vols. (Paris, 1705–1738), IV: 404, 420.

25. Cf. Germain Brice writing in 1698, cited by Louis Hautecoeur, *Histoire de l'architecture civile en France*, 7 vols. (Paris, 1943–1957), III: 46–47:

> Si ces entreprises continuent de la Sorte, la Ville de Paris, sans bornes, comme elle a été jusqu'à present, s'étendra à l'infini et pourra dans la suite des temps tomber dans la triste inconvénient de ces fameuses et superbes villes dont l'histoire fait mention, qui se sont détruits par le luxe immodéré et par leur grandeur extrême, telle que Thèbes, Memphys, Babylone, Eliopolis, Palmire, Persepolis, Leptis et Rome même, qui n'est plus a présent qu'un squelette de ce qu'elle était dans sa splendeur. Si l'on consulte la bonne politique, on ne doit pas souffrir qu'il se trouve une ville dans un Etat qui surpasse les autres par sa grandeur et par conséquent par sa puissance et par le nombre de ses habitants.

See also Piganiol de la Force, *Description historique de la ville de Paris*, new ed., 10 vols. (Paris, 1765), I: 25–26.

26. A good example of the denunciation of the city as the source and

locus of luxury and evil is Fougeret de Montbron, *La Capitale des Gaules, ou La Nouvelle Babilonne*, new ed. (La Haye, 1760).

27. Léon Cahen, "Recherches sur l'agglomération parisienne au XVIIIe siècle," *Vie Urbaine*, IV (1922): 131–145.

28. M–D France 1616, folios 173–192, Archives du Ministère des Affaires Etrangères, Paris.

29. G. de Bory, *Mémoire dans lequel on prouve la possibilité d'aggrandir la ville de Paris sans en reculer les limites* (Paris, 1774), p. 5.

30. See VD* 173, Archives de la Seine, for a claim made in 1790 that in the parish of La Madeleine, Ville l'Evêque, the number of deaths had never equalled the number of births in a given year and that there had never been an epidemic "properly so-called."

31. See, for example, the complaints about this failure made by Lefort de Saint Yenne, *L'Ombre du grand Colbert: le Louvre et la ville de Paris*, 2nd rev. ed. (Paris, 1752), p. 81n.

32. Jacques Dulaure (d'après Barbier), *Réclamation d'un citoyen contre la nouvelle enceinte de Paris élevée par les fermiers géneraux* (Paris, 1787). Hardy, ever sensitive to aesthetic considerations, thought that Parisians had all the more reason to protest as they were now deprived of the opportunity "to contemplate the verdant countryside" and "to breathe pure air on Sundays and holidays." Ms. Fr. 6685, folio 18, Bibliothèque Nationale.

33. J. H. Ronesse, *Vue sur la propreté des rues de Paris* (Paris, 1782), p. 75.

34. Pierre Lavedan, *Histoire de l'urbanisme*, 3 vols. (Paris, 1926–1952), II: 342–343.

35. Arthur Young, *Travels in France*, ed. Jeffry Kaplow (New York, 1969), pp. 13, 67–68.

36. J. Letaconnoux, "La Circulation parisienne," in J. Letaconnoux and Léon Cahen, eds., *La Vie parisienne au XVIIIe siècle* (Paris, 1914), pp. 32–33.

37. A. R., *The Curiosities of Paris in Nine Letters* (London, n.d. but written 1754–1755), pp. 25–26.

38. I am speaking here only of the day-to-day problems involved in supplying so great an urban center as Paris. The major cause of repeated *crises de subsistances* in old-regime France was the archaic nature of a still semifeudal agricultural system. See M. Morineau, "Y a-t-il eu une révolution agricole en France au XVIIIe siècle? *Revue Historique* CCXXXIX (1968): 299–326.

39. J. Junié, "Plan des paroisses de Paris, 1786," Carte N I Seine 56, Archives Nationales.

40. Anon., *Projet sur l'établissement de trottoirs pour la sûreté des rues de Paris et l'embellissement de la ville* (Paris, 1784).

41. François Boissel, *Discours contre les servitudes publiques* (Paris, 1786). p. 23.

42. Alfred Martin, *Etudes historiques et statistiques sur les moyens de transport dans Paris* (Paris, 1894), pp. 65–80.

43. Claude Antoine Joseph Leclerc de Montlinot, *Etat actuel du dépôt de moissons précédé d'un essai sur la mendicité* (Soissons, 1789), p. 49.

44. Arthur Young, *Travels in France*, p. 77.

45. J. Letaconnoux and L. Cahen, eds., *La Vie parisienne*, pp. 26–29. See also de Lamare, *Traité de la police*, IV: 122.

46. Menuret de Chambaud, *Essais sur l'histoire médico-topographique de Paris* (Paris, 1786), p. 93f.
47. A. P. Herlaut, *L'Eclairage des rues de Paris à la fin du XVIIe et au XVIIIe siècles* (Paris, 1916), reprinted from *Revue Historique*, CXXXIX (1922): 43–61, 202–223.
48. J. C. Nemeitz, *Séjour de Paris* (Leyden, 1727), pp. 118–120.
49. Siméon Prosper Hardy, *Mes Loisirs*, ed. Maurice Tourneux (Paris, 1912), p. 222.
50. Charles de Peysonnel, *Les Numéros*, 2nd ed., 3 pts. (Paris, 1783), III: 47; Poncet de la Grave, *Projet des embellissemens de la ville et fauxbourgs de Paris*, 3 pts. (Paris, 1786), II: 209ff. See also Anon., *Observations sur l'illumination de Paris* (Paris, 1789), p. 6f.
51. See the estimates of Expilly, *Dictionnaire*, V: 480–481; and L. Denis, *Pouillé historique et topographique du Diocèse de Paris* (Paris, 1767).
52. *Almanach de Paris, 1ère partie contenant les demeures, les noms et qualités de personnes de condition . . . pour l'année 1785* (Paris, 1785).
53. Expilly, *Dictionnaire*, V: 418–420.
54. François Furet, "Pour une définition des classes inférieures à l'époque moderne," *Annales: Economies, Sociétés, Civilisations*, XVIII (1963): 459–474.
55. Léon Cahen, "La Population parisienne au milieu du XVIIIe siècle," *Revue de Paris*, XVI, no. 17 (September 1, 1919); 146–170. Cahen relied too heavily on the tax registers of the Grand Bureau des Pauvres as his exclusive source. His figures should be used with discretion.
56. George Rudé, "La Population ouvrière parisienne de 1789 à 1791," *AHRF*, XXXIX, no. 187 (January–March, 1967): 15–33.
57. Messance, *Recherches sur la population des généralités d'Auvergne, de Lyon, de Rouen . . . depuis 1676 jusqu'en 1764* (Paris, 1766), pp. 184–185.
58. N. Karéiev, *La densité de la population des différentes sections de Paris pendant la Révolution* (Paris, 1912). See also Paul Meuriot, "Le Recensement de l'an II," *Journal de la Société Statistique de Paris*, LIX (1918): 34–56, 79–99; and Roger Mols, *Introduction à la démographie historique des villes d'Europe du XIVe au XVIIIe siècle*, 3 vols. (Gemb'loux, 1955–1956), II: 95, n. 3.
59. Large numbers of workers and artisans lived in the lodging houses of this section, particularly in the rues Tirechape, des Poulies and du Champfleury. On some streets (rues du Chantre, de Bauvais), there were both hotels for the bourgeois and rooming houses for the lower classes. Dossier C II 160^{114d}, C 260, Archives Nationales.
60. Marianne Picard, "La Section de la place Vendôme pendant la Révolution (unpub. D.E.S., Paris, 1963), pp. 20–25.
61. François Coqblin, "Le Faubourg Saint Marcel (La Section des Gobelins pendant la Révolution" (unpub. D.E.S., Paris, 1960); Brigitte Champ-Rigot, "L'Ile Saint Louis pendant la première année de la Révolution" (unpub. D.E.S., Paris, 1966), pp. 71–77. See also Denise Santi, "La Section de l'Ile Saint Louis pendant la période révolutionnaire" (unpub. D.E.S., Paris, 1966).
62. J. P. Cointet, "La Section de la Bibliothèque" (unpub. D.E.S., Paris, 1963), p. 95.
63. Yves Bonnaz, "La Section de l'Homme Armé" (unpub. D.E.S., Paris, 1960), p. 30.

64. Jean Lucien Gay, "L'Administration de la capitale entre 1770 et 1789," *Paris et l'Ile de France*, VII (1956): 299–370; *ibid.*, IX (1957–1958): 283–363; *ibid.*, X (1959): 181–247.

65. P. Bonnassieux, "Note sur l'ancienne police de Paris," *Bulletin de la Société de l'Histoire de Paris et de l'Ile de France*, XXI (1894): 187–192; Maxime de Sars, *Lenoir, lieutenant-général de police, 1732–1807* (Paris, 1948), passim.

66. Mercier, *Tableau*, I: 195.

67. Hugues de Montbas, *La Police parisienne sous Louis XVI* (Paris, 1949), p. 90ff.

68. Marc Chassaigne, *La Lieutenance générale de police de Paris* (Paris, 1906), pp. 253–256; Hardy, *Mes Loisirs*, pp. 24–25. For the range of police activities, see boxes 10034–91, Archives de l'Arsenal, Paris.

69. Poncet de la Grave, *Projet*, II: 139–141.

70. Charles Chassin, *Le Elections et les cahiers de Paris en 1789*, 4 vols. (Paris, 1888–1889), II: 411, 438–439.

71. Ms. Fr. 6680, Bibliothèque Nationale.

72. X^{2B} 1367, Archives Nationales.

73. For this and what follows, X^{2b} 1368, Archives Nationales; Collection Joly de Fleury, 1101, 1102, Bibliothèque Nationale; and A. P. Herlaut, "Les enlevements d'enfants à Paris en 1720 et en 1750," *Revue Historique*, CXXXIX (1922): 43–61, 202–223.

74. Collection Joly de Fleury, 1101, Bibliothèque Nationale.

75. Edmond Jean François Barbier, *Journal historique et anecdotique du règne de Louis XV*, 4 vols. (Paris, 1847–1856), III: 135, 138, 155–156.

76. Mercier, *Tableau*, XII: 136–137, reports that one woman, asked by a wounded policeman to fetch a confessor, replied: "Ah! Je le crois bien, vraiment; tu voudrois confesser pour aller en paradis? Non, non, point de confession: il faut que tu ailles droit en enfer." She then smashed his head with a paving stone.

Chapter [2]

1. Anon., *Letters on the French Nation by a Sicilian Gentleman Residing at Paris* (London, 1749), p. 42.

2. Philippe Hecquet, *La Médecine, la chirurgie et la pharmacie des pauvres*, 4 pts. in 3 vols. (Paris, 1740), I: xii–xiii.

3. Louis Chevalier has shown the impact the recognition that the *misérables* existed had on a later generation in his *Classes laborieuses et classes dangereuses* (Paris, 1958).

4. Cited by Jacques Peuchet, *Mémoires tirés des archives de la police*, 3 vols. (Paris, 1838), I: 204–210.

5. Ms. 1422, Bibliothèque d'Orléans, Orléans.

6. Jèze, *Etat ou tableau de la ville de Paris* (Paris, 1760), p. 335:

> Le titre de Savoyard est devenu dans Paris un nom générique que l'on donne à des jeunes enfants que la misère arrache de leurs patries, ou tire du sein de leur familles, pour venir dans cette grande ville chercher à vivre; ils y sont répandus dans les differents quartiers et dans les differentes rues, où ils rendent aux citoyens des services journaliers, et pro-

curent à peu de frais des facilités d'un usage très commode et très fréquent. . . . Les Savoyards proprement dits, c'est à dire ceux de ces jeunes gens qui sont réellement originaire de Savoye sont décrotteurs, frotteurs, scieurs de bois, ramoneurs de cheminée, commissionnaires, etc.

7. Edme Bouchardon's drawings, *Etudes prises dans le bas peuple, ou les cris de Paris*, of which five series were published between 1737 and 1746, are very informative in this regard. Many of them are reproduced by Marguerite Pitsch, *La Vie populaire à Paris au XVIIIe siècle* (Paris, 1949). See also François Boucher, *Le Pont Neuf*, 2 vols. (Paris, 1925).

8. Claude-Stephen Le Paulmier, *L'Orviétan* (Paris, 1892). See also Anon., *Observations sur le baume de vie composé par le sieur LeLievre* (Paris, 1758).

9. Abel Poitrineau, *La Vie rurale en Basse Auvergne*, 2 vols. (Paris, 1965), I: 56off.

10. Anon., *Les Rues de Paris avec les cris que l'on entend journellement dans les rues de la ville* (Troyes, 1724). This volume was published as part of the *Bibliothèque bleue*.

11. Edme de la Poix de Fréminville, *Dictionnaire ou traité de la police générale des villes, bourgs, paroisses et seigneuries de la campagne*, new ed. (Paris, 1771), p. 179.

12. Claude Marin Saugrain, *Dictionnaire universel de la France* 3 vols. (Paris, 1726), II: col. 939; Messance, *Recherches sur la population des généralités d'Auvergne, de Lyon, de Rouen . . . depuis 1676 jusqu'en 1764* (Paris, 1766), pp. 175–183; *Idem., Nouvelles recherches sur la population de la France* (Lyon, 1788), p. 75.

13. F^{20} 441, Archives Nationales; Jacques Necker, *De l'Administration des finances*, 3 vols. (Paris, 1784), I: 277.

14. Expilly, *Dictionnaire*, V: 401, 480–481.

15. AD XVI 10, Archives Nationales.

16. Louis Brion de la Tour, *Tableau de la population de la France* (Paris, 1789).

17. Léon Cahen, "La Population parisienne au milieu de XVIIIe siècle," *Revue de Paris*, XVI, no. 17 (September 1, 1919): 146–170; Marcel Reinhard, *Paris pendant la Révolution française*, 2 vols. (Paris, 1962–1965), I: 25–44.

18. "Mémoire concernant la situation des peuples du Royaume de France," 1745, M–D France 1767, Archives du Ministère des Affaires Etrangères, Paris. See also Mercier, *Tableau*, I: 140–142.

19. M–D France 1767, folios 14–15, Archives du Ministère des Affaires Etrangeres.

20. J. Ibanès, "La Population de la place des Vosges et de ses environs en 1791," in Commission d'Histoire Economique et Sociale de la Révolution, *Contributions à l'histoire démographique de la Révolution française*, 1st ser. (Paris, 1962), p. 88.

21. Letter of M. de Tournemire, subdelegate at Mauriac, to the intendant of Basse Auvergne in Départment du Puy-de-Dôme, *Inventaire sommaire des archives départementales antérieures à 1790*, ser. C, 7 vols. (Clermont Ferrand, 1893–1937), IV: 238.

22. Anon., "Appercu des causes et des effets de l'émigration dans des différentes parties de la province d'Auvergne et de l'état du peuple,"

1789, 4 C 33, Archives Départementales du Puy-de-Dôme, Clermont-Ferrand.

23. C 360, Archives Départementales de La Creuse, Gueret.
24. Remarks of Lamoignon de Malesherbes on a plan for ending beggary by Loménie de Brienne, AP II 154 (177 MI 158), Archives Nationales.
25. Friedrich Schulz, *Ueber Paris und die Pariser* (Berlin, 1791), p. 63.
26. G. Perrin, "La Section des Lombards" (unpub. D.E.S., Paris, 1963), p. 112ff; J. C. Goeury, "Evolution démographique et sociale du faubourg Saint-Germain," in Commission de'Histoire Economique et Sociale de la Révolution, *Contributions à l'histoire démographique de la Révolution française*, 2nd ser. (Paris, 1965), pp. 46–47; J. Ibanès, "Population," pp. 71–87.
27. François Coqblin, "Le Faubourg Saint Marcel (la section des Gobelins) pendant la Révolution" (unpub. D.E.S., Paris, 1960).
28. Pierre Jean Baptiste Legrand d'Aussy, *Voyage d'Auvergne* (Paris, 1788), pp. 3–6.
29. Cf. the remarks of the Prefect of the Cantal, circa 1810:

> A peine se souviennent-ils de leurs parents. De retour chez eux, ils ne reconnaissent plus leur autorité; les liens de famille se relâchent, l'amour de la patrie s'efface. Accoutumés à une vie errante et désordonnée ils ne peuvent se livrer à aucun travail assidu et s'ils ne deviennent pas le fléau de la société, ils en sont au moins une charge inutile. [Cited by Georges Mauco, *Les Migrations ouvrières en France au début du XIXe siècle* (Paris, 1932), p. 9.]

30. Des Essarts, *Dictionnaire de la Police*, 7 vols. (Paris, 1786–1788), VII: 458–464, article *"ouvriers."*
31. Ms. 1422, Bibliothèque d'Orléans.
32. Jean Baptiste Denisart, *Collection des Décisions nouvelles*, 14 vols., 8th ed. (Paris, 1783–1807), II: 224.
33. Jacques Savary, *Le Parfait négociant* (Paris, 1675), pp. 49–66. See also Jacques Savary des Bruslons, *Dictionnaire universel de commerce*, 4 vols. (Geneva, 1744).
34. Denisart, *Collection*, II: 225, citing an Arrêt du Parlement de Paris of March 14, 1730. In March, 1776, at a time of increasing labor unrest, the police forbade journeymen to leave their masters' employ until they had served one year, at least. See Ms. Fr. 6682, folio 191, Bibliothèque Nationale.
35. Minutier Central, August 30, 1778, étude 89, liasse 729, Archives Nationales.
36. Minutier Central, November 28, 1778, étude 89, liasse 732, Archives Nationales.
37. On apprenticeship in general, see Albert Soboul, "Problèmes du travail au XVIIIe siècle. L'Apprentissage: réalités sociales et nécessités économiques," *Studi Storici*, V (1964): 449–466.
38. Jèze, *Tableau*, pp. 211–237.
39. René de Lespinasse, *Les Métiers et les corporations de la ville de Paris*, 4 vols. (Paris, 1879–1897), II–IV: passim. François Olivier-Martin, *L'Organisation corporative de la France d'ancien régime* (Paris, 1938), p. 139, holds that the favor shown to sons of masters did not exclude journeymen from mastership altogether. No doubt, some did succeed. The question is: How many and at what price of time and struggle? The evidence is that their number was decreasing

as the old regime drew to a close. See also Collection des ordonnances de la police, Archives de la Préfecture de Police, Paris.

40. Paul Chauvet, *Les Ouvriers du livre en France des origines à la Révolution de 1789* (Paris, 1959), p. 247.

41. For the text of the edicts, see François A. Isambert, et al., *Receuil Général des anciennes lois françaises*, 29 vols. (Paris, 1821–1833), XXIV: 74–89.

42. Charles Chassin, *Les Elections et les cahiers de Paris en 1789*, 4 vols. (Paris, 1888–1889), II: 531. See also de Lespinasse, *Métiers*, III: 349–350: "Défense [aux maîtres cordonniers] d'acheter aucuns souliers aux compagnons chambrelans ou de faire aucuns ouvrages secretement en leur chambre." There were, in reality, two kinds of chambrelans: (1) legitimate masters too poor to have their own shops; and (2) apprentices, journeymen, and unqualified persons who practiced the trade clandestinely. Only the latter were subject to fines, confiscation of goods, and imprisonment. See Jacques Savary des Bruslons, *Dictionnaire*, 4 vols., 6th ed. (Geneva, 1750), I: 796.

43. Emile Coornaert, *Les Corporations en France avant 1789* (Paris, 1941), p. 244.

44. Cf. the development of guild socialism in the 1820s and 1830s.

45. Ms. Fr. 6682, folios 191, 194, Bibliothèque Nationale.

46. Restif de la Bretonne, *Les Nuits*, VIII: 1856. See also Pierre Verlet, *L'Art du meuble à Paris au XVIIIe siècle*, 2nd ed. (Paris, 1968), pp. 31–34.

47. Emile Coornaert, *Les Compagnonnages* (Paris, 1966); Agricol Perdiguier, *Livre du compagnonnage*, 2nd ed., 2 pts. (Paris, 1841); and République Française, Ministère du Commerce, Office du Travail, *Les Associations professionnelles ouvrières*, 4 vols. (Paris, 1899), I: 93–94, 118–120. On the role of ritual, see E. J. Hobsbawm, *Primitive Rebels* (Manchester, 1959), chap. 9.

48. An Arrêt du Parlement of November 12, 1778 forbidding associations and assemblies of journeymen made special mention of the *devoirs* and forbade publicans to aid or abet them in any way. This was particularly important because the members were in the habit of making their headquarters in a specific tavern whose owners were known as the *mère* and *père* of the *compagnons*. See Isambert, et al., *Anciennes Lois*, XXV: 452.

49. For example, the police repeatedly issued orders forbidding more than one-half of the journeymen in a master's employ to quit within a two-week period. Lespinasse, *Metiers*, II: 353 and III: 593ff.

50. Ordonnances de police, XL: 375ff, Archives de la Préfecture de police.

51. Report of Jacques Simon Dupuy, Commissaire du Châtelet, October, 1776, Y 12826, Archives Nationales.

52. Ms. Fr. 6682, folio 281, Bibliothèque Nationale.

53. Ms. Fr. 6685, folios, 149, 152, Bibliothèque Nationale.

54. Ordonnance de police, October 6, 1785, H^2 1968, Archives Nationales.

55. Marcel Rouff, "Une grève de gagne-deniers en 1786 à Paris," *Revue Historique*, CV (1910): 332–347; Germain Martin, *Les Associations ouvrières au XVIIIe siècle* (Paris, 1900), pp. 128–129; Ms. Fr. 6685, folios 262, 269, 274, Bibliothèque Nationale.

56. See police ordinances and orders of the Parlement in AD I 25^B, Archives Nationales.

57. Cited by Coornaert, *Corporations*, p. 169.
58. Cited by Patrice Courault, "La paternité des chansons folkloriques," *Bulletin Folklorique de l'Ile de France*, X (1948): 11–13.
59. Cited by A. Daumard and F. Furet, "Problèmes de méthode en histoire sociale. Réflexions sur une note critique," *Revue d'Histoire Moderne et Contemporaine*, XI (1964): 295.
60. Alfred Franklin, *Dictionnaire historique des arts, métiers et professions exercés dans Paris depuis le treizième siècle* (Paris, 1906), p. 352.
61. Savary des Bruslons, *Dictionnaire*, II: 537. See also Marie-Hélène Bourquin, "L'Approvisionnement de Paris en bois de la Régence à la Révolution" (unpublished doctoral dissertation Faculté de Droit, Paris, 1969), pp. 428–429.
62. Bourquin, "L'Approvisionment," pp. 421–423. See also S. H. Dubuisson, *Lettres du Commissaire Dubuisson au Marquis de Caumont, 1735–1741*, ed. A. Rouxel (Paris, n.d.), pp. 181–182.
63. Savary des Bruslons, *Dictionnaire*, II: 606.
64. Jean Martineau, *Les Halles de Paris des origines à 1789* (Paris, 1960), p. 184ff.
65. Mercier, *Tableau*, I: 145–146; Abbé Jaubert, *Dictionnaire raisonné universel des arts et métiers*, new ed., 4 vols. (Paris, 1773), II: 342–343 and III: 45–46.
66. For this and much of what follows, see R. F. du Breil de Pontbriand (d'après Barbier), *Projet d'un établissement déjà commencé pour élever dans la piété les Savoyards qui sont dans Paris* (Paris, 1735); Idem., *Progrès de l'établissement commencé depuis peu pour les Savoyards qui sont dans Paris* (Paris, 1737); Idem., *Suite du progrès de l'établissement pour l'instruction de tous les enfants et de tous les ouvriers des rues de Paris* (Paris, 1739).
67. Jaubert, *Dictionnaire*, I: 589.
68. Anon., *Les Rues de Paris*, pp. 73–76; F. Klein-Rebours, *Métiers disparus* (Paris, 1968), p. 63; A. Franklin, *Dictionnaire*, p. 237; and Jaubert, *Dictionnaire*, I: 589–590.
69. A. Franklin, *Dictionnaire*, p. 283; Savary des Bruslons, *Dictionnaire*, II: 607; Mercier, *Tableau*, V: 245–247.
70. See Anon., *An Agreeable Criticism of Paris and the French*, 2nd ed. (London, 1706), p. 19:

> Taylors have more trouble to invent than to stitch, and when a suit has lasted the Life of a Flower it appears decrepid. From hence is born a People call'd *Fripiers* (Brokers), vile Wretches, and descended from ancient Israel: They make a trade of buying and selling old second-hand suits, and they live splendidly by *stripping of some and Cloathing others*, a conveniency singular enough in a very large City! where those who are tired with wearing the same Habit long, may change it with moderate Loss, and where others, who are bare, have the means of clothing themselves with small Expence. In short, what is most incredible is, that if in one Day a Hundred Thousand Clients should be sent naked out of the Hands of the Attorneys, there are in this City shirts and suits enough to cover them.

In 1768, a tailor was accused by the guild of breaking the rules by selling new clothes at cut prices. His cheapest suit cost 34 livres, or almost a month's pay of a skilled or semiskilled worker. See J. B.

Darigrand, "Mémoire pour le Sieur Stouldré," 1768, D 5 Z 9, Archives de la Seine, Paris.

71. Mercier, *Tableau*, V: 245–247, and II: 253.
72. Quartier du Luxembourg, Etat des Hotelliers, 1754, Box 10245, Archives de la Bastille, Bibliothèque de l'Arsenal.
73. Y 9508, Archives Nationales.
74. Schulz and Kraus, *Beschreibung and Abbildung der Poissarden in Paris* (Weimar and Berlin, 1789), p. 8.
75. Ordonnances de police, February 5, 1762 and December 3, 1776, Y 9499, Archives Nationales.
76. Abbé d'Espagnac, *Précis sur délibéré pour les chaudronniers forains, Auvergnats, et autres contre la communauté des maîtres chaudronniers de Paris* (Paris, 1761). See also Anon., *Dialogue entre un citoyen de Lyon et un mendiant* (n.p., n.d., but circa 1788–1789).
77. Roger Mols, *Introduction à la démographie historique des villes d'Europe du XIVe au XVIIIe siècle*, 3 vols. (Gem'bloux, 1955–1956), III: 122.
78. Expilly, *Dictionnaire*, V: 402.
79. Tobias Smollett, *Travels through France and Italy*, 2 vols. (London, 1766), I: 85–86.
80. Mercier, *Tableau*, II: 199–202.
81. Jaubert, *Dictionnaire*, II: 562.
82. Fréminville, *Dictionnaire*, pp. 288–292.
83. Mercier, *Tableau*, I: 162–163.
84. Ms. 1422, Bibliothèque d'Orléans.
85. A case in point is that of François Etienne Cocu [!], age 15: "Arrêté sans passeport, il couchoit depuis plusieurs jours dans les bateaux et inquiète le public. Il a déclaré avoir son père domestique à Paris et avoir été renvoyé de chez son maître où il était en apprentissage." August, 1785, C 745, Archives Départementales de L'Aisne, Laon.
86. Des Essarts, *Dictionnaire de la police*, 7 vols. (Paris, 1786–1788), III: 467–485. Cf. Maille Dussausoy, *Le Citoyen désintéressé*, 2 vols. (Paris, 1767), II: 140: "Attirés par l'exemple de leurs camarades qui ont échangé une vie utile, honorable et pénible, pour des occupations vile et rampantes, ils [les domestiques] viennent s'énerver et se corrompre dans les grandes villes."
87. Messance, *Recherches et considérations sur la population de la France* (Paris, 1788), p. 113, wrote that, after all, domesticity was a very comfortable condition:

> C'est un des plus heureux [états], des plus favorisés, & où l'homme est le plus assuré de tout ce qui constitue le bien-être physique; souvent même lorsque les maîtres ont quelques privilèges attachés à leur état, les domestiques y participent, & sont exempts d'une partie des charges de la société, qu'ils seroient plus en état de supporter, que les malheureux sur lesquels on est forcé de les accumuler.

88. E. G. Cruickshank, "Public Opinion in Paris in the 1740s: The Reports of the Chevalier de Mouhy," *Bulletin of the Institute of Historical Research*, XXVII (1954): 66. See also Mercier, *Tableau*, II: 199–202.
89. Anon., *Avis à la livrée par un homme qui la porte* (Paris, 1789), pp. 11, 31:

Il faut donc, mes camarades, lorsque nos maîtres nous sondent, leur dé-
clarer franchement que nous sommes du peuple, et que nous n'abandon-
nerons point le peuple pour eux. . . . Nous avons . . . à défendre des
intérêts qui nous sont chers. Nous ne devons point trahir notre sang:
la raison nous le défend, aussi bien que la conscience.

90. AD I 25ᴮ, Archives Nationales; Karamzine, *Voyages en France,
   1789–1790*, ed. A. Legrelle (Paris, 1885), p. 92; Restif de la Bretonne,
   Les Nuits, I: 31, and II: 433–437.
91. Mercier, *Tableau*, III: 206–210.
92. D⁵ B⁶, 738, 983, 1105, 1309, 1966, 2160, 4203, Archives de la Seine.
93. C. E. Labrousse, *Esquisse du mouvement des prix et des revenus en
   France au XVIIIe siècle*, 2 vols. (Paris, 1933), II: 597–608.
94. Y 13322, X 2ᵇ 1367, Archives Nationales; "Journal de dépenses d'une
   bourgeoise," 1781–1783, Ms. 696, Bibliothèque Historique de la Ville
   de Paris; Victor Advielle, ed., *Journal professionnel d'un maître de
   pension de Paris au XVIIIe siècle* (Pont l'Evêque, 1868); J. C. Neimitz,
   Séjour de Paris (Leyden, 1727), I: 85.
95. Labrousse, *Des prix et des revenus*, II: 597–608. Visitors noted the
   price rise with dismay. Smollett wrote in 1763 that the cost of living
   had doubled in 15 years (*Travels*, I: 86), and Philip Thicknesse in
   1775 found "most articles . . . one-third dearer, and many double"
   compared with 10 years earlier (*A Year's Journey through France
   and Part of Spain*, 2 vols. [Dublin, 1777], II:150).
96. George Rudé, *The Crowd in the French Revolution* (Oxford, 1959),
   App. VII, Table I, p. 251.
97. Chassin, *Elections*, II: 426, 463.
98. Restif de la Bretonne, *Les Nuits*, VIII: 1808.
99. *Ibid.*, VIII: 1860.
100. Restif de la Bretonne, *Les Nuits*, VIII: 1806–1807.
101. Mercier, *Tableau*, IX: 173–179. A similar complaint came from the
   flower vendors in 1789. They claimed in their *cahier de doléances*
   that unless they were allowed a monopoly of the trade, some flower
   girls would be unable to make a living and would fall into "libertinage
   and debauchery." Chassin, *Les Elections*, II: 534–537.
102. Léon Abensour, *La Femme et le féminisme avant la Révolution*
   (Paris, 1923), pp. 186ff., 198.
103. Mercier, *Tableau*, II: 253.
104. Jaubert, *Dictionnaire*, II: 343; Savary des Bruslons, *Dictionnaire*, II:
   625, 733; Franklin, *Dictionnaire*, 616.
105. Abensour, *La Femme et le féminisme*, pp. 23–26.
106. François Olivier-Martin, *Histoire de la coutume de la prévôté et
   vicomté de Paris*, 2 vols. (Paris, 1922–1930), II: 224ff; Gabriel Lebras,
   La Famille dans l'ancien droit, 4th ed. (Paris, 1953), pp. 326–328,
   381–382. See also Eusèbe de Laurière, *Textes des coutumes de la
   prévôté et vicomté de Paris*, 3 vols. (Paris, 1777), II: 192, art. 223.
107. François Furet and Adeline Daumard, *Structures et relations sociales
   à Paris au milieu du XVIIIe siècle* (Paris, 1961). In 1749, 30 percent
   of the marriages in the faubourg Saint Antoine, presumably among
   the poorest, were celebrated without contracts.
108. Le père Féline, *Catéchisme des gens mariés* (Rouen, 1880), pp. 46–50.
   This book was originally published in 1782.

109. Cf. Robert Joseph Pothier, *Traité de la puissance maritale* (Paris, 1774), cited by Abensour, *La Femme et le féminisme*, p. 8: "Le Mari a pleine puissance sur sa femme et les biens de sa femme. Il a le droit d'exiger tous les devoirs de soumission qui sont dûs à un supérieur."
110. Féline, *Catéchisme de gens mariés*, pp. 6–7, 13, 35.
111. Valentin J. Renoul de Bas-Champs, *Traité de l'autorité des parents sur le mariage des enfants de famille* (London, 1773), pp. 87–90.
112. Anne Marie Sifflet, "La Vie quotidienne dans le faubourg Saint Antoine" (unpub. D.E.S., Paris, 1960), p. 42ff.
113. Mercier, *Tableau*, III: 210ff; Malvaux, *Moyens*, pp. 13–14.
114. Peuchet, *Mémoires*, III: 94–95. Note the propensity to blame the women rather than the men for living in sin. Eve, the eternal temptress.
115. Adeline Daumard, *La Bourgeoisie parisienne, 1815–1848* (Paris, 1963), p. 526, n. 2.
116. Ms. 678, folio 181, Bibliothèque Historique de la Ville de Paris.
117. For a discussion of these disabilities, see Renée Barbarin, *La Condition juridique du batard d'après la jurisprudence du Parlement de Paris, du concile de Trente à la Révolution française* (Mayenne, 1960), pp. 117–119.
118. Mercier thought this to be the case. *Tableau*, IX: 173–179.
119. Faydit de Tersac, *Supplément à l'ordre*, p. 22. Mercier, on the other hand, thought that *l'homme du peuple* had more feeling than the petits bourgeois, by which expression he meant those who stood just above the artisans on the social ladder. *Tableau*, XII: 100–101:

> Le petit bourgeois, moins sensible que l'homme du peuple, caresse à peine ses enfants. Quand ils sont un peu grands, il les oublie, songe à amasser un petit pécule; il croit avoir tout fait pour les siens, quand il leur a fait faire leur première communion, c'est pour eux l'éducation complète.

120. Restif de la Bretonne, *Nuits*, III: 532. This viewpoint is shared by J. Charon, *Lettre ou mémoire historique sur les troubles populaires de Paris en Août et en Septembre, 1788* (London, 1788), p. 45n, who thought that sending girls to work so early was a cause of prostitution.
121. Denisart, *Collection*, IX: 519–520, art. on *"grossesse."*
122. Ms. Fr. 6684, folios 133, 308, 358, 500, Bibliothèque Nationale.
123. F^{12} 2459, Archives Nationales; P. A. Alletz, *Tableau de l'humanité et de la bienfaisance, ou précis historique des charités qui se font dans Paris* (Paris, 1789), p. 64.
124. AD XVI 10, Archives Nationales. An average of 5,589 children died each year beween 1781 and 1783. There is a record of one child who was killed when his cradle fell out of the coach that was taking him to a nurse in the country. Ms. Fr. 6682, folio 275, Bibliothèque Nationale.
125. Camille Bloch and Alexandre Tuetey, eds., *Procès-verbaux du comité de mendicité de la constituante* (Paris, 1911), p. 31. This estimate may have been based on a minute of the administrators of the Hôpital Général of January 1, 1761, in which it was noted that one-third, perhaps even one-half of the foundlings were legitimate. In 1760, how-

ever, only 735 of 5,032 children admitted to the Hôpital des enfants-trouvés were legitimate (14.6 percent). See *Annuaire statistique de la ville de Paris, 1880* (Paris, 1880), pp. 469–470.

126. Y 13730, 13829, 13829 bis, Archives Nationales; C 196, Archives Départementales de L'Yonne, Auxerre. See also Mercier, *Tableau*, V: 52.

127. Camille Bloch, *Assistance et l'état en France, 1764–1790* (Paris, 1908), p. 105.

128. AD I 23ᵇ, Archives Nationales.

129. AD XVI 10, F¹⁵ 2459, Archives Nationales. See also H supp. 2577–2580, Archives Départmentales de L'Yvonne, Auxerre. A substantial number of these children came from the Generality of Dijon, where the authorities systematically refused to be burdened with them unless given a royal subsidy, which was not forthcoming.

130. F¹⁵ 2470, Archives Nationales; Léon Lallemand, *Histoire des enfants abandonnés et délaissés* (Paris, 1885), p. 207.

131. GG³, Archives de la Seine; see also Albert Dupoux, *Sur les pas de Monsieur Vincent* (Paris, 1958), p. 102.

132. Alletz, *Tableau*, p. 67.

133. F. Evrard, "Le Travail des enfants dans l'industrie (1780–1870)," *Bulletin de la Société d'Etudes historiques, géographiques et scientifiques de la région parisienne*, no. 37 (1936): 1–14. This practice was not limited to foundlings alone. Young inmates of *dépôts de mendicité* were also hired out in this manner, in order that (1) the crown might save money, and (2) the children might learn a trade instead of going back to begging upon release. Letter from Abbé Terray to the Intendant of Tours, September 4, 1771, C 304, Archives Départementales de l'Indre-et-Loire, Tours.

134. Register of petitions addressed to Santerre, inspector of the quartier Saint Denis, 1779–1786, Aᵇ 405, Archives de la Préfecture de Police. See also Y 13700, AP II 154 (177 M 125), Archives Nationales.

135. Y 13163, Archives Nationales. See also the anonymous plea in 1751 for the creation of a moderately priced asylum in which parents might lock up their "enfants malvez [mal éléves], dérégléz, libertins ou corrompus" in Collection Joly de Fleury 1310, folios 130–131, Bibliothèque Nationale.

136. Ms. 1421, Bibliothèque d'Orléans. It did happen, however, that too loose a tongue was punished by short-term imprisonment, as in the case of the petty merchant Claire Bablet, who found herself in jail because she had called her sister-in-law a whore. Y 10558, Archives Nationales.

137. For further evidence, see Fréminville, *Dictionnaire*, p. 405ff:

> Il n'est que trop ordinaire à des artisans grossiers, les revenderesses, les ouvriers, compagnons et domestiques de se quereller, et de se répandre en injures les uns contre les autres, et même d'insulter dans les marchés, foires et lieux destinés au commerce. . . .

Chapter [3]

1. Joseph Lavallée, *Les Dernières adieux du quai de Gesvres à la bonne ville de Paris* (London, 1787), pp. 28–29.

Notes

2. Adeline Daumard, *Maisons de Paris et propriétaires parisiens au XIXe siècle* (Paris, 1965), p. 90.
3. Madeleine Jurgens and Pierre Couperic, "Le logement à Paris aux XVIe et XVIIIe siècles," *Annales: ESC*, XVIII (1962): 488–500.
4. de Lamare, *Dictionnaire*, IV: 122; Pierre Bullet, *Architecture pratique* (Paris, 1788), p. xiii.
5. Q² 118 and Q² 117, 120, Archives Nationales.
6. Léon Cahen, "Recherches sur l'agglomération parisienne au XVIIIe siècle," *Vie Urbaine*, IV (1922): 144.
7. Johann Jacob Volkmann, *Neueste Reisen durch Frankreich*, 3 vols. (Leipzig, 1787), I: 175. See also Louis Hautecoeur, *Histoire de l'architecture civile in France*, 7 vols. (Paris, 1943–1957), vol. IV, *Architecture classique*, p. 406 and J. C. Villiers, Earl of Clarendon, *A Tour through Part of France* (London, 1789), pp. 89–90.
8. G. Perrin, "La Section des Lombards" (unpub. D.E.S., Paris, 1963), pp. 63–67; also printed in Commission d'Histoire Economique et Sociale de la Révolution, *Contribution à l'histoire démographique de la Révolution française*, 2nd ser. (Paris, 1965), pp. 70–72.
9. See plans in Charles Antoine Jombert, *Architecture moderne, ou l'Art de bâtir pour toutes sortes de personnes*, 2 vols. (Paris, 1764). See also Michel Gallet, *Demeures parisiennes—l'époque de Louis XVI* (Paris, 1964), pp. 77–82.
10. Anne Marie Sifflet, "La Vie quotidienne dans le faubourg Saint Antoine" (unpub. D.E.S., Paris, 1960), pp. 148–149, 171–172.
11. Bullet, *Architecture pratique*, p. 587; Jombert, *Architecture moderne*, I: 136.
12. Jean de la Monneraye, *La Crise du logement à Paris pendant la Révolution* (Paris, 1928), pp. 6–7. He cites the statement of the executive of an unidentified section in Brumaire, year III (October–November 1794), calling for a reduction of rents to the level of 1764: "C'est de ce temps où l'augmentation subite des baux fit suivre de près celle des denrées qui réduisit le peuple à cette affreuse misère qu'il ressent encore aujord'hui." [P. 11, n. 2.]
13. Arts. 161 and 171 of the Coutume de Paris allowed landlords to seize furniture for nonpayment of rent. See Antoine Babuty Desgodets, *Les Loix des batiments*, new ed. (Paris, 1787), p. 462ff.
14. Mercier, *Tableau*, X: 350–359, and I: 254–258.
15. Rents due the parish of Saint Roch, 1768, 3 AZ 114, Archives de la Seine; rents due the city of Paris, Q¹ 1099¹⁹⁴, 195–196, Archives Nationales.
16. Jèze, *Etat ou tableau de la ville de Paris* (Paris, 1760), pp. 31–70.
17. Anon., *Letters on the French Nation* (London, 1749), p. 26.
18. Ms. Fr. 6682, folio 452, Bibliothèque Nationale.
19. L. A. Caraccioli, *Lettre d'un indien à Paris*, 2 vols. (Paris and Amsterdam, 1789), I: 256. Earlier in the century, an Englishman testified: "Would you live incognito all your life? Go lodge in a House, where there's eight or ten Families. He that lies nearest to you shall be the last Man that knows who you are." [Anon., *An Agreeable Criticism of the City of Paris and the French*, 2nd ed. (London, 1706), p. 52.] This opinion was shared by Lapeyre, *Les Moeurs de Paris* (Amsterdam, 1747), p. 163: "Les gens à Paris sont logés jusques sur les toits, ceux qui ont demeuré lontemps dans la même maison ne

se conoissent point, on vit avec beaucoup de circonspection, on n'ose pas mettre sa confiance en personne. Si les amis sont rares partout, íls le sont encore plus à Paris qu'ailleurs."

20. Philippe Ariès, *Histoire des populations françaises et de leurs attitudes devant la vie* (Paris, 1948), pp. 276–278.

21. Robert Philippe, "Une opération pilote: l'étude du ravitaillement de Paris au temps de Lavoisier," *Annales: ESC*, XVI (1961): 564–568.

22. A similar criticism has been voiced by Albert Soboul in *AHRF*, XXXIII (1961): 418–419. For a more successful beginning in dealing with these questions, see Jean-Paul Aron, *Essai sur la sensibilité alimentaire à Paris au XIXe siècle* (Paris, 1967): 111–124 especially.

23. For most of what follows, see Léon Cahen, "L'Approvisionnement en pain de Paris au XVIIIe siècle et la question de la boulangerie," *Revue d'Histoire économique et social*, XIV (1926): 458–472; idem., "La question du pain à Paris à la fin du XVIIIe siècle," *Cahiers de la Révolution française*, I (1934): 51–76. There are slightly different figures in Paucton, *Métrologie ou traité des mesures, poids, et monnaies des anciens peuples et des modernes* (Paris, 1780), pp. 498–499.

24. P. J. Buch'oz, *L'Art de préparer les aliments*, 2nd ed., 2 vols. (Paris, 1787), I: 56.

25. Pierre-Jean-Baptiste Legrand d'Aussy, *Histoire de le vie privée des français*, 3 vols. (Paris, 1782), I: 81, 109, 112: "La police de Paris est si admirable que le bas peuple y mange du pain blanc."

26. Michel-Antoine Lair-Duvaucelles, *Mémoire sur le sujet proposé au concours par la municipalité et le conseil-général de la commune de Paris, relativement aux meilleurs moyens d'alimenter la capitale* (Paris, 1791).

27. Friedrich Schulz, *Ueber Paris und die Pariser* (Berlin, 1791), pp. 57–59.

28. Mercier, *Tableau*, V: 218–223.

29. On regulations governing the markets, see Jean Martineau, *Les Halles de Paris des origines à 1789* (Paris, 1960), pp. 176–233.

30. Y 12826, Archives Nationales.

31. Peysonnel, *Ley Numeros*, 2nd ed., 3 pts. (Paris, 1783), pp. 7–8.

32. Léon Cahen, "Le Pacte de famine et les spéculations sur les blés," *Revue Historique*, XLII (1926): 33–43.

33. The events of 1768 can be followed in Hardy, *Mes Loisirs*, entries for the months July through November.

34. Anon., *An Account of the Model in Relievo of the Great and Magnificent City and Suburbs of Paris by Monsieur Le Quoy, architect to his present most Christian majesty, Lewis the XVth* (London, 1771), pp. 27–28; Anon., *Essai sur le commerce de Paris, ou Abrégé historique et politique . . . par un ancien officier militaire* (Amsterdam, 1775), pp. 4–18. See also H 1952[1], Archives Nationales.

35. Jean Vidalenc, "L'Approvisionnement de Paris en viande à la fin de l'ancien régime," *RHES*, XXX (1952): 116–132.

36. Anon., *Essai sur le commerce*, pp. 44–49.

37. Ms. 1421, Titre 4, Bibliothèque d'Orléans.

38. Gustave Bienaymé, *Prix des principaux objets de consommation à Paris* (Paris, 1895); Hardy, *Mes Loisirs*, pp. 169, 178, 332. See also account book of M. de Chataux, wine merchant of the rue Royale, 1783, Y 13322, Archives Nationales.

39. Jean Vidalenc, "Une industrie alimentaire à Paris au XVIIIe siècle:

la préparation et la vente des tripes et abats," *Paris et Ile de France*, I (1949): 279–295.

40. Mercier, *Tableau*, V: 107. It also seems that butchers were able to charge the same price for better and poorer cuts of meat but that they reserved the former for the elite. See also Jean-Baptiste Michel de Chevigné *dit* Jaillot, *Lettres sur les embellissements de Paris* (Paris, 1778), p. 12.

41. Menon, *La Cuisinière bourgeoise* (Brussels, 1759). See also Menuret de Chambaud, *Essais dur l'histoire médico-topographique de Paris* (Paris, 1786), p. 93ff.

42. Mercier, *Tableau*, I: 206–207.

43. Ibid., XII: 128, and III: 201–204.

44. Ibid., III: 46–51.

45. Martineau, *Halles*, pp. 218–219; *Essai sur le commerce*, pp. 50–51, 135–142; Jaillot, *Lettres*, pp. 12–13. The regrattiers had been allowed by a ruling of 1694 to pursue their trade without joining the guild of the merchant fruiterers. See F. Oliver-Martin, *L'Organisation corporative de la France* (Paris, 1938), p. 106. See also Y 11037, 13163, Archives Nationales.

46. Amaury Duval, *Les Fontaines de Paris anciennes et nouvelles* (Paris, 1828), p. xi.

47. Some water carriers were privileged, that is, had the right to the exclusive use of certain fountains. This privilege was abolished by police ordinance on September 25, 1789, and a new rule was adopted whereby private citizens seeking water for personal use were to be served before the water carriers. H 1969, Archives Nationales.

48. J. J. Menuret de Chambaud, *Essais*, pp. 46–47, 93ff. See also A. Z. of the Middle Temple [William Lucas] *A Five Weeks Tour to Paris, Versailles, Marli*, etc. (London, 1750), p. 13, who warns against drinking water or "small wines, for so doing will most assuredly throw you into a violent looseness, and no place in the elegant and delicate world is so ill provided with conveniences for such a condition as Paris is. . . ."

49. Peysonnel, *Les Numéros*, 2nd ed., 3 pts. (Paris, 1783), II: 85–86; Darigrand, *Mémoire pour les habitans de la banlieue de Paris* (Paris, 1789), p. 44n.

50. Legrand d'Aussy, *Histoire*, III: 314–315. A *muid* contained 300 *pintes*.

51. De Sartine to the Syndics of the Commissaires du Châtelet, February 5, 1774, Y 15114, Archives Nationales.

52. Anon., *An Agreeable Criticism*, pp. 11, 24.

53. Roger Dion, *Histoire de la vigne et du vin en France des origines au XIXe siècle* (Paris, 1959), pp. 482, 510–511, 518. See also H² 1957, 1958, 1959, Archives Nationales.

54. J. Meuvret, "Les Crises de subsistances et la démographie de la France d'ancien régime," *Population*, I (1946): 643–650.

55. Messance, *Recherches sur la population des généralités d'Auverque* . . . (Paris, 1766), pp. 181–183.

56. Roger Mols, *Introduction à la demographie historique des villes d'Europe du XIVe au XVIIIe siècle*, 3 vols. (Gem'bloux, 1955–1956), II: 263–265.

57. Guillaume Daignan, *Tableau des variétés de la vie humaine*, 2 vols.

(Paris, 1786), II: 303. According to Kareiev, the section of Sainte Geneviève/Panthéon Français, which corresponded to the territory of the parish, had a population density of 320 per 1,000 square *toises*. This gave it 11th place among 48 sections. The 10 sections that had greater densities were all located on the Right Bank in the center of the city.

58. A. Chevallier and G. Lagneau, "Quelques remarques sur le mouvement de la population de Paris à un et deux siècles d'intervalle," *Annales d'Hygiène publique et de médicine légale*, 2nd series, XXXIX (Paris, 1873). See also the similar calculations by des Pommelles and Bertillon, cited by Mols, *Introduction*, II: 330, 332.

59. Dossier C II 160[114c, 114e], C 216, Archives Nationales; François Dupon, "Contribution à l'étude de la population de Paris à l'époque de la Révolution" (unpub. D.E.S., Paris, 1962). Note the similarities found by Martine Plessier, "La Population à Versailles en 1744," typescript in Archives Départementales, Seine-et-Oise, Versailles.

60. J. Bourgeois-Pichat, "Evolution générale," *Population*, VI (1951): 642, Table II. On January 1, 1967, the proportions were as follows: 33.9 percent under 20, 37.1 percent from 20 to 49, 11.2 percent from 50 to 59, and 17.6 percent over 60. *Annuaire statistique de la France*, LXXIII (1967): 32–33, Table IV.

61. Dupon, "La population de Paris"; Marianne Picard, "La Section de la place Vendôme pendant la Révolution" (unpublished D.E.S., Paris, 1963), pp. 46–54.

62. Buffon (1745–1766), Messance (1752–1761), Moheau (1768–1775), and des Pommelles (1789) all arrived at essentially similar results. See Mols, *Introduction*, II: 219–221, 289–290; Messance, *Recherches*, 137.

63. Antoine Deparcieux, *Essai sur les probabilités de la durée de la vie humaine* (Paris, 1746), p. 70.

64. Bourgeois-Pichat, "Evolution générale," p. 658. See also A. J. P. Paucton, *Métrologie*, p. 488.

65. Ms. 1421, Titre III, Bibliothèque d'Orléans. Duplanil added yet another reason for this state of affairs:

> Dans les grandes villes, les enfants, pour la plupart, périssent faute d'air pur. Les pauvres y vivent, dans des maisons basses et humides, dans lesquelles l'air extérieur ne peut point circuler. Quoique des hommes forts et robustes puissent exister dans de telles habitations, cependant elles deviennent nuisibles aux enfants, dont un petit nombre parvient à l'age viril, et qui, lorsqu'ils y sont arrivés sont foibles et mal conformés. Le peuple n'étant point en état de faire promener ses enfants en plein air, nous ne devons point être étonnes qu'il en périsse la plus grande partie. Mais les riches n'ont point d'excuses à alléguer.

See his translation of William Buchan, *Médecine domestique*, 2nd ed., 3 vols. (Paris, 1780), I: 72–73.

66. Philippe Hecquet, *Médecine, Chirurgie et la pharmacie des pauvres*, new ed., 3 vols. (Paris, 1742), II: 239, 291ff; Deparcieux, *Essai*, pp. 39–41. See also Menuret de Chambaud, *Essais*, new ed. (Paris, 1804), p. 98:

> . . . les [pauvres] sont presque forcés par la misère, par le besoin de travailler, par le défaut de logement, par le manque d'aides et de com-

modité de se décharger sur des femmes de la campagne de ce fardeau et de cet embarras. Les nourrices mercenaires emportent au loin ces petits êtres, ou ce qui est encore pis, les gardent dans la ville, enfermés dans des logemens étroits et mal aérés; la plupart les emprisonnent encore dans les liens serrés du maillot, presque toutes les gorgent de bouillie . . . et déposent ainsi journellement dans leur ventre le germe des gonflements et des obstructions, les principes du rachitis, qu'on observe si souvent chez eux.

67. There can be little doubt that mortality was high in the country. See the register of deaths of foundlings, Archives of the Public Assistance Administration, Paris.
68. Joseph Raulin, *De la conservation des enfants*, 2 vols. in 3 (Paris, 1769), II: 374ff. Rousseau gave his patronage to this campaign. See also Roger Mercier, *L'Enfant au XVIIIe siècle* (Dakar and Paris, 1961).
69. Raulin, *Conservation*, II: 275–276.
70. J. J. Gardane, *Détail de la nouvelle direction du Bureau des Nourrices de Paris* (Paris, 1775). The author advised the doctors not to scare potential nurses during the medical examination for

naturellement timides & même farouches, elles s'effrayent à la moindre question. C'est pourquoi il faut les interroger avec beaucoup de douceur & les rassurer; sans cela le saisissement qu'elles éprouvent les mettroit dans l'impossibilité de donner du lait & l'on concluroit souvent qu'elles n'en ont point ou qu'elles en manquent, lorsqu'elles en ont abondamment.

71. H 1963, Archives Nationales; troupes provinciales, 1778–1779, C 617, Archives Départementales du Jura, Lons-le-Saulnier; provincial regiment of Paris, 1756–1767, Y[13] C 112, Archives de la Guerre, Vincennes.
72. J. P. Leclerc, "Paris en 1773, Lettre d'une descendante des Huguenots," *La Cité*, III (1904): 50.
73. Restif de la Bretonne, *Les Nuits*, II: 246–247. Similar observations in Maille Dussausoy, *Le Citoyen désintéressé*, 2 vols. (Paris, 1767), II: 128, and Hester Lynch Piozzi, *Observations and Reflections Made on the Course of a Journey through France, Italy and Germany*, 2 vols. (London, 1789), I: 18:

I will tell nothing that I did not *see*; and among the objects one would certainly avoid seeing if it were possible is the deformity of the poor.— Such various modes of warping the human figure could hardly be observed in England by a surgeon in high practice, as meet me about this country incessantly.

74. Y[13] C 112, Archives de la Guerre, Vincennes. Hardy spoke of the "cruelles angoisses, les déchiremens de coeur qu'occasionnioent la perte d'enfans uniques enlevés à la fleur de l'age, et peut-être trop idolatrés pour pouvoir échapper aux justes décrets d'un dieu jaloux qui veut être aimé pardessus toutes choses." Ms. Fr. 6684, folio 4, Bibliothèque Nationale.
75. Mercier, *Tableau*, IV: 211–214.
76. See, for example, M. Geoffroy, "Constitution des années 1787 et 1788, avec le détail des maladies qui ont regné pendant ces deux années à Paris," *Histoire de la Société Royale de Médecine*, 2nd pt.: *Mémoires de médecine et physique médicale*, IX (1787–1788): [Paris, 1790],

pp. 1–46. A copy may be found in the library of the Académie de
Médecine, under call number 92466.

77. Joseph-Marie Audin-Rouvière, *Essai sur la topographie physique et
médicale de Paris* (Paris, an II [1793–1794]); C. Lachaise, *Topographie
médicale de Paris* (Paris, 1822); Menuret de Chambaud, *Essais sur
l'histoire médico-topographique de Paris* (Paris, 1786).

78. Joseph Levine, *Atlas métérologique de Paris* (Paris, 1921), p. 58,
Table X. There were occasional winters when the Seine remained
frozen for a month or two (1762–1763, 1788–1789, 1794–1795). See
also Menuret de Chambaud, *Essais*, pp. 17–20, 30; Lachaise, *Topographie*, pp. 45–46.

79. Report on the cemetery of the Holy Innocents by Louis Lemery,
François Joseph Hunauld (both doctors), and Claude Joseph Geoffroy
(an apothecary) in Collection Joly de Fleury, 1317, folios 61ff,
Bibliothèque Nationale. See also Jacques de Horne, *Mémoire sur
quelques objets qui intéressent plus particulièrement la salubrité de
la ville de Paris* (Paris, 1788), p. 4.

80. Y 9538, Archives Nationales.

81. J. J. Menuret de Chambaud, *Essai sur l'action de l'air dans les maladies
contagieuses* (Paris, 1781), pp. xx–xxi; de Horne, *Mémoire*, pp. 11–12,
and Anon., *Vœu général et particulier des habitants de la bonne ville de
Paris sur l'établisement indispensable des tueries générales au dehors
des ses barrières* (n. p., n. d.), where the muse is invoked to denounce
the horror:

> . . . Paris partout regorge
> De foyers d'où la mort décoche ses traits lents;
> Ces animaux, que, pour, nos aliments,
> L'insensible Boucher égorge
> Semblent pour le punir de sa ferocité,
> Se résoudre en vapeur mortelle;
>
> . . .
>
> Mais quel spectacle hideux! . . . de quelle horreur nouvelle
> Tous mes sens bouleversé à l'instant sont saisis?
> Des débris dégoûtants des bêtes égorgées
> Partout des voitures chargées
> Traînent l'infection, en inondent Paris. . . .

82. J. H. Ronesse, *Vue sur la propreté des rues de Paris* (Paris, 1782) pp.
31–36.

83. Audin-Rouvière, *Essai*, p. 26.

84. J. Rousset, "Essai de pathologie urbaine, les causes de morbidité et
de mortalité à Lyon aux XVIIe et XVIIIe siècles," *Cahiers d'Histoire*,
VIII (1963): 71–105.

85. William Buchan, *Médecine domestique*, II: 116.

86. J. B. N. Boyer, *Méthode à suivre dans le traitement des différentes
maladies épidémiques qui règnent le plus ordinairement dans la gén-
éralité de Paris* (Paris, 1761), p. 4.

87. Buchan, *Médecine Domestique*, I: 269.

88. M. Fosseyeux, *L'Hôtel-Dieu au XVIIe et au XVIIIe siècles* (Paris,
1912), p. 310.

89. Philippe Patissier, *Traité des maladies des artisans* (Paris, 1822). This is an adaptation and up-dating of Ramazzini's work, which had first been translated into French by de Fourcroy in 1777.
90. Lachaise, *Topographie*, p. 202.
91. Patissier, *Traité*, pp. 302–305; Lachaise, *Topographie*, p. 280.
92. Buchan, *Médecine domestique*, I: 116–117.
93. Anon., *Etat des médecins et chirurgiens de France* (Paris, 1772). In 1772, there were 152 docteurs-régens of the Faculty of Medicine of Paris (of whom 17 were nonresident) and 223 surgeons (20 nonresident). See also the pleas for the institution of a state medical service by D. N. Retz, *Motion d'une utilité remarquable proposée à l'assemblée des Etats-généraux* (Paris, 1789), p. 9: "... les seuls secours que les gens de la campagne, et le plus grand nombre des habitants des villes, puissent se procurer dans leurs maladies, sont ceux des chirurgiens qui font partout la médecine au rabais, ou des apothicaires qui ont coutume d'être consultés pour les maladies des pauvres, et qui ont la cruauté de vendre leurs avis comme leurs drogues."
94. [Arnault de Nobleville], *Le Manuel des dames de charité ou formules de médicamens faciles à preparer*, 4th ed. (Paris, 1758), *passim*, especially pp. xi, 5.
95. Ibid., pp. viii–ix.
96. Ms. Fr. 6684, folio 185, Bibliothèque Nationale.
97. Ms. Fr. 6684, folio 190, Bibliothèque Nationale. See also P. Alletz, *L'Albert moderne* (Paris, 1768), pp. 3, 127–129:

> ... si on prend six à sept gouttes [de cet elixir], on vit longtemps sans avoir besoin de saignée, ni d'autres médicamens. Il restitue les forces, anime les esprits vitaux, aiguise les sens, ôte les tremblements de nerfs, émousse les douleurs de rhumatisme et les douleurs de la goutte, l'empêche de remonter, nettoye l'estomach de toutes les humeurs crasses et gluantes, guérit les coliques, les indigestions, purifie le sang, est un contrepoison parfait, provoque les mois aux femmes, purge imperceptiblement et sans douleur, guérit les fièvres intermittentes: A la troisième dose, il est un préservatif contre les maladies contagieuses, fait pousser la petite vérole sans risque.

For another cure-all see Anon., *Observations sur le baume de vie composé par le sieur Lelievre* (Paris, 1758), copy available in Bibliothèque Historique de la Ville de Paris, call number 12237.
98. Mols, *Introduction*, II, 271, 273–274.
99. Buffon: III, 379–382, cited by Mols, *Introduction*, II: 278–279, III: 138.
100. Mols, *Introduction*, II: 325.
101. J. G. C. Blacker, "Social Ambitions of the Bourgeoisie in Eighteenth-Century France," *Population Studies*, XI (1957): 46–63.
102. See the articles by Philippe Ariès and Alfred Sauvy in Institut National d'Etudes Demographiques, *La Prévention des naissances dans la famille* (Paris, 1960).
103. Cited by Alfred Sauvy, "Some lesser-known French Demographers of the Eighteenth Century," *Population Studies*, V (1951–1952), pt. I: 4–5, 12.
104. Le Père Féline, *Catéchisme des gens mariés* (Rouen, 1880), pp. 8–9, 40–41.

Chapter [4]

1. F^{12} 245, 436, Archives Nationales.
2. F^{15} 2889, Archives Nationales.
3. Restif de la Bretonne, *Nuits*, II: 266–267.
4. For this and much of what follows, see P. A. Alletz, *Tableau de l'humanité et de la bienfaisance, ou Précis historique des charités qui se font dans Paris* (Paris, 1769).
5. Collection Joly de Fleury 2543, Bibliothèque Nationale.
6. F^{12} 245, Archives Nationales; Maurice Tourneux, ed., "Journal intime de l'Abbé Mulot (1777–1782)," *Mémoires de la Société de l'histoire de Paris et de l'Ile de France*, XXIX (1902): 71. See also papers of Guichard, procureur du roi en la chambre de commerce et administrateur de l'hospice de Vaugirard, T 930^2, Archives Nationales.
7. Jean Baptiste Charles Le Maire, *Détail sur quelques établissements de la ville de Paris demandé par Sa Majesté Impériale la Reine de Hongrie à M. Lenoir* (Paris, 1780), pp. 3–6, 13–17.
8. "Etat de l'Hôpital général de Paris," 1748, N. S. 41, Archives de l'Assistance Publique.
9. M. Fosseyeux, *L'Hôtel-Dieu au XVIIe et au XVIIIe siècles* (Paris, 1912), pp. 318–320.
10. Camille Bloch, *L'Assistance et l'état en France, 1764–1790* (Paris, 1908), p. 87.
11. Rondonneau de la Motte, *Essai historique sur l'Hôtel-Dieu de Paris* (Paris, 1787), p. 187; François Coguel, *La Vie parisienne sous Louis XVI* (Paris, 1882), pp. 50–51; Abbé de Récalde, *Traité sur les abus qui subsistent dans les hôpitaux* (Saint Quentin and Paris, 1786), pp. 48–49.
12. Anon., *Un Malade à l'Hôtel-Dieu de Paris, aux âmes sensibles* (Paris, 1787), p. 13:

> Quelle demeure affreuse! O honte! O ma Patrie!
> Toi, dont l'humanité charme tout l'univers,
> Vois ce triste cloaque où la Faux ennemie
> Fait de vastes moissons depuis cinq cents hivers;
> Maudissans les secours d'une charité dure,
> Vois tous ces Malheureux, par milliers amassés,
> Dans ce réduit infect, accusans la nature,
> Et sur un seul grabat l'un sur l'autre entassés,
> Respirans avec l'air le mélange funeste
> De poisons échapés au foyer de la peste.

13. Alletz, *Tableau*, p. 53; Récalde, *Traité sur les abus*, 53.
14. BB^{30} 70, Archives Nationales.
15. Eugene Sue, *Mystères de Paris*, 3 vols. (Paris, 1963), I: 49. This book was originally published in 1842.
Rodolphe asks the poor working-girl heroine, Fleur-de-Marie, what she wants out of life, and she answers:

> Ma liberté, vivre à la campagne, et être sûre de ne pas mourir à l'hôpital. . . . Oh! cela surtout . . . ne pas mourir là! Tenez, Monsieur Rodolphe, souvent cette pensée-là me vient . . . elle est affreuse!

> Ce n'est pas pour la misère . . . que je dis cela. . . . Mais après . . . quand on est morte. . . .
>
> Il y à une jeune fille que j'avais connue en prison . . . elle est morte à l'hôpital . . . on a abandonné son corps aux chirurgiens . . . murmura la malheueuse en frissonnant.

16. F^{15} 397, Archives Nationales: Yvonne Bézard, *L'Assistance à Versailles sous l'ancien régime et pendant la Révolution* (Versailles, 1924), p. 46; Messance, *Recherches et considérations sur la population de la France* (Paris, 1788), pp. 181–183.

17. Bloch, *L'Assistance et l'état*, p. 88.

18. Dupont de Nemours [d'après Barbier], *Idées sur les secours à donner aux pauvres malades dans une grande ville* (Philadelphia and Paris, 1786), *passim*, especially p. 43f.

19. Léon Cahen, "Les Idées charitables à Paris au XVIIe et au XVIIIe siècles," *Revue d'Histoire moderne et contemporaine*, II (1900–1901): 5–22.

20. Arrest de la Cour de Parlement servant de règlement pour les pauvres de la paroisse Saint Nicolas des Champs de Paris, 1764, art. 32, Collection Joly de Fleury 1570, Bibliothèque Nationale.

21. As in the parish of Saint Eustache. See Alletz, *Tableau*, p. 241.

22. Eléonore Marie Desbois de Rochefort, curé de Saint André des Arts, *Mémoire sur les calamités de l'hiver 1788–1789* (Paris, 1789), pp. 24–25.

23. Ibid., p. 7.

24. Faydit de Tersac, curé de Saint Sulpice, *Ordre d'administration pour le soulagement des pauvres de la paroisse de Saint Sulpice* (Paris, 1777).

25. Léon Cahen, *Le Grand bureau des pauvres de Paris au milieu du XVIIIe siècle* (Paris, 1904), pp. 26–27.

26. Ibid., pp. 18–20; Ms. N. S. 61, Archives de l'Assistance Publique.

27. Ms. N. S. 98, 1st bundle, 3rd and 4th registers, Archives de l'Assistance Publique.

28. It is curious to note that the Grand Bureau had a surplus at the very time that the situation of the *menu peuple* was worsening because of a rise in bread prices. J. J. Trudon, *avocat au Parlement* and *commissaire* of the Grand Bureau in the parish of Saint Paul, collected 4,731 livres in poor taxes in 1774 but distributed only 1,040 livres to the poor in 1775. The real state of the parish was not such as to warrant this kind of economy. See T ^{35} cote 5, Archives Nationales.

29. *Calendrier philanthropique*, année 1787 (Paris, 1787), p. xxxiv.

30. Tableaux de la comptabilité du Mont de Piété, année 1789 (Paris, 1789), copy in the Bibliothèque Historique de la Ville de Paris, call number 12834; Anon., *Aux Montagnards, aux vrais amis des sans-culottes* (Paris, an II [1794]), copy in the British Museum, call number 31* 2* (18). The word "capitalist" is used here to denote a usurer.

31. Y 13162, Archives Nationales.

32. Le Maire, *Détail*, p. 32.

33. F^{11} 1191, H^2 1959, 1960, Archives Nationales. The curé of Saint André des Arts further alleged that it would be difficult to get Parisians to cooperate in such a scheme, but the overwhelming number of applications for work proved him wrong. See Desbois de Rochefort, *Mémoire*, p. 27.

34. See F^{15} 3560, Archives Nationales, for figures concerning the expenses of the *atelier de filature des pauvres de Paris*, 1778–1789; see also Ms. Fr. N. A. 2799, 1767–1778, Bibliothèque Nationale, for money spent on wiping out beggary; see also papers of Bertier de Sauvigny, the last intendant of the Generality of Paris, 80 AP 12, Archives Nationales.
35. Ms. Fr. 6683, folio 13; and Ms. Fr. 6684, folio 409, Bibliothèque Nationale.
36. Police ordinance of July 1, 1718, 6 AZ 133, Archives de la Seine; Ms. Fr. 6684, folio 410, Bibliothèque Nationale.
37. René Baehrel, "Epidémie et terreur; histoire et sociologie," *Annales Historiques de la Révolution Française*, XXIII (1951): 113–146.
38. Restif de la Bretonne, *Nuits*, III: 651.
39. Edmond Jean François Barbier, *Journal historique et anecdotique du règne de Louis XV*, 4 vols. (Paris, 1847–1856), II: 283–284; F. Duval and A. Barroux, *Inventaire sommaire des archives communales [de Saint Denis] antérieures à 1790* (Saint Denis, 1923), col. 148.
40. Cf. Mercier, *Tableau*, I: 191: ". . . il n'y a guère de pendus que dans la classe de la populace: le voleur de la lie du peuple, sans famille, sans appui, sans protections, excite d'autant moins de pitié, qu'on s'est montré indulgent pour d'autres."
41. Ms. Fr. 6684, folio 494, Bibliothèque Nationale.
42. Mercier, *Tableau*, X: 3–4.
43. Marcel Fosseyeux, "Les Ecoles de charité à Paris sous l'ancien régime et dans la première partie du XIXe siècle," *Mémoire de la Société de l'histoire de Paris et de l'Ile de France*, XXXIX (1912): 225–366.
44. Ibid., p. 292; le citoyen Renaud, ancien instituteur, *Mémoire historique sur la ci-devant communauté des Ecoles Chrétiennes du faubourg Saint Antoine* (Paris, an XII [1803–1804]), a copy in the Bibliothèque Historique de la Ville de Paris, call number 959260.
45. Anon., *Règlement pour les Ecoles de charité de la paroisse de Saint Gervais* (Paris, 1710), pp. 3, 60.
46. *Ibid.*, pp. 5–20. On the matter of familiarity, children were expressly discouraged from calling each other "tu." Was this merely in conformity to the forms of the age? Or was the interdiction calculated to destroy a budding sense of community among the laboring poor, the lesson being: depend not on each other but only on the Church?
47. Ya 42, Archives de la Guerre, Vincennes.
48. A. P. Herlaut, "Les Abus du recrutement au XVIIIe siècle," *Revue du XVIIIe siècle*, I (1913): 294–301.
49. Paul d'Estrée, ed., "Journal intime du Lieutenant-général de Police Feydeau de Marville (1744)," from *Nouvelle Revue Retrospective* (April 10, 1897): 8, 20. These are notes by the Chevalier de Mouhy, a police spy.
50. Yc^{13} 112, Archives de la Guerre, Vincennes. See also Chevalier des Pommelles, *Tableau de la population de toutes les provinces de la France* (Paris, 1789), pp. 33–34, 52. He estimates that Paris furnished 6,000 to 7,000 recruits each year and that there were as many as 3,000 desertions annually (4,200 in 1766) throughout the kingdom. An anonymous letter of 1768 to Joly de Fleury tells the story of

conditions in the army (Collection Joly de Fleury 2075, Bibliothèque
Nationale):

> Sy on n'ose prendre la liberté de vous écrire c'est pour implorer votre
> secours au sujet du pauvre soldat. On le chagrine de tous côtés. Il est mal
> nourri, mourant presque de faim. Le pain est si cher qu'il n'est pas
> possible de vivre puisque il y a un soldat qui s'est pendu de désespoir.
> Monseigneur, à l'exercice on voit tomber les pauvres soldats de faim
> et de faiblesses. Sy les déserteurs étoient comme ils étoient auparavant sur
> les pays ennemis, on verroit des régimens entiers déserte parce[que] on
> meurt de faim par toute la France.

It appears that deserters could return to Paris and live there with a
certain degree of impunity because of the inefficiency of the maréchaussée in rounding them up. See letter from Maréchal de Segur to
the Prévôt-général de l'Ile de France, November 19, 1786, E 1806,
Archives Départementales de la Seine-et-Oise, Versailles.

51. A. P. Herlaut, *Le Recrutement de la milice à Paris en 1743* (Coulom-
    miers, 1921).
52. Antoine Delcer, "Les Arrêts de police du Parlement de Paris (1774–
    1790)" (Faculté de Droit, Paris, unpub. thesis DZ 1959/149), p. 26;
    Abbé de Boyer, *Principles de l'administration temporelle des parois-
    ses*, 2 vols. (Paris, 1786), I: 32. Even the small rentier could not
    always hope to become a vestryman, the preference usually going
    to a merchant of some wealth. In a popular parish like Saint Médard, a
    master artisan might occasionally be named to this post. See Mercier,
    Tableau, XII: 100–101; Marcel Brogniart, *La Paroisse Saint Médard
    au fauborg Saint Marceau* (Paris, 1951), p. 96.
53. *Statuts synodaux du diocèse de Paris* (1777 ed.), art. 27.
54. A. de Boislisle, ed., *Lettres de M. de Marville, lieutenant-général de
    police, au ministre Maurepas (1742–1747)*, 3 vols. (Paris, 1896–1905),
    I: 206.
55. Ms. Fr., 6683, folio 487, Bibliothèque Nationale.
56. *Journal encyclopédique*, October, 1775, p. 183, cited in *Bulletin de la
    Société de l'Histoire de Paris et de l'Ile de France*, XXXVIII (1911):
    297–298. The anonymous author of *Un Malade de l'Hôtel-Dieu* com-
    plained (page 18):

> Ah! Que fait-on du pauvre après des jours affreux?
> Son destin finit-il au séjour ténébreux [à l'hôpital]?
> Non . . . vois, coeur bienfaisant, jusqu'où va la misère
> De l'homme infortuné, ton image, ton frère:
> D'ossements entassés grossissant le monceau,
> Vois l'Inhumanité, sordide ménagère,
> A peine lui donner un linceul, un tombeau.
> Quand ses yeux pour jamais sont clos à la lumière,
> Dans un linge grossier, son corps porté sans deuil,
> Gît souvent par morceaux dans un peu de poussière:
> Vois cent Spectres errants demander un cercueil,
> Voilà donc, Indigents! vos tristes funérailles.

57. Ms. Fr. 6683, folios 219, 273, Bibliothèque Nationale.
58. Ms. Fr. 6681, folios 326, 378–379, Bibliothèque Nationale.

59. Mercier, *Tableau*, III: 185–188, and I: 191. See also Laliman, *Moyens propres à garantir les hommes du suicide* (Paris, 1779).
60. Mercier, *Tableau*, IV: 151 and X: 344.
61. Anon., *An Agreeable Criticism of the City of Paris and of the French*, 2nd ed. (London, 1706), p. 11.
62. Descriptions of the guinguettes and the goings-on there can be found scattered throughout the literature of the *genre poissard*. See, for example, André Charles Cailleau [d'après Barbier], *Le Goûté des Porcherons* (Paris, n. d., *circa* 1760), and Jean-Joseph Vadé, *La Pipe cassée—Poème épitragipoissardihéroicomique*, 3rd. ed. (Paris, 1755).
63. Anon., *Letters on the French Nation* (London, 1749), p. 16.
64. Peysonnel, *Les Numéros*, 2nd. ed., 3 pts. (Paris, 1783), I: 85–88.
65. Ibid., II: 118–119. See also Restif de la Bretonne, *Nuits*, VIII: 1705.
66. Anon., *Errors of Pronunciation and Improper Expressions used frequently, and chiefly by the Inhabitants of London, to which is added, Those in similar use, chiefly by the Inhabitants of Paris* (London, 1817), pp. 39, 49, 61–62.
67. A. P. Moore, *The Genre Poissard and the French Stage of the Eighteenth Century* (New York, 1935), p. 360.
68. Examples taken from Cailleau, *Le Goûté*; and Anon., *Code poissard* (Paris, n. d. but appears to be of the revolutionary period).
69. L. Sainéan, *Les Sources de l'argot ancien*, 2 vols. (Paris, 1912), I: 81.
70. Mercier, *Tableau*, V: 213–218.
71. Edme de la Paix de Fréminville, *Dictionnaire ou traité de la police générale des villes, bourgs, paroisses et seigneuries de la campagne*, new ed. (Paris, 1771), pp. 188–190; and "Sentence de police contre plusieurs particuliers pour avoir fait charivari," May 13, 1735, 6 AZ 133, Archives de la Seine. See also Anon., *Mémoire pour Nicolas Du Perret et al., tous charbonniers à Paris . . . contre le nommé Roblot, syndic & Jure des mes savetiers de Paris (1752)*. A copy may be found in the Bibliothèque Historique de la Ville de Paris, call number 134129.
72. Hardy, *Mes Loisirs*, 330–331; Bibliothèque Nationale, Ms. Fr. 6682, folios 326, 463; Ms. Fr. 6685, folios 58, 519. See also Hurtaut and Magny, *Dictionnaire historique de la ville de Paris*, 4 vols. (Paris, 1779, II: 72.
73. *Almanach du Palais Royal . . . pour l'année 1786* (Paris, 1786).
74. Ange Goudar, *L'Anti-Babylone* (London, 1759), pp. 21–23.
75. John Andrews, *A Comparative View of the French and English Nations in Their Manners, Politics and Literature* (London, 1785), p. 382. This book was first published in 1770.
76. Arthur Young, *Travels in France*, ed. Jeffry Kaplow (New York, 1969), p. 239.
77. Hester Lynch Piozzi, *Observations and Reflections Made on the Course of a Journey through France, Italy and Germany*, 2 vols. (London, 1789), I: 13–15.
78. Andrews, *Comparative View of the French and English Nations*, pp. 149–150; John Moore, *A View of Society and Manners in France, Switzerland and Germany*, 2nd ed., 2 vols. (Paris, n. d.), I: 36–37, 41–42. First published in 1779.
79. Mercier, *Tableau*, I: 52–54, 70.
80. Ms. 1421, Title 2, Bibliothèque d'Orleans.

Chapter [5]

1. On attitudes of the bourgeois to religious freedom, see Mercier, *Tableau*, III: 87–91.
2. Bernard Groethuysen, *Origines de l'esprit bourgeois en France* (Paris, 1927), pp. 15–17.
3. Anon., *An Agreeable Criticism of the City of Paris and the French*, 2nd ed. (London, 1706), pp. 35–36.
4. [J. C. Villiers, Earl of Clarendon], *A Tour through Part of France* (London, 1789), pp. 118–119.
5. Hester Lynch Piozzi, *Observations and Reflections Made on the Course of a Journey through France, Italy and Germany*, 2 vols. (London, 1789), I: 27–28. The trip was made in September, 1784.
6. Police ordinances to prohibit work on Sundays and holidays invariably went unobserved despite the heavy fines (ranging from 100 to 500 livres depending on the nature of the business) to which offenders were subject. The clergy also complained of the flouting of the law. See *Procès-verbal et cahier de l'assemblée du clergé de la paroisse royale de St. Paul . . . le 21 avril 1789*, art. III. Blue laws of this sort were periodically re-enacted, but after 1750 their enforcement was allowed to lag considerably. This matter is discussed at length by Yves Brisset de Morcour, *La Police séculière des dimanches et fêtes dans l'ancienne France* (Paris, 1938).
7. *Almanach spirituel pour l'année M.DCC. LXXIII* (Paris, 1773), p. 14.
8. A complete list may be found in L. Denis, *Pouillé historique et topographique de Paris* (Paris, 1767).
9. Abbé Expilly, *Dictionnaire*, V: 480, 515. One might add another 1,200 "ecclésiastiques séculiers non-attachés à aucune église particulière et répandus en différentes maisons de la ville." See also D. Farandjis, "Le Clergé de Paris en 1789" (unpub. D.E.S., Paris, 1961). For the distribution of the parish clergy, see *Almanach ecclésiastique* (Paris, new ed. each year in the eighteenth century).
10. Farandjis, "Le Clergé de Paris en 1789," pp. 9–10.
11. Gabriel Lebras, *Introduction à l'histoire de la pratique religieuse en France*, 2 vols. (Paris, 1942–1945), I: 98–99. We have found only one piece of evidence concerning the importance of Easter communion to Parisians. In a letter to Joly de Fleury dated March 24, 1762, Sartine wrote:

> . . . les habitants de la paroisse St. Leu commencent à murmurer beaucoup sur le défaut de prêtres nécessaires pour la desserte de cette église. . . . Quoique le service s'y fasse assés exactement, ils manquent néanmoins de confesseurs, et l'approche des fêtes de Pâques rendre cette disette encore plus frapante." Collection Joly de Fleury, 1568, folio 20, Bibliothèque Nationale.

12. First communion in the eighteenth century was taken considerably later than it is now, at between 15 and 18 years of age. *Le Pastoral parisien* published in 1786 by order of Le Clerc de Juigné recommended delaying it for some significant time after first confession because "il leur faut [aux enfants] une raison bien plus éclairée, qui leur fasse connaître ce qu'ils reçoivent dans ce sacrement." This view

of the matter has been attributed to Jansenist influence [Louis
Andrieux, *La Première communion* (Paris, 1911), pp. 155–156, 163].

13. Antoine Eléonor Léon Le Clerc de Juigné, *Le Pastoral parisien*, 3 vols.
    (Paris, 1786), III: 3–4, 510f.

14. Maupoint, avocat, [d'après Barbier], *Calendrier historique avec le
    journal des cérémonies et usages qui s'observent à la cour, à Paris et à
    la campagne* (Paris, 1737), *passim*; the quotation appears on p. 63.
    Also, Roger Vaultier, *Les Fêtes populaires à Paris* (Paris, 1946), pp.
    131ff.

15. *Almanach spirituel* (1773): 14–15. But who among the workers could
    allow themselves to take the time off? Perhaps those who were
    already unemployed?

16. R. F. du Breil de Pontbriand, *Progrès de l'établissement commencé
    depuis peu pour les Savoyards qui sont dans Paris* (Paris, 1737), pp. 15,
    28.

17. "Traité des fausses traditions et de superstitions spécialement de celles
    adoptées par le peuple de Paris," 1665, Ms. Baluze 213, no. 2, Bibli-
    othèque Nationale. See also Louis du Broc de Segange, *Les Saints
    patrons des corporations et protecteurs spécialement invoqués dans les
    maladies et dans les circonstances critiques de la vie*, 2 vols. (Paris,
    1887).

18. There were 71 confréries in 26 parishes in 1760. Arrêt du Parlement
    du 18 avril 1760 concernant les associations, congrégations et confréries,
    Collection Joly de Fleury, 1590, Bibliothèque Nationale.

19. Abbé Jean Gaston, *Les Images des confréries parisiennes avant la
    Révolution* (Paris, 1910).

20. Groethuysen, *Origines*, 22–23. Cf. the history of the Great Awakening
    and of the Chassidic movement among Jews in eighteenth-century
    Poland.

21. The virgin was the object of particular adoration among the Parisian
    masses. On July 3 each year a special ceremony was held on the rue
    aux Ours to commemorate a fifteenth-century incident in which the
    statue of the Virgin was supposed to have been insulted by a soldier.
    The philosophe Du Marsais attended once and overheard one woman
    telling another there was no need to push to get a better view of the
    Virgin, as she was present everywhere. He ventured to correct her
    by remarking that her statement was heresy, that only God was
    everywhere. She responded with insults and incited the crowd to
    do justice to "ce vieux coquin, cet Huguenot." Du Marsais had to
    take refuge with the police in order to escape their wrath. Peysonnel,
    Les Numéros, 2nd ed., 3 pts. (Paris, 1783), I: 63–66.

22. P. de Crousaz-Cretet, *Paris sous Louis XIV*, 2 vols. (Paris, 1922), II: 48.

23. Anon., *A Trip to Paris in July and August, 1792* (London, 1793),
    pp. 12–13.

24. Geneviève Bollème, *Les Almanachs populaires aux et XVIIe siècles*
    (Paris, 1969).

25. Albert Soboul, "Sentiments religieux et cultes populaire: Saintes
    patriotes et martyrs de la liberté," *Annales Historiques de la Révolu-
    tion Française*, XXIX (1957): 192–213.

26. Cited by Vaultier, *Fêtes*, pp. 230–231.

27. A similar observation of the disinclination of the poor to accept change

has been made by Thérèse Jean Schmitt, *L'Organisation ecclésiastique et la pratique religieuse dans l'archidiaconé d'Autun de 1650 à 1750* (Dijon, 1952), p. 243.

28. Ms. Fr. 6684, folio 322, Bibliothèque Nationale.
29. Ms. Fr. 6685, folio 329, Bibliothèque Nationale.
30. Christopher Hill, *Society and Puritanism in Pre-revolutionary England* (London, 1964), pp. 30–123.
31. *Statuts synodaux du diocèse de Paris renouvellés et confirmés par Mgr. Christophe de Beaumont* (Paris, 1777), arts. 13 and 14.
32. We need a good study of the sermon as an instrument of social control. Unfortunately, the standard works on eighteenth-century preaching are concerned exclusively with literary accomplishments and eloquence in the pulpit. See A. Bernard, *Le Sermon au XVIIIe siècle* (Paris, 1901), and A. de Coulanges, *La Chaire française au XVIIIe siècle* (Paris, 1901).
33. See for example: Anon., *L'Ange conducteur dans les prières et exercises de piété très propres aux âmes dévotes pour s'assurer la bienheureuse éternité* (Liége, 1734).
34. Lorenzo Scupoli, *Le Combat spirituel* (Angers, 1785), p. 11. Originally written in Latin and published as *Pugna spiritualis* at the beginning of the seventeenth century, Barbier notes that this book went through more than 200 editions in French translation before 1785.
35. Joseph Lambert, *Introductions courtes et familières sur les évangiles des dimanches et des principales fêtes de l'année en faveur des pauvres, et particulièrement des gens de la campagne* (Paris, 1721), introduction.
36. Ibid., pp. 483ff. The same sentiment is expressed in another book of popular devotions, Anon., *L'Ame élevée à Dieu par les réflexions et les sentiments*, 2nd ed. (Liége, 1785), p. 188.
37. Lambert, *Introductions*, pp. 185–187; and Anon., *Cantiques spirituels à l'usage des retraites que l'on fait pour tous les ouvriers des rues de Paris* (Paris, 1750), pp. 18–21:

> INSTRUCTION POUR LES OUVRIERS
>
> Vous qui vivez dans les travaux
> Qui souffrez l'indigence;
> Apprenez à rendre vos maux
> Dignes de récompense
>
> Ayez toujours, chers Ouvriers,
> Ayez dans la mémoire,
> Que c'est par de maux passagers,
> Qu'on arrive à la gloire
>
> · · ·
>
> Pourvu qu'enfin nous parvenions
> A la Sainte Patrie;
> Qu'importe que nous endurions
> Divers maux dans la vie.

The same kind of advice was to be found in nonreligious items of popular culture like *L'Etat de servitude ou la misère des domestiques* (Troyes: Bibliothèque Bleue, 1720), in which much is made of the sufferings of domestics, but they are nonetheless counseled to be patient and resigned:

> Mais pour vous qui servez, ressouvenez-vous bien,
> Que pour gagner un maître il faut n'omettre rien;
> Secret, discrétion, propreté, vigilance,
> Grande assiduité, petits soins, complaisance;
> Attachez vous toujours à servir de bon coeur,
> Etudiez d'un maître et l'esprit et l'humeur,
> Et n'oubliez jamais qu'il faut pour lui complaire
> Quelque raison qu'on ait, avoir tort et se taire;
> Ceux de vous qui pourront ainsi se ménager,
> Rendront leur sort plus doux et leur joug plus léger,
> Car qui n'est pas heureux, c'est qu'il ne veux pas l'être,
> Puisque le bon valet fit toujours le bon maître.

38. See, for example, Dom Augustin Calmet, *Dissertations sur les apparitions des esprits*, 4th ed. (Paris, 1751). I am inclined to agree with Groethuysen when he remarks that popular superstition, however scandalous to the noble and bourgeois, was often only "faith applied to the small facts of life." *Origines*, pp. 22–23.

39. Hardy, *Mes Loisirs*, pp. 163–164, 166.

40. Ms. Fr. 6682, folio 331, Bibliothèque Nationale.

41. Ms. 1421, Bibliothèque d'Orléans.

42. Jacques Louis Ménétra, "Mémoires écrits par lui-même," Ms. 678, folio 13, Bibliothèque Historique de la Ville de Paris:

> Dans cest temps [1750] le bruit couroit que l'on prenoit les jeunne garson et que l'on les seigneoit et qu'il étoit perdue pour jamais et que de leurs sangs servoit pour baigné une princesse ataquée d'une maladie quy ne pouvoit être que guérit avec du sangs humain. Sela fit beaucoup de rumeurt dans Paris. Mon père vint me cherchée à l'écolle comme bien d'autre avec sept fort garson tonnelier quy portoit chacun un levier sur l'épaule. La rumeur fut si forte que les vitres des comissaire fure cassé et que l'on asomma plusieurs malheureux et même que l'on en brula un en place de grève que l'on avoit prie resembland à un mouchard. L'on ne laissoit plus sortir les enfant. Il eu trois misérable quy fure pendue en place de grève pour fair justice et pour rendre le calme dans Paris.

43. Ms. 1421, Bibliothèque d'Orléans.

44. Ms. Fr. 6682, folio 375, Bibliothèque Nationale.

45. Ms. Fr. 6683, folios 139–140, Bibliothèque Nationale. Cf. the case of Johanna Southcott in England a generation later, in Edward Thompson, *The Making of the English Working Class* (London: Penguin edition, 1969), pp. 420–428.

46. Collection Joly de Fleury 1292, Bibliothèque Nationale.

47. Restif de la Bretonne, *Nuits*, I: 53.

48. Schulz and Kraus, *Beschreibung und Abbildung der Poissarden in Paris* (Weimar and Berlin, 1789), p. 4.

49. A. de Boislisle, ed., *Lettres de M. de Marville, lieutenant-général de police, au ministre Maurepas (1742–1747)*, 3 vols. (Paris, 1896–1905), II: 212–214.

50. Léon G. Pelissier, "Une lettre de Paris (1772)," *Bulletin de la Société Historique de Paris*, XXVI (1899): 61–64. See also Mercier, *Tableau*, II: 285n.

51. René Taveneaux, *Jansénisme et politique* (Paris, 1965), pp. 7–50.
52. R. A. Knox, *Enthusiasm* (Oxford, 1950), pp. 378–379.
53. Ibid., pp. 2–3, 209–210.
54. Edmond Jean François Barbier, *Journal historique et anecdotique du règne de Louis XV*, 4 vols., ed. A. de la Villegille (Paris, 1847–1856), I: 219–220. For an examination of medical evidence concerning these cures, see Paul Richer, *Etudes cliniques sur la grande hysterie ou hystéro-épilepsie* (Paris, 1885), pp. 866–888.
55. P. F. Mathieu, *Histoire des miraculés et des convulsionnaires de Saint Médard* (Paris, 1864), pp. 117–119, 136–137. See also Louis Basile Carré de Montgeron, *La Vérité des miracles*, 2 vols. (Paris, 1737–1741).
56. Barbier, *Journal*, I: 282, 287–288, 352–354, 393; Mathieu, *Histoire des miraculés*, pp. 218–219.
57. Barbier, *Journal*, I: 287–288, 352–353.
58. Taveneaux, *Jansénisme*, p. 49.
59. Anon., *Plan général de l'oeuvre des convulsions*, cited by Mathieu, *Histoire*, p. 278.
60. P. Mitchal [d'après Barbier], *Idée de l'oeuvre des secours, selon les sentiments de ses légitimes défenseurs* (Paris, 1786), pp. 17–18. See also Barbier, *Journal*, II: 4–5, and IV: 298, 339–340.
61. Mitchal, *Idée l'oeuvre des secours*, pp. 31–32. The author assures us that "the breast being always covered," this was done "with the greatest decency."
62. Collection Joly de Fleury, 1567, Bibliothèque Nationale.
63. Eric J. Hobsbawm, *Primitive Rebels* (Manchester, 1959).

Chapter [6]

1. Sir William Mildmay, *The Police of France* (London, 1763), pp. 76–77.
2. Collection Joly de Fleury 1308, Bibliothèque Nationale.
3. "Etat des mendiants et vagabonds qui ont été renfermés dans les dépôts de mendicité établis dans le royaume . . . pendant l'année 1773 et précédentes," Ms. Fr. 8129, Bibliothèque Nationale. As of December 31, 1773, 1,419 persons were imprisoned in the *dépôts* of the Generality of Paris. The total number of persons arrested in all of France during this period was 71,760 or 72,025. The difference between the two estimates we have seen is of no importance.
4. F15 2811, Archives Nationales. For each beggar arrested and sent to prison, the police inspectors received 15 sous, and 10 sous for each person arrested but not detained. The result of this system was a rash of unjustified arrests. In 1782, 799 of 2,145 persons arrested were released without further proceedings being taken against them. In 1783, the figure was 817 of 1,944, or 37 and 42 percent respectively.
5. Jacques Necker, *De l'Administration des finances*, 3 vols. (Paris, 1784), III: 166. The figures here cited do not, by definition, give any idea of the number of beggars who escaped the attention of the authorities. The lieutenants-general of police Sartine and Lenoir often complained that they did not have sufficient manpower to control beggars and criminals adequately.

6. Agenda de police, November 30, 1769, Y 13700, Archives Nationales.
7. Y 9514, ibid.
8. Jacques Peuchet, *Mémoires tirés des archives de la police*, 3 vols. (Paris, 1838), III: 55–56.
9. Christian Paultre, *De la Répression de la mendicité et du vagabondage en France sous l'ancien régime* (Paris, 1906), pp. 385–386.
10. Bibliothèque Nationale, Ms. Fr. 8129, and N.A. 2799—Mémoire sur la mendicité, 1778.
11. Guillaume François Letrosne, *Mémoire sur les vagabonds* (Soissons and Paris, 1764), p. 8.
12. Claude Antoine Joseph Leclerc de Montlinot, *Etat actuel du dépôt de Soissons précédé d'un essai sur la mendicité* (Soissons, 1789), p 22. See also Maille Dussausoy, *Le Citoyen désintéressé*, 2 vols. (Paris, 1767), II: 150f.
13. Denis Laurian Turmeau de La Morandière, *Police sur les mendiants* (Paris, 1764), pp. 64–65.
14. Friedrich Schulz, *Ueber Paris und die Pariser* (Berlin, 1791), p. 206.
15. Mercier, *Tableau*, III: 210.
16. For a description of the Cour des Miracles, see Henri Sauval, *Histoire et recherches des antiquites de la ville de Paris*, 3 vols. (Paris, 1724), I: 511–516. See also Maurice Vloberg, *De la Cour des miracles au gibet de Montfaucon* (Paris, 1928), pp. 51–57, 221–222.
17. Papers of the seigneurial court of Saint Médard, April 10, 1781, H² 1955 and Z² 3699, Archives Nationales.
18. Abbé Malvaux, *Les Moyens de détruire la mendicité en France*, new ed. (Chalons, 1780), p. 323. Also, Albert Soboul, "Problèmes du travail en l'an II," *Annales Historiques de la Révolution Française*, XXVIII (1956): 236–254.
19. Letrosne, *Mémoire sur les vagabonds*, pp. 2–3.
20. Jean Pierre Gutton, "Les Mendiants dans la société parisienne au début du XVIIIe siècle," *Cahiers d'Histoire*, XIII (1968): 131–141. The author argues, very plausibly it seems to me, that (1) artisans resented the competition they had to suffer from the workshops of the Hôpital Général staffed by captured beggars, and (2) that their anti-police action was a sign of their lack of submissiveness to authority. On the second point, I would say, and one of the major purposes of this book is to show, that the values of the laboring poor were, even when not consciously formulated, different from those of their rulers, but that they were capable of challenging the established order only in a limited and sporadic way and always at a very low level.
21. Leclerc de Montlinot, *Etat actuel*, pp. 10–11.
22. Ibid., p. 2.
23. Ms. N.S. 110, No. 168, Archives de l'Assistance Publique. The total comes to 415, as we lack information on the place of origin of six prisoners. Note that Paris was not, for certain regions, the only pole of attraction. Migrants from the southwest went to Bordeaux, and Bretons traditionally took to the sea and the colonies (notably Quebec). See also J. P. Poussou, "Aspects de l'immigration pyrénéenne (Bèarn, Bigorre, Comminges, Ariège) à Bordeaux au milieu et à la fin du XVIIIe siècle," *Bulletin de la Société des Sciences, Lettres et Arts de Pau*, série 4, I (1966): 99–116.

24. Registre . . . [de] Jean Christophe subdélégué de M. l'intendant de Paris à St. Denis . . . [qui] doit servir à l'enregistrement des mendiants, etc., 1786, FF 16, Archives de la Municipalité de Saint Denis. See also "Captures de mendiant par la prévôté de l'hôtel à Versailles," 1781–1789, O¹ 3707, Archives Nationales.

25. Letter from Montlinot, October 7, 1786, C 747, Archives Départementales de l'Aisne, Laon.

26. C 1119, Archives départementales de Puy-de Dôme, Clermont-Ferrand. See also C 1116, 1120, 1123, 1143. The request for verification of identity of Auvergnats accused of beggary invariably elicited the same response from their native villages: they had left the province to look for work but had never been known to beg.

27. Examples from 1769, C 116, ibid.

28. Dépôt de mendicité of Angers and Tours, list of persons arrested in Paris, 1787, C 303, Archives Départementales d'Indre-et-Loire, Tours.

29. List of beggars arrested in Versailles, 1788, for the evidence of their inability to sign their names, I B 112, Archives Départementales de Seine-et-Oise.

30. C 94, Archives Départmentales de la Sarthe, le Mans.

31. Sacheverell Stevens, *Miscellaneous Remarks made on the spot in a late seven year tour through France, Italy, Germany and Holland* (London, 1756).

32. See the section on popular Jansenism below, pp. 121–126.

33. Bernard Groethuysen, *Origines de l'esprit bourgeois en France* (Paris, 1927), pp. 1–5, 12–36

34. Edmond Jean François Barbier, *Journal historique et anecdotique du règne Louis XV*, ed. A. de la Villegille, 4 vols. (Paris, 1847–1856), I: 114–116.

35. G. Parker, *A View of Society and Manners in High and Low Life: Being the Adventures in England, Ireland, Scotland, Wales, France, etc. of Mr. G. Parker*, 2 vols. (London, 1781), II: 214–215.

36. The question was posed by Mercier, *Tableau*, I: 195.

37. Barbier, *Journal*, I: 79–80, 113–114, 232.

38. A. C. Cailleau [d'après Barbier], *Vie privée et criminelle d'Antoine François Desrues* (Avignon and Paris, 1777), p. 128.

39. Georges Claretie, *Derues l'empoisonneur* (Paris, 1906), passim, but especially pp. 288–325.

40. The popular biography of Cartouche is entitled *Histoire de la vie et du procès de Louis Dominique Cartouche et de plusieurs de ses complices*, with slight variations from edition to edition. I have consulted the "third edition" published at the Hague by Jean Heaulme, 1722 and another published in Amsterdam by Gertrude de Royter, 1737. An early nineteenth-century variant was published in Paris by Vve. Demoraine et Bourquin, no date, under the title *Les Amours et la vie de Cartouche, ou Aventures singulières et galantes de cet homme*. Defoe's translation is *The Life and Actions of Lewis Dominique Cartouche* (London, 1722). The Russian edition is M. Kamarov, *Obstoyatelnaya I Vernaya Istorii Dvukh' Moshenikov, Pervovo Rossiskovo Yelavnovo Vora . . . Vani Kaina . . . Vtorovo Frantzuskovo Moshenika Kartusha I Yevo Sotovarishché* (St. Petersburg, 1779).

41. Frantz Funck-Brentano, *Les Brigands* (Paris, 1904), pp. 181–220.

42. Anon., *Historie de la vie* (1772), p. 29.

43. Note the words attributed to him in the nineteenth-century edition of his biography: he worked only in the Marais, the faubourgs Saint Germain, Saint Denis, and Saint Martin. "Le faubourg Saint Marceau ne valant rien, je le laissai aux fripons subalternes." [pp. 55–56].

44. Anon., *Histoire de la vie* (1737), pp. 95–96.

45. Nicolas Ragot de Grandval, père [d'après] Barbier, *Le Vice puni, ou Cartouche*, new ed. (Paris, 1726), pp. 2–3. Compare the popularity of more avowedly social bandits; for example F. Funck-Brentano, *Mandrin, Capitaine général des contrebandiers de France* (Paris, 1908).

46. Barbier, *Journal*, IV: 287–289.

47. H. Monin, *L'Etat de Paris en 1789* (Paris, 1889), pp. 89–92. See also the collection of printed *arrêts* in AD III 15, AD XIV 15, Archives Nationales.

48. Y 10648, Y 13614, Archives Nationales. Bicêtre in the 1770s had a complement of about 900 male prisoners at any given time, jailed for various offenses, of which the three major ones were murder, theft, and libertinage.

49. A^B 392, folio 18 *verso*, November 23, 1747, Archives de la Préfecture de Police.

50. The police archives show that one of the most common offenses was the return to the city before the expiration of the ban. See, for example, the reports of the Guet in the Tocqueville Archives, AP II 154 (177 M 125), Archives Nationales.

51. Barbier, *Journal*, III: 148–149.

52. Anon., *Projet d'établissement d'un bureau de consultation d'avocats pour les pauvres* (Paris, 1763), p. 6.

53. See the list of names and trades of prisoners detained at Bicêtre from 1780 to 1788 in A^B 339, Archives de la Préfecture de Police. It is noteworthy that almost every one of the prisoners identified himself as having a trade. Perhaps because they hoped such identification would gain them better treatment at the hands of the law than if they simply admitted to parasitism.

54. Ms. 1421, Bibliothèque d'Orléans.

55. Ms. Fr. 6682, folios 387, 390, Bibliothèque Nationale.

56. Hardy, *Mes Loisirs*, p. 81.

57. Reports of the Guet to Malesherbes, 1782, AP II 154 (177 M 160), Archives Nationales. See also for fraud at the barriers, Y 9535.

58. Leon Radzinowicz, *A History of English Criminal Law and Its Administration from 1750*, 4 vols. to date (London, 1948–1968). See also, P. Linebaugh, "Crime in London Between 1720 and 1740: A Survey of the Historical Evidence" (M. A. Essay, Columbia University, 1969).

59. A^B 391–393, 401, Archives de la Préfecture de Police; Y series, Archives Nationales.

60. Jean Claude Gégot, "Etude par sondage de la criminalité dans le bailliage de Falaise (XVIIe–XVIIIe siècles). Criminalité diffuse ou société criminelle?" *Annales de Normandie*, XVI (1966): 103–164; Bernadette Boutelet, "Etude par sondage de la criminalité dans le bailliage de Pont-de-l'Arche (XVIIe–XVIIIe siècles)," idem., XII (1962): 235–262.

61. Barbier, *Journal*, I: 401.

62. Thefts in churches, 1751, Collection Joly de Fleury 1310, Bibliothèque

Nationale. Theft in church of Saint Germain en Laye, March 15, 1787, Y 10480, Archives Nationales.

63. A. de Boislisle, ed., *Lettres de M. de Marville, lieutenant-général de police au Ministre Maurepas* (1742–1747), 3 vols. (Paris, 1896–1905), I: 29. See also A^B 393, folio 318 *recto*, Archives de la Préfecture de Police.

64. See above, pp. 131–132.

65. Robert Dauvergne, "Paris, foyer d'émigration au cours des âges," *Bulletin de la Société d'Etudes historiques, géographiques, et scientifiques de la région parisienne*, XXXV (1961), no. 1–7, 112–113.

66. Collection Joly de Fleury 2074, Bibliothèque Nationale.

67. March 21, 1769, Y 10300, Archives Nationales.

68. Hardy, *Mes Loisirs*, pp. 89, 398–399.

69. As early as 1742, Marville had expressed his own displeasure at the inefficiency of the courts: ". . . depuis les longeurs qu'il faut essuyer pour l'instruction des affaires criminelles, de dix coquins que l'on juge il y en a neuf qui échappent à la justice par le dépérissement des preuves. D'ailleurs, les juges supérieurs sont trop indulgents, et l'on ne prononce que des bannissements, et un homme banni est un voleur de plus dans Paris." [A. de Boislisle, ed. *Lettres de M. de Marville, lieutenant-général de police, au ministre Maurepas (1742–1747)*, 3 vols. (Paris, 1896–1905), I: 73–74.]

70. Barbier, *Journal*, II: 337.

71. *Ibid.*, III: 358–359. See also Ms. Fr. 6682, folio 435, Bibliothèque Nationale.

72. Ms. Fr., 6685, folios 4, 8, 11, Bibliothèque Nationale.

73. A^B 392, folio 35 *verso*, Archives de la Préfecture de la Police.

74. Of Cartouche's marriage, it was said: "Il est vrai qu'on n'appella ni notaire ni prêtre, mais aussi ces sortes d'alliance durent souvent si peu, qu'il est besoin de moins de formalités pour les contracter." *Histoire de la vie* (1722), p. 25. See also our remarks on family stability, pp. 60–63.

75. July 2, 1779, Y 10400, Archives Nationales.

76. A. J. B. Parent-Duchâtelet, *De la Prostitution dans la ville de Paris*, 3rd ed., 2 vols. (Paris, 1857), I: 27–28. See also Nicolas Edme Restif de la Bretonne, *Le Pornographe, ou Idées d'un honnête homme sur un projet de reglement pour les prostituées* (London and the Hague, 1769).

77. Mercier, *Tableau*, III: 214; Restif de la Bretonne, *Les Nuits*, I: 59.

78. H. Montbas, *La Police parisienne sous Louis XVI* (Paris, 1949), pp. 154–167; L. P. Berenger, *De la Prostitution, cahier de doléances d'un ami des moeurs* (Paris, 1790), art. XXV.

79. Anon., *Code ou Nouveau reglement sur les lieux de prostitution dans la ville de Paris* (London, 1775), pp. 76ff. The definitions of the categories mentioned were as follows:

Les boucaneuses. Ces filles vivent . . . chez des Maquerelles . . . mais elles sont au premier venu, et raccrochent pour elle-mêmes. Elles courent de mauvais lieu en mauvais lieu.

Les raccrocheuses. Elles sont assez mal logées en chambres garnies, et sujettes à bien des inconvénients du côté de la police. Celles-ci sont quelquefois chez des Maquerelles de leur classe. Le tout n'est pas fort en sûreté.

Les barboteuses. Ce sont des malheureuses qui se trouvent le long des maisons dans les rues peu frequentées où elles exercent effrontément leur impudique métier, qui n'ont pour logement que des galetas dans les fauxbourgs, où elles ne conduisent personne volontairement. Elles sont très dangereuses pour les hommes de peine qui s'y arrêtent, et qu'elles infectent du poison vénerien.

80. See the case of Potvin le Petit, arrested on this charge (January, 1746) in A^B 392, folio 5, *verso*, Archives de la Préfecture de Police. Another instance is found in Michel Vovelle, "De la mendicité au brigandage: les errants en Beauce sous la Révolution française," *Actes du 86e Congrès des Sociétés Savantes . . . 1961* (Paris, 1962), pp. 483–512. For examples of the argot, see the dictionary printed as an appendix to Grandval, *Vice puni*, and Leclerc de Montlinot, *Etat actuel*, p. 55.
81. Francisque Michel, *Etudes de philologie comparée sur l'argot* (Paris, 1856), p. xvi.
82. A brilliant illustration of how professional criminals find it in their interest to persecute individual deviant behavior is to be found in Fritz Lang's motion picture, *M*.
83. In this connection, it is important to note the large number of soldiers and deserters among the criminals. The soldiers concerned came from the militia, the *garde françaises*, and the regular regiments. Before one can say anything definite about the influence of military life on the development of criminality, one would have to know whether individual criminal activity preceded or followed the first enlistment. On the one hand, persons suspected of an offense were allowed to escape prosecution by joining the militia. On the other, to be a soldier meant that one was removed from one's usual environment and hence also from traditional community restraints. For the role of soldiers in Parisian crime, see examples in Y 9650, Archives Nationales, and A^B 392, Archives de la Préfecture de Police. A letter addressed to Cardinal Fleury *circa* 1740 (Ms. 713, folio 54 Bibliothèque Historique de la Ville de Paris) specifically complained of the large number of soldiers who were both thieves and pimps, attributing this state of affairs to the fact that their pay of six or seven sous a day was not enough for subsistence. In 1753 (Ordonnances de police, XL, folio 236 Archives de la Préfecture de Police), the police ordered all soldiers on leave in Paris to register with the lieutenant-general of police as a means of discouraging their raucous and dangerous behavior.

Chapter [7]

1. E. J. Hobsbawn, *Bandits* (London, 1969), p. 46.
2. Mercier, *Tableau*, I: 59–60.
3. Schulz and Kraus, *Beschreibung und Abbildung der Poissarden in Paris* (Weimar and Berlin, 1789), p. 5.
4. Ms. Fr. 6684, folio 42, Bibliothèque Nationale.
5. For what follows, see Jules Flammermont, *Remontrances du Parlement de Paris*, 3 vols. (Paris, 1888–1898), introductions. Also, Léon

Cahen, *Les querelles religieuses et parlementaires sous Louis XV* (Paris, 1913).

6. See above, pp. 121–126.

7. Hardy, *Mes Loisirs*, pp. 20–21.

8. Edmond Jean François, Barbier, *Journal historique et anecdotique du règne de Louis XV*, ed, A. de la Villegille, 4 vols. (Paris, 1847–1856), III: 381.

9. Ibid., III: 470: "L'on compte que cela fait vingt mille personnes de moins à Paris pour la consommation."

10. Hardy, *Mes Loisirs*, I: 254–255, 319.

11. Barbier, *Journal*, IV: 30, 34.

12. Ms. Fr. 6681, folio 409; Collection Joly de Fleury, 1413; Bibliothèque Nationale.

13. Henri Carré, "Les Fêtes d'une réaction parlementaire," *Révolution Française*, XXIII (1892): 5–35; Abbé Baudeau, "Chronique secrète de Paris sous le règne de Louis XVI," *Revue Retrospective*, 1st series, III (1833): 39, 282, 402–407. See also Ms. Fr. 6681, folios 445–448, Bibliothèque Nationale.

14. Note the following bit of testimony: "During the exile of the Parlement [1754], all Sorts of Provisions were dearer than common, as they regulate the Markets, and fix a stated Price occasionally, upon all Commodities exposed publicly to Sale; though this were an inconsiderable Inconveniency to others, which the Parisians suffered by their Banishment." [A.R.], *The Curiosities of Paris* (London, n. d.), pp. 95–96.

15. In September 1763, an Order in Council forbade the Parlements to publicize their remonstrances and orders "pour instruire les peuples des démarches qu'ils faisoient en leur faveur, contre les diverses dispositions des ministres, et pour se les rendre favorables." Barbier, *Journal*, IV: 469.

16. Mercier, *Tableau*, X: 281–283, and III: 93–94. For an excellent example of this mentality, see A. C. Cailleau, *Le Cri du Coeur* (Paris, 1774), and his *L'Allégresse publique sur le nouveau règne* (Paris, 1774).

17. Rudé, *The Crowd in the French Revolution* (New York, 1959), chapters III–V.

18. Jacques Charon, *Lettre ou mémoire historique sur les troubles populaires de Paris en août et septembre, 1788* (London, 1788), pp. 7–8.

19. Rudé, *Crowd*, p. 46.

20. Mercier, *Tableau*, VI: 22–26.

21. Ibid., XII: 6.

22. Charles Chassin, *Les Elections et les cahiers de Paris en 1789*, 4 vols. (Paris, 1888–1889), I: 333ff.

23. CC 67, Archives de la municipalité de Saint Denis.

24. Chassin, *Elections*, II: 331.

25. Anon., *Pétition de cent cinquante mille ouvriers et artisans* (Paris, 1789), pp. 4–5.

26. Chassin, *Elections*, II: 451–452, Cahier du district de St. Joseph, Quartier des Halles, art. 25. See also Jean Vidalenc, "Les Revendications économiques et sociales de la population parisienne en 1789 d'après les cahiers de doléances," *Revue d'Histoire Economique et Sociale*, XXVII (1949): 273–287.

27. Chassin, *Elections*, II: 47, Cahier du district de St. Laurent.

28. Jean François Lambert, *Le Cahier des pauvres* (Paris, 1789), pp. 3–4, 14–15.
29. Rudé, *Crowd*, p. 43.
30. Ibid., p. 39.
31. Anon., *Les Casques de Ségovie, Eloge des habitans du faubourg Saint Antoine & Saint Marcel* (Paris, 1789), defended artisans against charges of wanton murder and massacre, attributing all such incidents to *agents provocateurs, jeunes élégants*, or dockworkers. This is testimony not only to a long-standing mutual distrust between constituent elements of the laboring poor, but also to a new political consciousness. The *envoi* is of some interest:

> Ne blâmez donc plus ces héros, & songez que si la pauvreté [dans le sens de la médiocrité honnête] est l'apanage des Casques de Ségovie [i.e., artisans], ce glorieux apanage est l'école de la vertu & des bonnes moeurs, comme le disoit Aristophane; & les richesses, selon Euripide, sont pleines de vices, mais la pauvreté est accompagnée de sagesse, & tous les gens de bien se contentent des choses nécessaires, combien les Casques de Ségovie, qui ne souffrent aucune bassesse parmi eux. [P. 8]

32. Mercier, *Tableau*, XII: 323–326.
33. Leclrec de Montlinot, *Etat actuel*, p. 54, n. 5.
34. Anon., *Paris aujourd'hui, ou Idées diverses d'un citoyen du tiers état sur le commerce, l'opulence, et la pauvreté actuelle des habitants de cette ville* (Paris, 1789), p. 11.
35. François Furet, "Définition," *Annales: ESC*, XVIII (1963): 459–474.
36. Mercier, *Tableau*, XII: 137:

> Tant que le pain de Gonesse ne manquera pas . . . la commotion ne sera point générale; mais si le pain de Gonesse venait à manquer dans deux marchés de suite, le soulèvement seroit universel; et il est impossible de calculer à quoi se porteroit cette grande multitude, réduite aux abzois, quand il faudroit se délivrer de la famine, elle et ses enfans.

37. Oscar Lewis, "The Culture of Poverty," *Scientific American*, CCXI (1966): 19–25.
38. Nicole H. Courtine, "Etude du costume masculin populaire à Paris de 1789 à 1794" (Unpub. D.E.S., Paris, 1961).
39. Restif de la Bretonne, *Les Nuits*, I: 230, and VIII: 1907. Schulz, *Ueber Paris und die Pariser* (Berlin, 1791), p. 231, noted that (master?) artisans like shoemakers, tailors and workers in the luxury trades would think it a shame to be seen in the *guinguettes*. Instead, they took their families to the boulevards, the Champs Elysées, to a picnic in the several royal gardens, or in the countryside along the Seine.
40. Ms. Fr. 6681, folio 348, Bibliothèque Nationale.
41. Ms. Fr., 6681, folio 361, Bibliothèque Nationale.
42. Oscar Lewis, "Culture," p. 24.

INDEX

Workers (*cont'd*)
  tions of, 119–120; treatment of,
  96; types, 11, 19–20, 29, 45; united,
  43; unmanageability of, 40; un-
  organized, 34, 39, 153; unskilled,
  39, 41, 43; values, 138; virtues,
  131; wages, 38, 53, 54, 162, 165;
  women, 55–57

Workhouses, 97, 143
Workshops, 37

❧ Y ❧

Yonne, 39
Young, Arthur, 15, 17, 109